AQUACULTURE AND FISHERIES ENVIRONMENT

AQUACULTURE
AND
FISHERIES ENVIRONMENT

Edited by

Dr. Sanjay Kumar Gupta
M.F.Sc., Ph.D., (ARS Scientist)
Directorate of Cold Water Fisheries (DCFR)
Experimental Fish Farm and Field Centre
(ICAR, Govt. of India)
Champawat (Uttarakhand), India
E-mail: sanfish111@gmail.com

&

Dr. Pawan Kumar 'Bharti'
M.Sc., Ph.D., PGDISM, FASEA
Centre for Agro-Rural Technologies (CART-India)
20, Jamaalpur Maan, Raja Ka Tajpur
Bijnore (UP) - 246 735 (India)
Email: gurupawanbharti@rediffmail.com

DISCOVERY PUBLISHING HOUSE PVT. LTD.
NEW DELHI-110 002

Published by:
Tilak Wasan

DISCOVERY PUBLISHING HOUSE PVT. LTD.
4383/4B, Ansari Road, Darya Ganj
New Delhi-110 002 (India)
Phone : +91-11-23279245, 43596064-65
Fax : +91-11-23253475
E-mail : discoverypublishinghouse@gmail.com
sales@discoverypublishinggroup.com
parul.wasan@gmail.com
web : www.discoverypublishinggroup.com

First Edition: **2014**

ISBN: 978-93-5056-408-0

Aquaculture and Fisheries Environment

Printed at:
Aditi Fine Art Press
Delhi

Preface

Aquaculture and fisheries have made significant contributions to the world economy and to the health of the poor people as a major source of animal protein especially in developing countries. Aquaculture is the fastest growing food production sector with an average growth rate of about 8.8% accounting about 47% of the world's fish supply (FAO 2012). Fisheries sector contribute over 1.0 % of the National GDP and 5.3% of the agricultural GDP in India. The role of inland aquaculture in particular is gaining increasing importance to enhance the overall fish production of the country.

In aquaculture practices, fishes are subjected to a wide variety of environmental and anthropogenic stressors. Environmental pollutants, disease, and various factors involved are some of the examples of these stressors experienced by fishes in captivity. Monitoring of adverse effects of pollutant is extremely important to regulate and remediate toxicity. To test the toxicity, biomarkers/bioindicator is applied to detect even low level of contaminants. Fishes serve as an excellent model for the assessment of pollution and play significant roles in evaluating potential risk associated with pollutants in aquatic environment. Additionally, fish, like other vertebrates, have evolved strategies to counteract effects of stressors by eliciting coordinated set of hormonal, physiological and consequent behavioral changes which are cumulatively termed as the 'stress response'. One of the important components of the stress response at the cellular level is the induction of evolutionarily conserved heat shock proteins (HSPs). Endocrine disrupting chemicals, a diverse group of synthetic industrial and agricultural chemicals compounds can affect endocrine system of the fish through mimicking the effects of endogenous hormones, antagonizing the effects of endogenous hormones, altering the pattern of synthesis and metabolism of normal hormones and modifying hormone receptor levels.

Pearl farming, one of the world's largest aquaculture activities in terms of value, practiced in the freshwater aquaculture environment. Indian pond mussel, *Lamellidens marginalis* is the major species used in pearl aquaculture. Central

Institute of Freshwater Aquaculture (CIFA), Bhubaneswar has taken the lead initiative to disseminate the technology of freshwater pearl culture to the fish farming communities, entrepreneurs, researchers and students of the country. This book provides the comprehensive coverage to briefly discuss about indigenously developed technology of pearl farming in freshwater.

Pond bottom soil plays a pivotal role in determining pond productivity. India has about 90% red-lateritic soils of its total area and majority of acid soils have pH below 5.6. Management of this problematic red soil based upland aquaculture system is of paramount importance. Present book briefly discusses the methodology developed for ameliorating the acidic soil and water and the need of soil specific fertilization especially for acidic soils to enhance aquaculture productivity.

The Brahmaputra River is the fourth largest river in the world in terms of average flow discharge, flow through the Assam of North-east India furnishing huge ichthyofaunal diversity to the region. Authors has made an attempt to assess the ecological requirements (water quality features) of the lower stretch of the Brahmaputra river for the survival and growth of fish fauna.

Success of Indian Major Carp farming exclusively relies on the primary food production in the natural pond environment. Both phyto and zooplanktons is the natural food items in freshwater fish ponds. Study on diversity of both phytoplankton and zooplankton community are essential to learn plankton dynamics in ponds through enrichment of autotrophic and heterotrophic pathways to enhance fish production. To increase the production of shrimps (a highly price commodity in the Global trade), bioremediation (bioaugmentation) technology is being employed which is gaining considerable attention in recent years depending on the nature of the products used and competition between species or strains of bacteria.

Land degradation described as an environmental phenomenon affecting dry lands, a long-term decline in ecosystem function and productivity. Intensification of sustainable aquaculture can be implemented to reduce the ecological effect without affecting the productivity through management of deforestation, irrigation, urban sprawl, mining and quarrying and land reclamation. Further, authors have briefly described the importance of local and global policies and regulations imperative to control the land degradation in order to increase the aquaculture production. With population increase and economic growth, water demands for cities and for the industry are growing much faster than those of agriculture. More focus should be on sustainable management of water resources for optimal agricultural production. This necessitates the exploration of opportunities for multiple use of water in agriculture through farming system approach. Integrated farming system involving multiple use of water could be an answer to resource scarce conditions in changing climatic scenario.

The editors have tried hard to make comprehensive coverage of the fundamental principles, current practices and trends in the field of aquaculture and fisheries environment. This book updates the subject matter, illustrations and problems to incorporate new concepts and issues related to aquaculture and fisheries environment. Editors have made all possible efforts to avoid any omissions and errors but still some may appear after publication. It is hoped that those oversights will not detract the readers from the wealth information presented by the authors within this volume.

Publication of the document has been possible through enthusiastic support, assistance and cooperation of dedicated scientists/workers from different institutions working in the field and also in other areas of aquaculture and fisheries. The processing and editing of various articles has taken long time, we express our sincere gratitude to all the contributors for bearing with us.

We wish this book would be of immense benefit to researchers, scientists, students, entrepreneurs and fishers working in the field of aquaculture, limnology, freshwater ecology, aquatic ecosystem, environmental pollution and fisheries.

Sanjay Kumar Gupta

Pawan Kumar 'Bharti'

Contents

List of Contributors

A.K. Prusty, Scientist, Project Directorate for Farming System Research (PDFSR), Meerut, Uttar Pradesh - 250 110, India.

Alkesh Das, Pursuing Masters Programme from Division of Aquaculture, Central Institute of Fisheries Education, Versova, Mumbai - 400 061, India.

Asim K. Pal, Joint Director, Central Institute of Fisheries Education, Versova, Mumbai - 400 061, India.

Bhaskar J. Saud, Research Scholar, Central Inland Fisheries Research Institute (CIFRI), Regional Centre, HOUSEFED Complex, Dispur, Guwahati - 781 006.

Biji Xavier, Scientist, Visakhapatnam Regional Centre of Central Marine Fisheries Research Institute, Visakhapatnam - 530 003, India.

Biswajit Dash, Scientist, Visakhapatnam Regional Centre of Central Marine Fisheries Research Institute, Visakhapatnam, India.

Chandra Prakash, Sr. Scientist, Aquaculture Division, Central Institute of Fisheries Education (Deemed University), Versova, Mumbai - 400 061, Maharastra, India.

Debtanu Barman, College of Fisheries, Central Agricultural University (Imphal), Lembucherra, West Tripura - 799 210, India.

D.K. Meena, Scientist, Central Inland Fisheries Research Institute (CIFRI), Barrackpore, Kolkata 700 120, India.

J. Mohanty, Principal Scientist, Central Institute of Freshwater Aquaculture Kausalyaganga, Bhubaneswar - 751 002, Odisha, India.

J.P. Singh, Project Directorate for Farming System Research (PDFSR), Meerut, Uttar Pradesh - 250 110, India.

Loveson L. Edward, Scientist, Visakhapatnam Regional Centre of Central Marine Fisheries Research Institute, Visakhapatnam - 530 003, India.

M.V. Hanumantha Rao, Visakhapatnam Regional Centre of Central Marine Fisheries Research Institute, Visakhapatnam - 530 003, India.

Madhumita Das, Scientist, Visakhapatnam Regional Centre of Central Marine Fisheries Research Institute, Visakhapatnam, India.

Mitali Chetia, Department of Zoology, Gauhati University, Guwahati - 781 014, India.

Mrinal Kanti Datta, Assistant Professor, College of Fisheries, Central Agricultural University, Lembucherra, Tripura (West), Pin - 799 210, India.

Muktha Menon, Scientist, Visakhapatnam Regional Centre of Central Marine Fisheries Research Institute, Visakhapatnam - 530 003, India.

N Rajendra Naik, Visakhapatnam Regional Centre of Central Marine Fisheries Research Institute, Visakhapatnam - 530 003, India.

Poonam Kashyap, Scientist, Project Directorate for Farming System Research (PDFSR), Meerut, Uttar Pradesh - 250 110, India.

P. Jayasankar, Director of CIFA, Central Institute of Freshwater Aquaculture Kausalyaganga, Bhubaneswar - 751 002, Odisha, India.

Pralaya Ranjan Behera, Scientist, Visakhapatnam Regional Centre of Central Marine Fisheries Research Institute, Visakhapatnam - 530 003, India.

Prem Kumar, Scientist, [a]Central Institute of Brackishwater Aquaculture (CIBA) 75- Santhome High Road, R.A. Puram, Chennai, India.

P. Priya, SRM, University, Potheri, Kattankulathur, Kancheepuram, Tamil Nadu 603203, India.

Rishikesh S. Dalvi, Assistant Professor, Department of Zoology, Maharshi Dayanand College of Arts, Science and Commerce, Shri Mangaldas Verma Chawk, Dr. S.S. Rao Road, Parel, Mumbai - 400 012, India.

Ritesh Ranjan, Scientist, Visakhapatnam Regional Centre of Central Marine Fisheries Research Institute, Visakhapatnam - 530 003, India.

S.K. Gupta, Scientist, Directorate of Coldwater Fisheries Research, Chhirapani Fish Farm, Champawat, Uttrakhand - 262 523, India.

S. Khogen Singh, Research Scholar, College of Fisheries, Central Agricultural University (Imphal), Lembucherra, West Tripura - 799 210, India.

Sagar C. Mandal, Assistant Professor, College of Fisheries, Central Agricultural University (Imphal), Lembucherra, West Tripura - 799 210, India.

Shailesh Saurabh, Scientist, Central Institute of Freshwater Aquaculture Kausalyaganga, Bhubaneswar - 751 002, Odisha, India.

Shubhadeep Ghosh, Sr. Scientist, Visakhapatnam Regional Centre of Central Marine Fisheries Research Institute, Visakhapatnam - 530 003, India.

U.L. Mohanty, Technical Officer (T-6), Central Institute of Freshwater Aquaculture Kausalyaganga, Bhubaneswar - 751 002, Odisha, India.

Hussein Abdel-Hay Kauod, Veterinary Hygiene and Environmental Pollution Department of Veterinary Hygiene and Management, Faculty of Veterinary Medicine, Cairo University (Egypt).

1

Biological Indicators of Aquatic Environment

S.K. Gupta; Alkesh Das
Akriti Gupta and A.K. Prusty

ABSTRACT

Bioindicators are organisms or communities of organisms used to determine the healthiness of ecosystem on the basis of sensitiveness to the abiotic stressors in their surrounding environment. Bioindicators are assessed through their presence or absence, relative abundance, reproductive success, composition and diversity, trophic structure of community or any combination existing. An ideal bioindicator species provide continuous assessment over a wide range and intensity of stresses such as pollution, climate change, disease and competition, should be inexpensive to be assessed by the non professionals, indicates early warning signal of natural responses to environmental impacts. Various type of bioindicator has been in vogue to assess the safety of ecosystem and includes mainly algae, bacteria, fungi, protozoa, aquatic invertebrates and fishes. Fishes are by far one of the most recognized bioindicator of environmental health representing the status of polluting, improving or degrading aquatic ecosystem. Fishes serve as an excellent model for the assessment of pollution and play significant roles in evaluating potential risk associated with pollutants in aquatic environment. Fish constantly reside in the water and amalgamate the chemical, physical, and biological properties of the water in long run due to their longer life span. Stressors like fluctuations in seasonal temperature, thermal effluents, industrial waste discharge or physical habitat modifications are expressed in the fishes at molecular and biochemical levels. Biomarkers data are generated due to exposure to environmental stressors are usually expressed at the suborganismal level of biological organisation which includes: genetical, physio-biochemical, haemato- immunological and histopathological alterations. Biological indicator studies have shown marked improvements in the health of fishes during last decades as they play pivotal role in prioritizing stressors and deciding control measures. Over all, bioindicators are an excellent tool for monitoring the health of biological populations and ultimately assessing the potential hazards of environmental contaminant on human health. This would further help to formulate appropriate management plan for evaluating the effectiveness of remedial actions for restoration of degraded habitat.

Keywords: Bioindicator, fish, aquatic, environment, stressors, monitoring.

INTRODUCTION

Biological indicators are species used to assess the healthiness of an environment or ecosystem, and termed as bioindicator or biomarkers or biomonitoring or biodetector species. Indicator organisms which are ideal for biomonitoring programme are also called as sentinel organisms. They are any biological group of species whose function, population, or status can be used to determine ecosystem or environmental integrity. The term "Bioindicator species" was coined by Kolkwitz in 1908 regarding the impact of organic pollution (i.e. sewage) on aquatic organisms (Rosenburg & Resh 1996). Presences of biological indicator species give first hand information on the fitness of a specific ecosystem such as reservoirs, river, beels, stream, lake, wetland and estuary. Bioindicators are assessed with their presence or absence, health condition, survivality and abundance, maturity status, community composition and diversity, trophic structure or any combination existing thereof (Hellawell 1986, Landres et al. 1988). Organisms co-existing and interacting with one another in a specific ecosystem are generally considered as the most reliabe indicators for conservation biology since inferences can be drawn at the ecosystem level, individual species level or population level (Kovacs et al. 1992).

In the rapidly changing environmental condition, it is not only difficult but also very expensive to monitor frequently the health of the ecosystem for data recording purpose. Recording water quality parameters at regular interval provides information on conditions at that point of time only (Spellerburg 1991, Resh et al. 1996). Measurements of abiotic (i.e. aquatic pollution) or biotic (i.e. introduced species) variables are imperative since it provides insight into ecological effects, while considering the synergistic effects of multiple factors. Lack of complete understanding of synergistic interactions is the biggest hurdle (Paoletti 1999, Hilty & Merenlender 2000, US EPA 2002a). Measuring abiotic parameters may provide incomplete or inaccurate information on the state of an ecosystem. Therefore, monitoring of bioindicator species helps in setting-up guidelines for safety and security of aquatic environment.

Bioindicators are an excellent tool for monitoring the health of biological populations, assessing the potential hazards of environmental pollution to human health and determining if industry is complying with regulations, and evaluating the effectiveness of remedial actions. The fate of the human working in coal mines served as a bioindicator of pollutant toxicity that could threaten human health and possibly cause death, therefore newly opened part of the mine would test the toxicity level of gases. Genotoxic and mutagenic potential of the river contamination may cause a serious distress to aquatic organisms, especially to fish, and ultimately to human beings. Hence, bioindicators have to play an important role in prioritizing stressors and deciding control measures besides assessing the effectiveness of remedial measure. Bioindicators are used to evaluate the potential efficacy of management actions for restoration of degraded habitat which would further help in protecting the important wildlife species, such as fish species (trouts, carps, bluegill, catfish, and striped bass) and other macro invertebrates living in or near these waterways. In total, the levels of pollutants like pesticides, heavy metals and radionuclides can be measured in animals due to bioaccumulation or biomagnifications. This chapter attempts to summaries the different types of biological indicator of aquatic environment with special emphasis to fish.

TYPES OF BIOLOGICAL INDICATORS

Habitat Indicator Species

Habitats are based primarily on natural communities which are composed of combinations of communities and provide useful information about the quality of their physical condition, thereby effectively functions as biological litmus paper (Hellawell 1986). Riparian and stream habitat are the two types of habitat indicator. Former represents width, continuity, extent of shading and species composition whie later represents the measures of the extent of scouring and bank erosion and the presence of woody debris (fallen trees, etc) that provide important habitat for many species.

Population Indicator Species

Based on the sensitivity of species to the particular eco-climatic condition, population indicator species are selected and differentiated from the population of similar species on the basis of environmental circumstance (Landres et al. 1988, Caro & O'Doherty 1999). Species inhabitating in the particulatar environment express their responses to alterartions and mechanisms of population control. Sensitivity of the species to disease resistance and their declination may increase the number of other species due to free access to limited resources (Landres et al. 1988, Caro & O'Doherty 1999). Researchers have shown to exist the correlation between the indicator species and its guild member except prey and predators relationship (Mannan et al. 1984, Szaro et al. 1986).

Biodiversity Indicator Species

Biodiversity is the diversity of individual species, the genetic diversity within species and the variety of ecosystems that support them. The biodiversity indicators are used to monitor the progress of ecosystem in order to reduce the loss of biodiversity. Therefore, convention of biological diversity (CBD) and its associates organisations are working strongly with biodiversity indicators partnership (BIP) to construct an over-arching anecdote of global biodiversity. Biodiversity indicators have been used to infer lower taxon (i.e. species) richness by surveying higher taxonomic levels (i.e. family) (Oliver & Beattie 1993, Gaston 2000). The presence of threatened or endangered species at areas of high biodiversity does not corresponds either to species at risk (Bonn et al. 2002) or poor indicators of rare or endemic species (Reyers et al. 2000). The necessity for various taxa and substantiation within each region removes the initial perceptive appeal of bioindicators as a quick and easy answer for assessing biodiversity. To ensure the validity and accuracy of the indicator taxon, it is essential to identify and select habitat or population which is resource intensive.

Aquatic Invertebrates as Bioindicators

Aquatic invertebrates are small creatures, such as insects, crustaceans, mollusks and worms which thrive well in surrounding water among the logs, rocks and gravel. Most of the aquatic invertebrate commences their life cycle in the water. Aquatic invertebrates are useful as water quality indicator as they are easy to collect and identify without involvement of trained personnel and specific equipment. Fishes require sufficient dissolved oxygen from the water but sometimes depletion in the dissolved oxygen of water compels them for surface movement to gulp atmospheric oxygen. On the contrary, some aquatic invertebrates generally cannot move around very much like fish, and respond quickly to transforming environment, thus invertebrates are generally regarded as better bioindicator than vertebrates (Pearson & Cassola 1992, Weaver 1995). Long lived invertebrates found attached to the rocky bottom are frequently used to recognize the location of a particular environmental stress. During seasonal variation, substrate availability, patchy distribution and dispersal, it becomes difficult to collect the specimen for recording and examination purposes (Hellawell 1986). Aquatic macro- invertebrates are the most frequently used taxa for monitoring habitat quality (Hellawell 1986), with a well developed body of information for lotic systems (Birge et al. 2000, Giggleman & Bocanegra 2000, Braukmann 2001). The benthic invertebrates are one of the most important elements of the continental water ecosystems and used as indicator of water pollution, as it reacts quickly to minor environmental changes.

Odonates as Bioindicators

Odonates are portrayed as excellent habitat indicators of present and past (long-term) environmental conditions in aquatic habitats (Samways & Stetler 1996,

Stewart & Samways 1998). Odonates exhibit biphasic life cycle dweling both in terrestrial and aquatic habitats therefore reflect disturbance to the riparian buffer than other strict wetland obligates. Odonates have been utilized as habitat indicators rarely in lotic systems(Samways & Stetler 1996, Stewart & Samways 1998), but regularly in lentic systems (Choanec & Raab 1997).

Characteristics of Ideal Indicator

- Extensive distribution
- Numerically abundant
- Provide continuous assessment over a wide range and intensity of stresses such as pollution, climate change, disease and competition
- Taxonomically easy to identify
- Known ecological requirements
- Indicates early warning of natural responses to environmental impacts
- Point out the source of change rather than simply the existence of change
- Inexpensive to assess even by the non professionals involved in the monitoring (Kriesel, 1984; Davis, 1989; di Castri et al., 1992).

Organisms used as Biological indicators of environmental pollution include:

- Algae
- Bacteria
- Fungi
- Protozoa
- Fish

Algae

Algae constitute an integral component of biological monitoring programmes to evaualte the quality of water. During the summer time excessive increase in the population of colonial blue green algae takes place on the surface of water bodies in the form of algal mats termed as algal blooms. Formation of algal bloom has been particularly useful as an indicator of high nutrient status, which is a key component of various trophic indices. On the other hand, increase in populations of unicellular blue-green algae represents the oligotrophic to mesotrophic conditions. Desmids are attractive green algae, found in freshwater bodies and are excellent indicators for water quality. In the marine environment, various photosynthetic algae particularly seaweeds have been used as bioindicators to monitor the pollutants. Ubiquitous and global distribution of marine algae along the seashore could be used for monitoring the health of ecosystem in a time bound response. Both micro and macro alga are important tools to monitor the physiological changes of the organisms due to exposure of various toxicant such as pesticide and heavy metal.

Serum cortisol level is widely used as a primary stress response to exposure of pollutants, handling and space restriction such as confinement, air exposure and crowding (Tejpal et al., 2008). Elevated cortisol levels upon different environmental stressors in teleost fishes were reported by many workers (Brown et al., 1984; Bleau et al., 1996). Basal circulating cortisol levels show diurnal and seasonal fluctuations and interspecific differences and therefore the normal ranges are highly variable in aquatic vertebrates including fish. Complement reactive protein (CRP) acts as secondary stress response parameter and considered as reliable biomarker for aquatic toxicity studies (Dincel et al., 2009). Toxic agents increase the non antibody proteins, namely CRP levels, in fish as a first line defense towards environmental pollutants. This increased presence of CRP in the acute phase response of invertebrate and some fish suggests that they may have an important role in overall host mechanism to toxicity exposure, directing attention to the apparently reciprocating relationship between immune and chemical detoxifying systems (Paul et al.,1998; Sinha et al., 2001).

Histopathological Biomarkers

Histopathological alterations or cellular changes in tissues and organs of fishes represent a useful tool to assess the degree of pollution, particularly for lethal effects. Pathological changes in fish are powerful indicator of exposure to environmental contaminant. Results of the histological analysis are prominently displayed in the gills and liver tissues. Gill is the unique organ which plays a very important physiological function in case of fish and major route for the entry of different substances because of the intimate and continuous contacts with the water. Thus gills are directly or indirectly affected by various types of toxic substances (Ramachandra Mohan, 2003) exposure. Gill tissue of fish exposed to contaminant exhibits moderate congestion of primary lamellae, excessive mucous secretion, erosion of secondary gill lamellae, destruction of denticular structures, loss of uniformity of gill rackers, breakage of epithelial layer as well as fusion and clumping of gill lamellae.

Histo-architechural changes in fish liver are useful biomarkers to indicate exposure to environmental toxicants. Changes that have been noticed in the liver, the first organ to be exposed by the portal circulation after enteric uptake of pesticide by Wester (1988), were enlargement of hepatocytes with vacuualation.

Macrophage aggregates are excellent indicators of exposure to sediments contaminated with organics or low dissolved oxygen (Myers and Fournie 2002) in fishes collected from contaminated sites (Fournie et al., 2001). Macrophage aggregates are focal accumulations of macrophages found in the spleen, head kidney, liver, and sometimes testes.

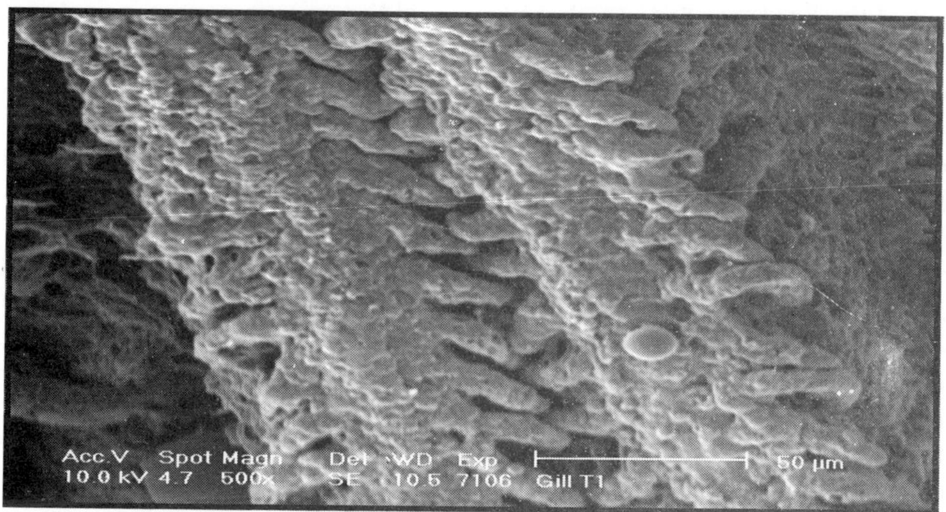

Fig. 1.1: Scanning Electron Microscope (SEM) Photpgraph of Gill Tissue of Common Carp Fry Exposed to Sublethal Toxicity of Pesticide. Damaged Gill Lamellae, Loss of Uniformity of Gill Racker. Breakage of Epithelial Layer, Fusion of Gill Lamellae as well as Clumping of Gill Lamellae was Discernible

FEW COMMONLY USED FISH SPECIES AS THE BIOINDICATOR

Rainbow and Brown Trout

Rainbow and brown trout are the two important species which dwells in the clean and fast flowing waterways having high content (>8 ppm) of dissolved oxygen and are free from any pollutant and suspended matter. Both species are very sensitive to fluctuating temperature and severely affected when water heats up and considered as more tolerant of higher temperatures than many of its relatives. Metallothionein (MT) have been evaluated as a good bioindicator of heavy metal pollution in brown trout (*Salmo trutaa fario*) (Linde et al., 2001) whereas rainbow trout (*Oncorynchus mykiss*) have been used as model organism to study the behavioral dysfunctions due to exposure of cholinesterase-inhibiting chemicals. Marked proliferative, degenerative and inflammatory lesions of gills, liver and kidney were observed due to influence of the sewage waste water in both species. Prominent degenerative and inflammatory reactions in the liver of trout exposed to sewage water have been noticed in rainbow trout. The physiological oxidative stress biomarkers in rainbow trout from selenium-impacted streams in a coal mining region revealed that rainbow trout appear to be very sensitive to Selenium.

vulnerable to such conditions and can be considered as an important indicator of environmental stressors (Kumar et al. 2013). Chemical like pesticeds and heavy metals get entry into the body of fish through ingestion or direct contact with skin, scales or mucus and thus responsible for stressful conditions even at sub lethal concentration (Elia et al. 2002; Wan et al. 2005). Various species of fish have been reported to have deleterious effects when exposed to pesticides (Khangarot et al. 1988; Areechon & Plump 1990).

Stressors like fluctuations in seasonal temperature, thermal effluents, inductrial waste discharge or physical habitat modifications are expressed in the fishes at molecular and biochemical levels. Sublethal stress is generally first manifested at the suborganismal level, where effects can be measured via alteration in cellular components. Deleterious effects of the stressors leads to reduction in the growth, alters physio-iochemcal responses and impairs reproduction. The parameters like haematological alterations and variations in different enzyme activities of fishes can be used as good biomarkers of pollution in the water bodies. Biomarkers are functional measures of exposure to environmental stressors, which are usually expressed at the suborganismal level of biological organisation (Adams, 2002).

The level of change is measurable and often related to the severity of the exposure. Evidence of biological exposures has been defined by the USEPA (1991) as those endpoints that measure the apparent effects of stressors, including chemical water quality criteria and tissue residues. Since there are multiple stressors acting simultaneously and animal responses to mixtures of stressors are often different from those by individual chemicals (de Souza-Bueno et al., 2000). It is not possible to measure the impact by chemical stressors individually or the mixtures, without biological and physical stressor impacts. Addionally, biomarkers that are sensitive and specific only to the particular stressors/chemicals are unusual (Sorensen et al.,2003). Consequently, the biomarker choice strategy was directed across various levels of biological organisation in the fishes.

Biomarker data generated on these biological levels of organisation includes: Genetic, physio-biochemical, haemato- immunological and histopathological.

Genetic biomarkers: Developtment of micronucleus (MN) test and Alkaline Comet assay has received considerable attention in the view of its importance of coastal fisheries biomonitroirng programmes around the world in order to assess the genotoxicity caused due to multiple sources of pollution and are reflected in the peripheral blood cells of fishes. Alterations or fragmentations in genomic DNA due to water borne contaminants are the most commonly used biomarker for genetic and toxicological studies. Adverse affects of the pollutants leads to enhanced frequency of chromosomal aberrations or the alteration of the primary structure of DNA (DNA damage) or the change in the base sequence (mutation) (Potters et al., 2002) In severe cases, alteration at germ cell level becomes heritable due to exposure of mutagens or carcinogens. It has proved that a strong correlation exists between DNA damage and the development of cancer, infertility and poor sperm quality (Whittier & McBee 1999; Choi & Meier 2000; Gielazyn et al., 2003)

Physio-biochemical Parameters Used as Biomarkers

Sublethal exposure of pollutants produces considerable alterations in the biochemical responses, resulting into delayed adverse health effects and ultimately death of fishes. Acetylcholine esterase (AChE) is one of the most widely used enzyme as a biomarker for environment pollution studies. In general, fish can tolerate about 70-80% inhibition of AChE activity before death as reported by Sarma (2003), but Devraj et al. (1991) showed 80% inhibition of AChE activity in *Oreochromis mossambicus* without recording mortality; however both observed same behavioral changes like sluggish movement, loss of balance etc.

Significant increase of Aspartate amino tansferase (AST) activity in liver and muscle tissues of fishes indicates stress conditions in general and induce elevation in transamination pathway (Awasthi et al., 1984). Involvement of alternate pathways like aminotransferase reactions are also possible due to inhibition of oxidative enzymes like MDH, a situation also demonstrated by Ghosh (1989). Alkaline phosphates (ALP) a zinc-containing metallo-enzyme, plays an important role in phosphorus metabolism and malate dehydrogenase (MDH), an enzyme of TCA cycle are inhibited due to exposure to pollutants (54 and mine). The increase in antioxidant enzymes like Catalase and super oxide dismutase (SOD) in the liver of fish demonstrates that liver has an important role in the detoxification of pollutants.

Haemato-immunological Parameters Used as Biomarkers

Blood cells are the mediators of defense mechanisms in animals, and WBCs are key components of innate immune defense (Jenkins and Ourth, 1993) where defense responses are measurable and influenced by stressors (Adams, 2002). Increase of WBC count in pollutant exposed fishes indicates the hypersensitivity of WBC which may be due to immunological reactions to produce antibodies to cope up with stress. Increase in WBCs count can be correlated with an increase in antibody production which helps in survival and recovery of animals exposed to pesticides (Joshi & Smith, 2002). Decrease in the haemoglobin contents may be resulted from rapid oxidation of haemoglobin to methaemoglobin or release of O_2^- radical due to the toxic stress of contaminant. Changes in blood glucose have been suggested as sensitive indicator of stress in teleost (Nemcsok & Boross 1982). Increase in the blood glucose level in the fishes might be resulted from gluconeogenesis to provide energy for the increased metabolic demands imposed by stressors. Decreased serum protein level may be attributed to stress mediated mobilization to accomplish an increased energy demand by the fish to cope up with stress (Jenkins et al., 2003). However, Neff (1985) has suggested that decline in protein content may be related to impaired food intake, increased energy cost of homeostasis, tissue repair and detoxification mechanism during stress.

Bacteria

Bacteria are very sensitive to even slight fluctuations in environmental condition and are promising early indicator of envinmamental degradation and some of their attributes make them excellent tools for monitoring the early signs of degradation as they show great deal of temporal and spatial variation. Bacteria have ability to tolerate high concentration of heavy metals and capacity to survive well in diverse condition and therefore considered as bioindicators for metal contamination. Based on the environmental attributes like pH, temperature and dissolved oxygen, bacteria are the most preferred species of bioindicator than the algae and fungi which has not been utilized until now. Aerobic bacterial is a potentially valuable for detecting the early signs of degradation in wetland ecosystem.

Fungi

The hyphae and mycorrhizae of fungi easily reflect changes in the environment due to their proloferaration ability in the soil and vegetation. Fungi may be used as sensitive bioindicator to assess the effects of SO_2, O_3 and CO_2 in terrestrial ecosystems. Based on the report available, macro fungi have adaptative mechanisms to sustain heavy metal toxicity and therefore used as bio-marker of heavy metal pollution. Fungal growth mainly of *Penicillium* and *Aspergillus* with concomitant release of conidia and fragments into the atmosphere represents the air pollution. Mycorrhizal roots of the fungi exhibit ectotrophic symbiosis and is a very sensitive bioindicator of air pollution. Evaluation of membrane-bound sterol ergosterol present in the fungi holds significant promise as quantitative indicator of fungal response to water quality.

Protozoa

Protozoa are heterotrophic organisms and an essential component of marine, freshwater and soil ecosystems which enhance nutrient cycles and energy flow for the benefit of microorganisms, plants and animals. Mostly, protozoa are not replaceable by higher animals as indicator organisms as they have unique physiological properties, consume more food, have shorter generation and life times and reproduce much faster. Ciliate (Protozoa) communities have rampant availability and are highly sensitivity to pollutants, which makes them useful as biological indicators of the sediment environment. Additionally, ciliates are widely used as bioindicators for assessing water quality. Ciliates have been used to assess the sediment quality of mangrove sewage belt. Soil protozoa could provide powerful means to evaluate natural environmental changes and to monitor the environmental pollution brought by anthropogenic activities

Fish as Bioindicator Species

Fishes have an important ecological role as they occupy top position of food chain in aquatic environment and are important source of supplying protein rich food, recreation and also source of livelihood security for poor. Fishes are by far one of the most recognized bio-indicator of environmental health which represents the status of polluting, improving or degrading aquatic ecosystem. Depending on the type of species, fishes display a variety of physio-biochemical responses to natural disturbances such as habitat alterations, organic enrichment, pesticides and heavy metal toxicity as well as thermal fluctuations. Pollution tolerance level in fishes varies depending on the type of species, therefore we can characterize water quality on the basis of presence or absence of pollution-tolerant or pollution-intolerant species hence, they are vital components of any bio-monitoring programme. Similarly, fish constantly reside in the water and amalgamate the chemical, physical, and biological properties of the waters in long run due to their longer life span.

Table 1.1: Advantages and Disadvantages of Fish as Bio-indicators

Advantages	Disadvantages
Ample and extensive database on fish behaviour, occurrences, habits and habitate are available.	Specific sampling methods with fastidious gears (elecrtric fishing trawling, dipnets etc.) are employed to catch particular fishes, which leads to sampling biasness.
Fishes are omnipresent occur in a wide variety of ecosystem.	Migratory behaviors of some species provide misleading data.
Some species exhibit long life span to show short and long term impacts.	Atleast 2-3 persons are required to effectively sample fish with sampling equipments.
Some fishes possess ability to survive in the fluctuating environmental condition. Eg. Common carp	Some fishes are very sensitive to altering environmental condition. Eg. Coral reef fishes.
Well-known species are easily identified	Requires fish taxonomist for correct identification of particular species.

Many researchers have considered various biological measures to assess the quality of surface water in their biomonitoring programme (Adams, 2002). Since each life stage of fishes remain in close association with the sediments and environmental media and their physiological response integrates with several biological response mechanisms and therefore portrays the biological and ecological condition of aquatic systems. As a comparative animal model, a large amount of informations have been generated using different species of fishes in aquatic toxicology and in environmental monitoring studies during the last two decades and further facilitated in formulating appropriate management action plan in order to control the degrading environmental environment.

Use of chemical stressors are increasing day by day which can have adverse impact on aquatic ecosystem. Chemicals employed in the agricultural practices, find their way into freshwater bodies (Bhatnagar et al. 1992) and affect various non target organisms including fishes even at sublethal concentrations (Prusty et al. 2011). Fishes are one of the most important groups of aquatic organisms, which are

Rainbow Trout ***(Orcorhynchus mykiss)***

Brown Trout ***(Salmo trutta fario)***

Brook Trout.*(Salvelinus fontinalis)*

Brook trout (*Salvelinus fontinalis*) are the only trout that are native to Eastern United States, therefore also called as eastern brook trout. Since brook trouts require cold, clean and silt free bottom, they serve as indicators of the health of the aquatic environment they inhabit and display that stream or river ecosystem is healthy and water quality is excellent if their population is high. When habit/habitat is damaged due to urbanization or anthropogenic activities, brook trout are one of the first to decline in their population. A decline in populations can serve as an early caution that the health of an entire aquatic system is at risk. The brook trout is more sensitive to changing environmental conditions and higher temperatures than the rainbow and brown trout. Severe damages in the gill, liver and kidney tissue of brook trout have been noticed due to exposure of pollutant like pesticide and ammonia present in the stream water. Brook trout have evolved to be the most tolerant of the trout species to acidic conditions, and adult fish can tolerate pH levels as low as 5.0. and all the brook trout population would perished away i f the pH falls down below 5.0. Brook trout require relatively high concentrations of dissolved oxygen in water compared to other fish and even other trout species.

Common Carp

Among the different species of fish cultured throughout the world, Common carp (*Cyprinus carpio*) is the most extensively cultured species owing to its tolerance to diseases, superior growth, prolific breeding and capability to sustain wide fluctuations in environmental conditions such as low dissolved oxygen levels, thermal stress, turbidity and pollution. Several state and regional tolerance classifications rank the carp as a "tolerant" species. Common carp has been used as potential biomarkers of metals contamination, DNA damage, Cytochrome P450 induction, vitellogenesis, alteration in haematological, histological, serum glucose, serum cortisol and different enzymatic parameters in various selected organ. Significant reduction of larval body total length in the common carp has been reported as sensitive indicator of the diazinon exposure.

Common carp (*Cyprinus carpio*) has been used as indicator of hypoxia condition when exposed to 1 - 2 ppm dissolved oxygen for 1 week and showed a significant reduction in feeding rate, respiration rate, faecal production and nitrogenous excretion. Both specific growth rate and RNA/DNA ratio were significantly reduced when common carp were exposed to severe hypoxia (0.5 ppm) for 4 weeks (Zhou et al., 2001). Deltamethrin pollution may have an adverse effect on embryos and larvae of common carp which should be considered as biomarkers when this chemical is employed in agricultural areas near aquatic ecosystems.

Air Breathing Fish

Several species of air breathing fishes have been in vogue to assess the impact of various pollutant on the health of different aquatic ecosystem. Airbreathing catfishes are hardy in nature and inhabit well in swampy or muddy condition, generally deficient in dissolved oxygen. Cat fishes (*Clarias batarachus, Heteropneustes fossilis*) respire atmospheric oxygen through specialized accessory respiratory organ. Effect of heavy metal toxicity in the *Clarias batarachus* has been evaluated which alters the physio-biochemical responses and affect the growth rate and reproduction resulting in disturbance to whole community and tropic levels of food .chains, ultimately the ecosystem. Histopathological changes induced by the acute toxicity of mercuric chloride on the epidermis and on the mucocytes of a fresh water catfish- *Heteropneustes fossilis* have been evaluated by (Rajan et al., 1991). Similarly, histopathological analysis due to toxic affect of zinc chloride on the respiratory organs of *Heteropneustes fossilis* and air breathing murrel, *Channa striata* has been reported as indicator of the heavy metal pollution (Hemlatha and Banerjee 1997 a & b; Chandra and Banerjee 2003).

CONCLUSION

Biological indicator presents early cautioning indications of potential health effects of contaminants of aquatic ecosystem. Fish serve as useful model for the assessment of pollution in aquatic ecosystems and further play significant roles in

Resh, V.H. Meyers, M.M. Hannaford, M.J. (1996): Macroinvertebrates as Biotic Indicators of Environmental Quality. In, Methods in Stream Ecology, Hauer, F.R. Lamberti, G.A. (eds). *Academic Press, San Diego, CA*. pp. 674.

Reyers, B. van Jaarsveld, A.S. Kruger, M. (2000): Complementarity as a Biodiversity Indicator Strategy. Proceedings of the Royal Society of London, Series B: *Biological Sciences,* 267(1442): 505-513.

Rosenburg, D.M. Resh, V.H. (1996): Use of Aquatic Insects in Biomonitoring. In, An Introduction to the Aquatic Insects of North America (3rd ed.). Merritt, R.W. Cummins, K.W. (eds). Kendall/Hunt Publishing Company, Dubuque, IA. pp. 862.

Samways, M.J. Stetler, N.S. (1996): Dragonfly (Odonata) Distribution Patterns in Urban and Forested Landscapes, and Recommendations for Riparian Management. *Biological Conservation,* 78(3): 279-288.

Sarma, K. (2003): Biochemical Responses of *Channa punctatus* to Endosulfan and its Implication in Environmental Monitoring, Ph.D., Dissertation, Central Institute of Fisheries Education, Mumbai, India.

Sinha, S. Mandal, C. Allen, A.K. Mandal, C. (2001): Acute Phase Response of C-reactive Protein of *Labeo rohita* to Aquatic Pollutants is Accompanied by the Appearance of Distinct Molecular Forms. *Archives of Biochemistry and Biophysics*, 396: 139-150.

Sorensen, M. Autrup, H. Moller, P. Hertel, O. Jensen, S.S. Vinsents, P. Knudsen, L.E. Loft, S. (2003): Linking Exposure to Environmental Pollutants with Biological Effects. *Mutation Research,* 544: 255-271.

Spellerburg, I.F. (1991): Monitoring Ecological Change. *Cambridge University Press, Cambridge, UK.* pp. 334.

Stewart, D.A.B. Samways, M.J. (1998): Conserving Dragonfly (Odoanta) Assemblages Relative to River Dynamics in an African Savanna Game Reserve. *Conservation Biology,* 12(3): 683-692.

Szaro, R.C. (1986): Guild Management: An Evaluation of Avian Guilds as a Predictive Tool. *Environmental Management,* 10: 681-688.

Tejpal, C.S. Pal, A.K. Sahu, N.P. Kumar, J.A. Muthappa, N.A. Vidya, S. Rajan, M.G. (2008): Dietary Supplementation of L-tryptophan Mitigates Crowding Stress and Augments the Growth in *Cirrhinus mrigala* Fingerlings. *Aquaculture,* 293(3-4): 272-277.

U.S. Environmental Protection Agency (EPA), (2002a): Methods for Evaluating Wetland Condition. Office of Water, U.S. Environmental Protection Agency, Washington, DC. EPA-822-R-01-014.

U.S. Environmental Protection Agency (EPA), (1991): Environmental Monitoring and Assessment Programme, EMAP-surface Waters Monitoring and Research Strategy – Fiscal Year 1991.

Van Der Oost, R. Beyer, J. Vermeulen, NPE. (2003): Fish Bioaccumulation and Biomarkers in Environmental Risk Assessment: A Review. *Environ Toxicol Pharm,* 13: 57-149.

Wan, MT. Kuo, JN. Pasternak, J. (2005): Residues of Endosulfan and Other Selected Organochlorine Pesticides in Farm Areas of the Lower Fraser Valley, British Columbia. *Canada J Environ Qual,* 34: 1186-1193.

Weaver, J.C. (1995): Indicator Species and Scale of Observation. *Conservation Biology,* 9: 939-942.

Whittier, J.B. McBee, K. (1999): Use of Flow Cytometry to Detect Genetic Damage in Mallards Dosed with Mutagens, *Environmental Toxicology and Chemistry*, 18: 1557-1563.

Zhou, B.S. Wu, R.S.S. Randall, D.J. Lam, P.K.S. (2001): Bioenergetics and RNA/DNA Ratios in the Common Carp (*Cyprinus carpio*) Under Hypoxia. *Journal of Comparative Physiology B,* 171(1): 49-57.

Ghosh, TK. (1989): Influence of Cypermethrin on the Oxidative Metabolism of Fish *Labeo rohita. Proc Ind Natl Sci Acad* B 55:115-120.

Giggleman, C.M. Bocanegra, O.R. (2000): The Impact of Petroleum Hydrocarbon and Brine Contaminants to Macroinvertebrate Communities Inhabiting Lotic Systems at Hagerman National Wildlife Refuge, Grayson County, Texas 1999. pp. 23.

Gielazyn, M.L. Ringwood, A.H. Piegorsch, W.W. Stancyk, S.E. (2003): Detection of Oxidative DNA Damage in Isolated Marine Bivalve Hemocytes Using the Comet Assay and 44 formamidopyrimidine Glycosylase (Fpg): *Mutation Research-Genetic Toxicology and Environmental Mutagenesis*, 542: 15-22.

Hellawell, J.M. (1986): Biological Indicators of Freshwater Pollution and Environmental Management. In, Pollution Monitoring Series, K. Mellanby (ed). *Elsevier Applied Science Publishers, London, UK.* pp: 546.

Hemlatha, S. Banerjee, T. K. (1997a): Histopathological Analysis of Sublethal Toxicity of Zinc Chloride to the Respiratory Organs of the Air-breathing Catfish *Heteropneustes fossilis* (Bloch). *Biol. Res,* 30: 11-21.

Hemlatha, S. Banerjee, T. K. (1997b): Histopathological Analysis of Acute Toxicity of Zinc Chloride to the Respiratory Organs of the Air-breathing Catfish *Heteropneustes fossilis* (Bloch). *Vet. Arhiv,* 67: 11-24.

Hilty, J. Merenlender, A. (2000): Faunal Indicator Taxa Selection for Monitoring Ecosystem Health. *Biological Conservation,* 92: 185-197.

Jenkins, J.A. Ourth, D.D. (1993): Opsonic Effect of the Alternative Complement Pathway on Channel Catfish Peripheral Blood Phagocytes. *Veterinary Immunology and Immunopathology*, 39: 447-459.

Jenkins, F. Smith, J. Rajanna, B. Shameem, U. Umadevi, K. Sanhya, V. Madhavi, R. (2003): Effect of Sublethal Concentration of Endosulfan on Hematological and Serum Biochemical Parameters in the Carp, *Cyprinus carpio. Bulletin of Environmental Contamination and Toxicology*, 70(5): 993-997.

Joshi, P. Deep, H. Smith, J. (2002): Effect of Lindane and Malathion Exposure to Certain Blood Parameters in a Freshwater Teleost Fish *Clarias batarachus. Pollution Research*, *21*: 55-57.

Kenan Koprucu, Rahmi Aydin (2004): The Toxic Effects of Pyrethroid Deltamethrin on the Common Carp (*Cyprinus carpio* L.) Embryos and Larvae. *Pesticide Biochemistry and Physiology*, 80 (1): 47-53.

Khangarot, B.S. Ray, P.K. Singh, K.P. (1988): Influence of Copper Treatment on the Immune Response in an Air Breathing Teleost *Saccobranchus fossilis. Bull Environ Contam Toxicol,* 41: 222-226.

Kovacs, M. Podani, J. Tuba, Z. Turcsanyi, G. Csintalan, Z. Meenks, J.L.D. (1992): Biological Indicators in Environmental Protection. Ellis Horwood, London, UK. pp. 207.

Kriesel, W. (1984): Representation of the Environmental Quality Profile of a Metropolitan Area. *Environ. Monit. Assess.* 4: 15-33.

Kumar, A. Prasad MR. Srivastava, K. Srivastav, SK. Suzuki, N. Srivastav, AK (2013): Cyto-histopathological Alterations in the Liver of Azadirachtin Treated Catfish, *Heteropneustes fossilis. Proc Nat Acad Sci India Sect B Biol Sci doi,* 10.1007/s 40011-013-0169-7.

Landres, P.B. Verner, J. Thomas, J.W. (1988): Ecological Uses of Vertebrate Indicator Species: A Critique. *Conservation Biology*, 2: 316-328.

Linde, AR. Sanchez-Galan, S. Valles-Mota, P. Garcia-Vazquez, E. (2001): Metallothionein as Bioindicator of Freshwater Metal Pollution: European eel and Brown Trout. *Ecotoxicology and Environmental Safety,* 49(1): 60-63.

Lopez-Barea J (1996): Biomarkers to Detect Environmental Pollution. *Toxicol Lett,* 88: 77-7.

Mannan, R.W. Morrison, M.I. Meslow, E.C. (1984): The Use of Guilds in Forest Bird Management. *Wildlife Society Bulletin,* 12: 426-430.

Myers, M.S. Fournie, J.W. (2002): Histopathological Biomarkers as Integrators of Anthropogenic and Environmental Stressors, *in* Adams, S. M., ed., Biological Indicators of Aquatic Ecosystem Stress, American Fisheries Society, Bethesda, Maryland, 221-288.

Neff, J.M. (1985): Use of Biochemical Measurement to Detect Pollutant-mediated Damage to Fish, *In.* R.D. Cardwel, R. Purdy, R.C. Bahner. Philadelphia (Eds.) Aquatic Toxicology and Hazard Assessment, American Society for Testing Materials. pp. 155-181.

Nemcsok, J. Boross, L. (1982): Comparative Studies on Sensitivity of Different Fish Species to Metal Pollution. *Acta Biologica Academiae Scientiarum Hungaricae, 33*(1): 23-27.

Oliver, I. Beattie, A.J. (1993): A Possible Method for the Rapid Assessment of Biodiversity. *Conservation Biology,* 7(3): 562-568.

Paoletti, M.G. (1999): Using Bioindicators Based on Biodiversity to Assess Landscape Suitability. *Agriculture, Ecosystems and Environment,* 74: 1-18.

Paul, I. Mandal, C. Mandal, C. (1998): Effect of Environmental Pollutants on the C-reactive Protein of a Freshwater Major Carp *Catla catla. Developmental and Comparative Immunology*, 22(5-6): 519-32.

Pearson, D.L. Cassola, F. (1992): World-wide Species Richness Patterns of Tiger Beetles (Coleoptera: Cincindelidae): Indicator Taxon for Biodiversity and Conservation Studies. *Conservation Biology*, 6(3): 376-391.

Potter, A.J. Gollahon, K.A. Palanca, B.J.A. Harbert, M.J. Choi, Y.M. Moskovitz, A.H. Potter, J.D. Rabinovitch, P.S. (2002): Flow Cytometric Analysis of the Cell Cycle Phase and Pecificity of DNA Damage Induced by Radiation, Hydrogen Peroxide and Doxorubicin: *Carcinogenesis,* 23: 389-401.

Prusty, A.K. Kohli, M.P.S. Sahu, N.P. Pal, A.K. Saharan, N. Mohapatra, S. Gupta, S.K. (2011): Effect of Short Term Exposure of Fenvalerate on Biochemical and Haematological Responses in *Labeo rohita* (Hamilton) Fingerlings. *Pesticide Biochemistry and Physiology*, 100: 124-129.

Rajan, M.T. Banerjee, T.K. (1991): Histopathological Changes Induced by the Acute Toxicity of Mercuric Chloride on the Epidermis of a Fresh Water Catfish- *Heteropneustes fossilis* (Bloch). *Ecotoxicol. Environ. Safety,* 22: 139-152.

Rajan, M.T. Banerjee T. K. (1994): Effect of Mercuric Chloride on the Mucocytes of the Air sac and Skin of the Air-breathing Catfish, *Heteropneustes fossilis. J. Freshwater Biol,* 6: 253-258.

Ramachandra. M.M. (2003): A Composite Approach for Evaluation of the Effect of Malathion on Gobid Fish *Glossogobius giuris* (ham). *Poll. Res*, 19(1): 45-47.

evaluating potential risk associated with pollutants in aquatic environment since they are directly exposed to chemicals, carcinogen and mutagen resulting from surface run off of agricultural land or indirectly through the food chain of the ecosystem (Cavas and Ergene- Gozukara 2005).The chemical substances bring deleterious effect, resulting in to their endocrine, reproductive, and metabolic dysfunction, alteration in histo-architechture, hormone levels, haematological and nutritional imbalances, DNA damage and cancerous lesions in non target aquatic organism in general and fishes in particular. Biological indicator studies have shown marked improvements in the health of fish populations in the stream at several levels of biological organisation and as a result a number of pollution-sensitive species of fish are now beginning to flourish.

Future Direction

Further research with toxicity testing methods in same or other species of fish would give more comprehensive picture which would be of great importance in monitoring possible ecotoxicological risk assessments of contaminants. However, further studies are required to investigate the biological consequences of DNA damage in aquatic organisms due to detrimental effects of polluted water of river and also to plan appropriate management approaches for safety and security of aquatic animals and also to determine what to monitor and how to interpret. Bioindicators and pollutant data generated would be helpful for human health and ecological risk assessments to guide the regulators in determining the extent of environmental restoration required as well as their effectiveness for restoration programme.

REFERENCES

Adams, S.M. (2002): Biological Indicators of Aquatic Ecosystem Stress: Bethesda, MD. *American Fisheries Society*. pp. 644.

Areechon, N. Plump, J.A. (1990): Sub Lethal Effects of Malathion on Channel Cat Fish, *Ictalaurus punctatus*. *Bull Environ Contam Toxicol*, 44: 435-442.

Awasthi, M. Shah, P. Dubale, M.S. Gadhia, P. (1984): Metabolic Changes Induced by Organophosphates in the Piscine Organs. *Environ Res*, 35(1):320-325.

Bhatnagar, M.C. Bana, A.K. Tyagi, M. (1992): Respiratory Distress to *Clarias batarachus* (Linn.) Exposed to Endosulfan- A Histological Approach. *Journal of Environmental Biology*, 13: 227-231.

Birge, W.J. Price, D.J. Shaw, J.R. Spromberg, J.A. Wigginton, A.J. Hogstrand, C. Kapustka, L.A. (2000): Metal Body Burden and Biological Sensors as Ecological Indicators. *Environmental Toxicology and Chemistry,* 4: 1199-1212.

Bleau, H. Daniel, C. Chevalier, G. Van-Rra, H. Hontela, A. (1996): Effect of Acute Exposure to Mercury Chloride and Methylmercury on Plasma Cortisol, T_3, T_4, Glucose and Liver Glycogen in Rainbow Trout (*Onchorynchus mykiss*). *Aquatic Toxicology*, *34* (3): 221-235.

Bonn, A. Rodrigues, A.S.L. Gaston, K.J. (2002): Threatened and Endemic Species: are they Good Indicators of Patterns of Biodiversity on a National Scale? *Ecology Letters,* 5: 733-741.

Braukmann, U. (2001): Stream Acidification in South Germany: Chemical and Biological Assessment Methods and Trends. *Aquatic Ecology,* 35(2): 207-232.

Brown, S.B. Eales, J.G. Evans, R.E. Hara, T.J. (1984): Interrenal Thryroidal and Carbohydrate Responses of Rainbow Trout (*Salmo gairdneri*) to Environmental Acidification. *Canadian Journal of Fisheries and Aquatic Sciences, 41*(1): 36-45.

Caro, T.M. Doherty, G. O. (1999): On the Use of Surrogate Species in Conservation Biology. *Conservation Biologyqw,* 13: 805-814.

Cavas T, Ergene-Gözükara, S. (2005): Micronucleus Test in Fish Cells: A Bioassay for in situ Monitoring of Genotoxic Pollution in the Marine Environment. *Environ Mol Mutagen,* 46: 64-70.

Choanec, A. Raab, R. (1997): Dragonflies (Insects, Odonata) and the Ecological Status of Newly Created Wetlands: Examples for Long-term Bioindication Programmes. *Limnologica,* 27(3-4): 381-392.

Chandra, S. Banerjee, T.K. (2003): Toxic Impact of the Inorganic Salt Zinc Chloride on the Skin (An Accessory Water Breathing Organ) of the Air Breathing Murrel, *Channa striata. Res. J. Chem. Environ,* 7: 18-23.

Choi, K. Meier, P.G. (2000): Implications of Chemical-based Effluent Regulations in Assessing DNA Damage in Fathead Minnows (*Pimephales promelas*) when Exposed to Metal Plating Wastewater. *Bulletin of Environmental Contamination and Toxicology,* 64: 716-722.

Davis, G.E. (1989): Design of a Long-term Ecological Monitoring Programme for Channel Islands National Park, California. *Nat. Areas J,* 9: 80-89.

De Souza-Bueno, M.A. de Bragança Pereira, C.A. Rabello-Gay, M.N. (2000): Environmental Genotoxicity Evaluation Using Cytogenic End Points in Wild Rodents, *Environmental Health Perspectives,* 108: 1165-1169.

Devraj, P. Selvarajan, VR. Durairaj, S. (1991): Relationship Between Acetyl Cholinesterase and Monoamine Oxidase in Brain Regions of *O. mossambicus* Exposed to Phosalone. *Ind J Exp Biol,* 29: 790-792.

Dincel, A.S. Benli, A.C.K. Selvi, M. Sarýkaya, R. Sahin, D. Ozkule, I.A. Erkoc, F. (2009): Sublethal Cyfluthrin Toxicity to Carp (*Cyprinus carpio* L.) Fingerlings: Biochemical, Hematological, Histopathological Alterations. *Ecotoxicology and Environmental Safety, 72*(5): 1433-39.

Di Castri, F. Vernhes, J. R. Younés, T. (1992): Inventoring and Monitoring Biodiversity: A Proposal for an International Network. *Biol. Internat,* 27: 1-27.

Elia, AC. Waller, WT. Norton, SJ. (2002): Biochemical Responses of Bluegill Sunfish (*Lepomis macrochirus*, Rafinesque) to Atrazine Induced Oxidative Stress. *Bull Environ Contam Toxicol,* 68: 809-816.

Fournie, J.W. Summers, J.K. Courtney, L.A. Engle, V.D. Blazer, V.S. (2001): Utility of Splenic Macrophage Aggregates and an Indicator of Fish Exposure to Degraded Environments. *Journal of Aquatic Animal Health,* 13: 105-116.

Gaston, K.J. (2000): Biodiversity: Higher Taxon Richness. *Progress in Physical Geography,* 24: 117-127.

2

Stress Responses in Fish
Potentials of Heat Shock Proteins for Bio-monitoring and Disease Control

Rishikesh S. Dalvi and **Asim K. Pal**

ABSTRACT

Fish are subjected to a wide variety of environmental and anthropogenic stressors. Environmental pollutants, disease, and various factors involved in aquaculture practices are some of the examples of these stressors experienced by fishes in captivity. Fish, like other vertebrates, have evolved strategies to counteract effects of stressors by eliciting coordinated set of hormonal, physiological and consequent behavioural changes which are cumulatively termed as the 'stress response'. One of the important components of the stress response at the cellular level is the induction of evolutionarily conserved proteins called the heat shock proteins (HSPs). The HSPs are a suite of highly conserved proteins of varying molecular weight (16–100 kDa) produced in all cellular organisms. Different families of HSPs have diverse physiological functions, and their induction is regulated at the transcriptional level, which is mediated by the activation of heat shock factors. As molecular chaperones HSPs play vital roles in protein metabolism during normal and stressful conditions such as, preventing aggregation or improper folding of proteins, membrane translocation, localization of proteins to their appropriate cellular compartment or degradation of misfolded protein. HSP-mediated cross-protection is regarded as a fundamental protective mechanism that decreases cellular sensitivity to damage due to environmental protuberances. Moreover, their expression can be enhanced by various stressors such as anoxia, ischaemia, pesticides, hypoxia, acidosis and microbial infection, and therefore HSPs are potential biomarkers for assessing stress state in fish. However, since the HSP responses may vary considerably according to tissue, family of HSP, organism, developmental stage and stressor, effects of other variable stressors should also be comprehensively evaluation before using HSPs for environmental monitoring. In aquatic animals HSPs have been shown to play an important role in health, particular in the development of immune responses against bacterial and viral infections. HSPs offer several advantages over current methods of disease treatment and they are being increasingly exploited for enhancing disease and stress tolerance in commercially important aquatic organisms. HSP based vaccines have been produced for use in aquaculture either by supplying exogenous prokaryotic HSPs or by supplying exogenous HSP stimulation factor. The present chapter briefly describes the generalized stress responses in fish, and emphasis is given on the HSPs with particular reference for their potential use as biomarkers for environmental monitoring and for enhancing the disease resistance and health in fin-fishes.

Keywords: Fin-fishes, stress response, Heat shock proteins, bioindicator, pathogenic infections, HSP vaccines.

INTRODUCTION

Fishes are exposed to biotic and abiotic stressors in their natural habitat, as well as in captivity. The physiological systems of fish can be challenged or stressed, by a wide range of biological, chemical or physical factors. The factors that cause stress are called stressors. Stressors produce effects that threaten or disturb the homeostatic equilibrium in fish. Environmental stressors may include changes in water quality such as dissolved oxygen, ammonia, hardness, pH, and temperature which can cause stress in fish. Waters contaminated with metals such as, copper, cadmium, zinc, and iron, and other contaminants such as arsenic, chlorine, cyanide, various phenols, and polychlorinated biphenyls, can cause severe stress and even death in fish. Other potential environmental stressors include insecticides, herbicides, fungicides, and defoliants which are routinely used in aquaculture. These contaminants can also be added to the environment through industrial, domestic, and agricultural activities and can affect fish at all life stages. Stressors that disturb the fish physically and psychologically include handling, crowding, confinement, transport, or other forms of physical disturbance encompass the pathophysiological stressors, and are mostly practiced in the intensive culture of fish. Massive mortalities due to disease and outbreaks can occur in nature as well as in cultured fish. Similarly, plankton blooms in the wild as well as in aquaculture facilities can cause stress and kill fish. Therefore pathogens, parasites and harmful plankton blooms can be considered as biological stressors.

The concept of biological stress has stimulated numerous, formal definitions in the scientific literature, the variety of which bearing testimony to the difficulty of establishing a single, comprehensive definition. Selye (1950) defined stress as, "The sum of all physiological responses by which an animal tries to maintain or re-establish a normal metabolism in the face of a physical or chemical force". Brett (1958), defined stress as " A state produced by any environmental factor which extends the normal adaptive responses of an animal, or which disturbs the normal functioning to such an extent that the chances of survival are significantly reduced". Esch and Hazen (1978) defined stress as "The effect of any environmental alteration or force that extends homeostatic or stabilizing processes beyond their normal limits, at any level of biological organisation". Chrousos and Gold (1992) defined stress as, "A condition in which the dynamic equilibrium of organisms called homeostasis is threatened or disturbed as a result of the actions of intrinsic or extrinsic stimuli". Chrousos (1998) defined stress as "a state of threatened homeostasis that is re-established by a complex suite of adaptive responses". These definitions depict that stress is the sum of the physiological responses by which an animal tries to maintain metabolic homeostasis.

Stressors provoke a coordinated set of hormonal, physiological and consequent behavioral responses in fish which are cumulatively termed as the 'stress response'. The term stress response is defined as "a response by cells, tissues and organisms to any physical, chemical or biological factor(s), which initiates a series of biological events that facilitate and promote counteraction, adaptation and survival" (Demirovic and Rattan, 2013). The physiological and biochemical changes take place in three phases, (*i*) an alarm reaction in which Catecholamine and Corticosteroids "stress hormones" are released, (*ii*) a stage of resistance during which adaptation occurs, (*iii*) a stage of exhaustion if adaptation is lost because the stress was too severe or long lasting (Wedemeyer and Mcleay, 1981). During chronic conditions the stress response loses its adaptive value and become dysfunctional, which may result in inhibition of growth, reproductive failure and reduced resistance to pathogens. Thus stressor is the causative factor and stress is the response of the animal, and can be applied to the whole animal as well as at the cellular level in the organism.

One of the important aspects of stress response that has been extensively studied in various animal models including fish and shellfish is the 'cellular stress response'. Cells generally respond to stress by up-regulating a group of highly conserved proteins known as the heat shock proteins (HSPs). HSPs are synthesized in response to a variety of stresses, including extremes of temperature, cellular energy depletion, and extreme concentrations of ions, other osmolytes, gases, and various toxic substances. These stresses, if sufficiently intense, induce HSP expression. Although not all HSPs are stress-inducible, activation of various intracellular signaling pathways results in HSP expression. Accordingly, HSPs are equally well termed as stress proteins, and their expression is termed the stress response (Feder and Hofmann, 1999). A common aspect of the HSP inducing stressors is that they result in proteins having non-native conformations (Somero, 1995), which is consistent with the function of HSPs as molecular chaperones. Owing to its responsiveness to diverse forms of stressors, HSPs are especially useful biomarkers and has a widespread application in biomonitoring and environmental toxicology (dePomerai, 1996). It has been suggested that HSPs, produced in response to stressful conditions, are not only constitute the stress response but are also integral part of the host defenses against chronic pathogens (Srivastava, 2002). Therefore, a complete understanding of the relationship between HSP functions in stress response and disease may facilitate application of HSP technology in aquaculture.

Generalized Stress Responses in Fish

When fish and other aquatic organisms experience stress, the effect may be dramatic. Only a general understanding exists of the sequence of physiological and behavioral alterations that occurs as fishes attempt to maintain themselves in the face of short or long term stress. Exposure of fish to stressors induces a characteristic series of endocrine, and other responses that are termed as primary, secondary and tertiary stress responses depending upon the level of biological organisation monitored (Figure 2.1).

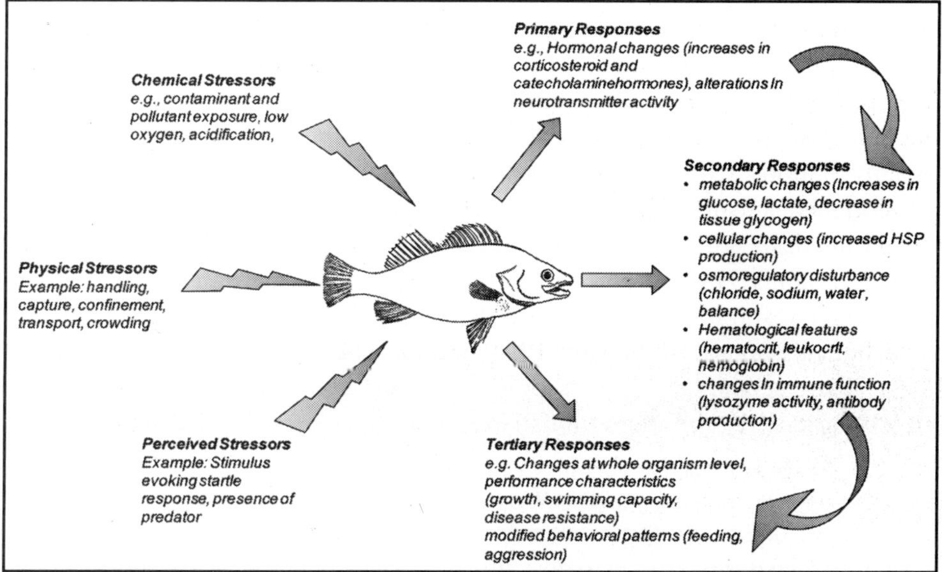

Fig. 2.1: Overview of Stressors and Stress Responses in Fish. (Modified from Barton 2002)

Though these stress responses show a general vertebrate pattern, stress response in fish has many characteristics that are unique to this group. Fishes respond to harmful chemicals and many other stressors at intensities far below than those that can be perceived by terrestrial animals. This is due to the intimate contact of fishes with their surrounding water through gills where the stressor affects the branchial structure and hydromineral balance. Another reason is the great variety and exquisite sensitivity of the sensory system of the integument.

Stress responses in fish are documented in detail by Wendelaar Bonga (1997) and Barton (2002). Sensory perception of stress is a prerequisite for stress response in animals. In fish, an adverse condition stimulates the afferent neural pathway that run in the synaptic nervous system from the hypothalamus to the chromaffin tissue of the head of kidney. Direct stimulation of the chromaffin tissue leads to the release of catecholamines. Other neurons, within the hypothalamus that run to the adenohypophysis of the pituitary glands, secrete a neuropeptide that stimulates the pituitary to produce and release adrenocorticotropic hormone (ACTH). ACTH released in the blood stimulates the inter-renal cells of the head of the Kidney to produce corticosteroid hormone particularly cortisol. This results in rapid elevation of plasma catecholamines and cortisol that leads to secondary stress responses. In fish, cortisol enters liver cells where it binds to nuclear receptor, resulting in activation of genes that produce a series of enzymes that have a range of metabolic effects. This results in a suite of biochemical and physiological changes, which may include hyperglycemia, hyperlacticaemia, depletion of tissue glycogen reserves, lipolysis and inhibition of protein synthesis. Other changes may include the osmotic and ionic disturbances, due to diuresis and loss of electrolyte from the blood, and change in haematology, with erythrocytic changes and reduction of white blood cells (leucopenia). Catecholamines in particular, have marked influence on cardiovascular functions; leading to change of blood circulation, gill perfusion and oxygen carrying capacity of blood. Corticosteroids on the other hand are known to stimulate the ion-transport mechanism in the gill and kidney. Secondary responses include changes in plasma and tissue ion and metabolite levels, hematological features, and heatshock or stress proteins (HSPs), all of which relate to physiological adjustments such as in metabolism, respiration, acid-base status, hydromineral balance, immune function and cellular responses (Pickering, 1981; Iwama et al., 1998, 1999; Mommsen et al., 1999). These secondary stress responses are believed to be adaptive mechanisms and are particularly important for fish to recover from stress, by maintaining oxygen supply to the tissues, to regain osmotic and ionic equilibrium and to meet the increased energy demands imposed by the stressor. Typically these changes persists only for few hours or days, following acute exposure to the stressor, and do not therefore result in any deleterious effect to the animal. In contrast, chronic exposure to stressors provokes tertiary stress responses that result in a number of pathological changes and reduction in reproductive success, depression of growth rate and decreased disease resistance. Thus, when fish are exposed to environmental stressor, array of responses are initiated, and if the stress is severe or long lasting, successively higher levels of biological organisation gets affected. This signifies that, the primary responses are the changes at the endocrine level, where as the tertiary responses refer to those changes that can be easily seen by observing the animal (Jobling 1995). A fish's or fish population's tolerance to environmental alterations thus depends at least in part, upon the individual fish's ability to regulate stabilizing processes so as to accomplish the required physiological or behavioral adaptation (Elliott, 1981).

Such a generalized stress response also occurs at the cellular level and is called the cellular stress response. It is characterized by increased levels of highly conserved group of proteins called the heat shock or stress proteins (HSPs). The HSPs, a group of highly conserved intracellular proteins, are induced in response to variety of stressors such as temperature change, salinity variation, pesticides and disease (Iwama et al. 1998; Feder and Hofmann 1999). They play a central role in the maintenance of cellular homeostasis by preventing aggregation or improper folding of proteins, membrane translocation, localization of proteins to their appropriate cellular compartment or degradation of misfolded protein (Lindquist and Craig, 1988; Yamashita et al. 2010). HSPs are suitable biomarkers for assessing the organism's response to environmental stressors because their accumulations indicate the intensity of the stressors (Hightower et al. 1980, Sanders 1993).

The Cellular Stress Response: Heat Shock Proteins

As part of the cellular stress response the cell naturally responds to stressors by increasing the concentration of highly conserved intracellular proteins classes of HSPs. Activation (puffing) of specific chromosomal loci of *Drosophila* in response to heat shock was first described by Ritossa (1962). These observations were pivotal for research on heat induced molecular response in organisms. Later, Ashburner and Bonner (1979) the identified the specific genes and their proteins induced during heat stress coined the term heat shock proteins (HSPs). Further research showed similar phenomena in prokaryotes and other eukaryotes (Kelley and Schlesinger, 1978; Lemaux et al., 1978; McAlister and Finkelstein, 1980), which suggested that the heat shock response is a universal and ancient mechanism. The HSPs were first thought to be merely as products of genes whose expression is induced by heat stress. However, it is now known that HSPs are induced by a variety of biotic and abiotic factors and are commonly referred to as 'stress proteins'. HSPs are known to play important role as molecular chaperones, as they perform numerous functions in cells and assist with a variety of cellular processes. HSPs function as molecular chaperones in regulation of cellular homeostasis and promoting survival. As molecular chaperones they play vital roles in protein metabolism during normal and stressful conditions such as, preventing aggregation or improper folding of proteins, membrane translocation, localization of proteins to their appropriate cellular compartment or degradation of misfolded protein (Lindquist and Craig, 1988; Bukau and Horwich 1998; Kregel 2002).

HSPs normally represents 5-10% of the total protein in most cells, and are increased to two or threefold when cells are exposed to stressors such as extremes of temperature, nutritional deficiencies, oxygen deprivation, disease, cellular energy depletion, and extreme concentrations of ions, other osmolytes, gases, and various toxic substances (Lindquist and Craig 1988; Morimoto and Santoro 1998; Pockley 2003). Extensive studies have revealed diverse forms of heat shock protein which are broadly classified into different families on the basis of their sequence homology and molecular weight such as, HSP100, HSP90, HSP70, HSP60, HSP40, and small HSP (sHSP) families. In eukaryotes, many families comprise multiple members that differ in their intracellular localization and function (Table 2.1). Most members of the HSP families have isomforms, referred to as heat shock cognates (Hscs). The Hscs are expressed in the cell under normal/non-stress conditions and play an important role in the regulation of normal protein synthesis in the cell.

Table 2.1: Cellular Localization and Functions of the Major Heat Shock Protein Families

Protein Family	Members	Cellular Localization	Function
(1)	(2)	(3)	(4)
HSP100	ClpA, ClpB ClpC HSP104	Cytoplasm, nucleolus, nucleus, chloroplast	Protein disaggregation, folding and destruction; assists in stress tolerance; long-term spore viability
HSP90	HSP82 Grp94, HtpG Grp94/gp96 HSP90 (α and β)	Cytoplasm, nucleus	Essential for viability; folds nascent and denaturing proteins; prevent aggregation of refolded peptide, interacts with kinases and other regulatory molecules; protein degradation, assists the maintenance of the HSF1 monomeric state in non-stressful conditions.
HSP70	Cognate/constitutive: Inducible: HSP70, HSP70hom Hsc70 DnaK, grp78/BiP, mtHSP70/Grp75	Cytoplasm, nucleus, mitochondria, chloroplasts, endoplasmic reticulum	Chaperone required for nascent protein folding, secretion and import into organelles; thermotolerance and cross-protection; protein degradation; growth at high temperature; HSF1 activity ATP binding; ATPase activity; HSP70 downregulates; protects against stresses including bacterial infection.

(Contd...)

(1)	(2)	(3)	(4)
HSP40	DnaJ HSP47	Cytoplasm, nucleus, endoplasmic, reticulum	Regulates the activity of HSP70; binds to non-native proteins. Processing of pro-collagen; processing and/or secretion of collagen.
HSP60	GroEL, HSP65, cpn60, Rubisco-binding protein	Mitochondria, chloroplasts	Chaperonin, bind to partly folded polypeptides and assist correct folding. Folding of complex multi-domain nascent proteins, promotes oligomer formation; high concentration required for growth at elevated temperature
Small HSPs (sHSPs)	α-B-crystallin HSP27 Haem oxygenase, HSP32	Cytoplasm, nucleus	Protect proteins from irreversible denaturation during stress, apoptosis inhibition, cytoskeleton stabilization

Source: Lindquist, 1992; Pockley, 2003; Roberts et al. 2010; Sung and MacRae, 2011.

Cross-protection, also known as cross-tolerance, is the ability of one stressor to transiently increase the resistance of an organism to a subsequent heterologous stressor, a capability acquired through concomitant accumulation of the HSPs. Cross-protection may be an important feature of the cellular stress response especially in an environmental context. Earliest studies of cross-protection in fish were reported by Brown et al. (1992). These researchers showed that exposure of the renal epithelium of winter flounder (*Pleuronectes americanus*) to mild heat shock increased the levels of HSP28, HSP70, and HSP90 in the cell and protected these cells against the deleterious effects of a subsequent extreme temperature or chemical challenge. Subsequent work demonstrated that heat stressed Atlantic salmon (*Salmo salar*) that had artificially elevated levels of branchial and hepatic HSP70 were able to tolerate an osmotic challenge and consistently display the highest survival, relative to control fish (DuBeau et al., 1998). Studies of cross-tolerance indicate that aquatic organisms acquire protection against environmental change by regulating endogenous HSPs. Since HSPs synthesized in response to abiotic stressor may confer cross-tolerance to biotic stressors, they may help in devising strategies to enhance disease tolerance in aquatic organisms (Sung et al., 2011).

One of the most extensively studied family among the heat shock proteins the HSP70. The HSP70 family is very large with most organisms having multiple members, found in a variety of cellular compartments and is involved in protein folding and several other cellular functions. Some of the better known mammalian members of HSP 70 are the constitutive cytosolic member HSC70 (or HSP73); the stress-induced cytosolic form HSP70 (or HSP72), the endoplasmic reticulum form BiP (or Grp78), and the mitochondrial form mHSP70 (or mito-HSP70, or Grp75) (Fink, 1999). HSP70 is highly conserved protein and shows 50% similarity at amino acid level between *E. coli* and human (Gupta and Golding, 1993). The HSP70 chaperones help in protein folding and unfolding and confer acquired thermotolerance in cell and organisms on exposure to heat stress. The HSP90 and HSP70 families are critical to the folding and assembly of other cellular proteins (Gething and Sambrook 1992), and have a wider role in relation to the immune, apoptotic and inflammatory processes (Ellis 1990; Moseley 2000; Srivastava 2002; Pockley, 2003). Another important outcome of the HSP function, which is relevant to aquaculture, is the acquisition of thermotolerance in fish and other organisms (Clegg et al. 2000; Basu et al. 2002). The HSPs that are induced by a particular stressor can protect against several environmental perturbations suggesting its fundamental role in survival (Sun et al. 2002; Rahman et al. 2004; Todgham et al. 2005).

Pathway of HSP70 Synthesis in Cell

At the molecular level HSP induction results from the binding of the heat shock transcription factor (HSF) to the key promoter region, called the heat shock element (HSE), in front of the heat shock gene. Since the major heat shock gene does not contain introns the messenger RNA can be immediately translated in few minutes of exposure to the stressor. The heat shock factors, from various plants and animals studied, show a high degree of structural similarity. There is a DNA-binding domain of about 100 amino acids at the amino terminus; adjacent to this domain is a region containing three leucine zipper repeats, which are key to the trimerization of the HSF1. Stress does not change the amount of HSF1, but transforms the HSF1 to transcriptionally active state that results in expression of HSP70. The cause and mechanism of HSF1 activation and nature of sensors of the stressors in the cell is unknown. However, stressors that act by damaging native proteins inside the cell, and involve HSP70 as the key sensor and mediator of the essential event lead to the production of HSP70. HSF is found as a monomer complex with HSP70 in the cytosol of unstressed cells. As the result of a stressor, the misfolded or damaged proteins sequester HSP70 and other chaperone proteins to aid their repair or destruction. The HSP70 that is normally bound to the monomeric form of cytosolic HSF is dissociated away from such protein complexes. This results in the translocation of HSF1 into the nucleus and a change from the latent monomeric form to a trimeric state, owing to interactions among the oligomerization domains of HSF1. The trimeric form is able to bind to the promoter regions of the heat shock gene, but remains trancriptionally inactive until stress-induced phosphorylation of HSF1 takes place. Upon phosphorylation of HSF1, HSP70 is expressed through the normal transcription and translation processes. During recovery such free HSP70 would come both from the newly formed protein as well as from those that were bound by the damaged proteins that may have released them as a result of repairs or destruction. These free HSP70 will bind to the HSF1 for the release of HSF1 bound to HSE of the DNA, and subsequently dissociate from the trimeric form back to the inactive monomers that move back into the cytoplasm (Figure 2.2).

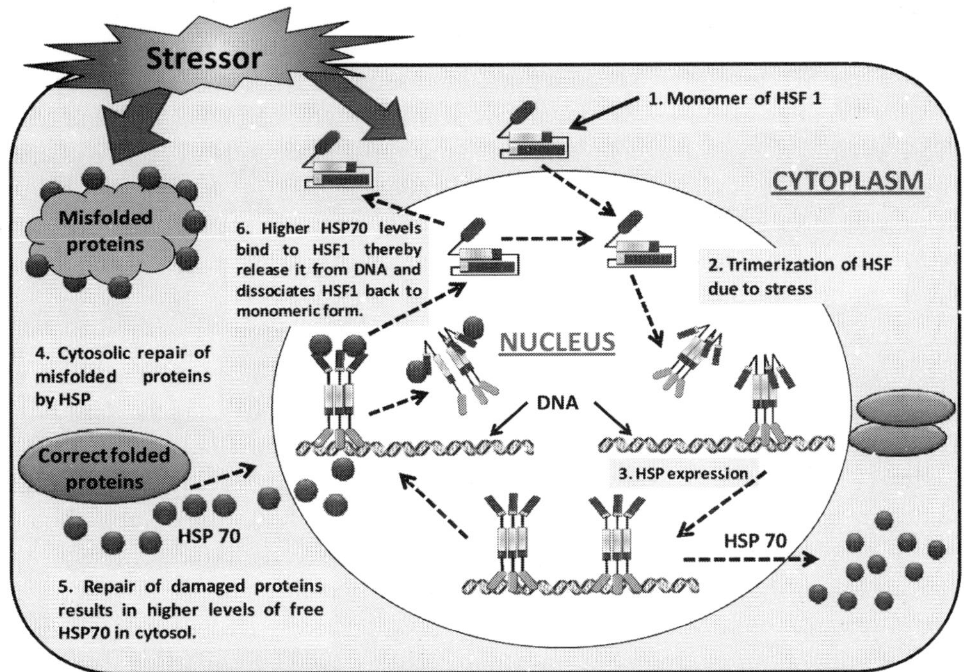

Fig. 2.2: Synthesis of HSP70 within a Cell (Modified from, Iwama et al., 1998)

HSPs as Indicators of Stress in Fish

Several efforts have been made to validate the use of the HSP response as an indicator of stressed states in fish. The majority of studies on HSPs in fish are limited to the in vitro experiments conducted in laboratory conditions. Functional significance of HSPs in various aspects of fish physiology, including development and aging, stress physiology and endocrinology, immunology, environmental physiology, acclimation and stress tolerance has been reviewed by many authors (Iwama et al., 1998; Basu et al., 2002, Roberts et al., 2010; Sung and MacRae 2011, Sung et al., 2011). It has been reported that various environmental stressors can induce the HSP synthesis in fish. Elevation in environmental temperature is an important abiotic stressor of many aquatic organisms. Increased expression of HSP in various tissues of fish exposed to elevated temperatures has been reported in *Fundulus heteroclitus* (Koban et al., 1991), Fathead minnow (Dyer et al., 1991), *Gillichthys mirabilis* (Dietz and Somero, 1992), *Enophrys bison*, *Leptocottus armatus*, *Citharichhthys stigmaeus*, *Parophrys vetulus* (Dietz and Somero, 1993), *Carassius auratus* (Kikuchi et al., 1993), *Labeo rohita* (Das et al., 2006) and *Cirrhinus mrigala* (Das et al., 2005), *Horabagrus brachysoma* (Dalvi et al., 2012). The temperature at which the heat shock response is induced and the time required for HSP synthesis vary according to tissue and species under investigation, and are determined by the acclimation temperature, the thermal tolerance capacity of the organisms and the environmental conditions in which the organisms reside. Increase in HSPs levels have been reported in tissues of fish exposed to industrial effluents (Vijayan et al., 1998), polycyclic aromatic hydrocarbons (Vijayan et al., 1998), several metals such as copper, zinc and mercury (Sanders et al., 1995; Williams et al., 1996; Duffy et al., 1999), pesticides (Sanders, 1993; Hassanein et al., 1999) and arsenic (Del Razo et al., 2001). These studies demonstrate that HSP70 have potential for using as a biomarker of cellular stress and the increase in concentrations of these proteins in the tissue may indicate physiological stress.

However, several studies have also shown that the HSP response can vary according to tissue (Rabergh et al., 2000; Smith et al., 1999), HSP families (Smith et al., 1999) and stressor under investigation (Airaksinen et al., 2003), and the sensitivity of HSP expression can also differ with according to the season (Fader et al., 1994), species (Basu et al., 2001; Nakano and Iwama, 2002), developmental stage (Santacruz et al., 1997; Lele et al., 1997; Martin et al., 2001). Moreover it should also be noteworthy that common forms of hatchery-related stressors such as, exposure to anesthesia, formalin, hypoxia, hyperoxia, capture stress, crowding, feed deprivation and cold stress, did not alter levels of gill HSP30, HSP70 and HSP90 in Atlantic salmon (*Salmo salar*) (Zarate and Bradley, 2003). Similarly, it has been reported in rainbow trout that handling stress rainbow trout (*Oncorhynchus mykiss*) does not alter levels of hepatic HSP70 (Vijayan et al., 1997), and levels of muscle, gill, heart and hepatic HSP60 (Washburn et al., 2002). It is also important to consider that some fish species may not show a heat shock response e.g. temperature stress did not induce HSP70 in Antarctic fish (*Trematomus bernacchi*) (Hofmann et al., 2000). These studies indicate that HSPs may not be a sensitive indicator of stressed states when physical stressors are applied in aquaculture operations.

The potential application of HSPs as biomarkers continues to be an important subject of research in environmental physiology of fish. However, since many different stressors can induce HSPs, it is difficult to attribute changes in HSP expression to any particular stressor. Thus, generalizations cannot be made on the HSP response and more knowledge is required so as to know when a specific HSP family can be used as a stress indicator in fish. Therefore it is suggested that stressor- and species-specific approach should be made if HSPs are to be used as indicators of the stress response in fish (Iwama et al., 1998). In their natural condition organisms often experience multiple stressors simultaneously and the interactions between these stressors may result in significant HSP expression even when none of the single monitored toxicant is at harmful levels. On the contrary, HSPs induced by another stress can enhance tolerance of a toxicant whose presence is being monitored. Therefore further knowledge on the response of fish exposed simultaneously to multiple stressors or to sequential stressors (Schreck, 2000).

HSPs for Control of Diseases in Fish

Disease occurs as a result of infection by pathogenic and opportunistic microbes including bacteria, protozoa, fungi and viruses in all fish and shrimp at all life stages (Lightner and Redman, 1998), and constitutes a major obstacle to further increase aquaculture production. HSPs chaperone intra-cellular peptides released from dead or damaged cells following infection and stimulate a concomitant inflammatory response by presenting these peptides, as complexes, to antigen presenting cells for activation of T-lymphocytes (Srivastava 2002; Kulkarni et al., 2011). This is a particularly significant process, which facilitates the subsequent host response to the pathogens responsible for the necrosis (Pockley 2003). Cho et al. (1997) reported induction of HSP90 during an *in vitro* challenge of the Chinook salmon embryo cell line with infectious hematopoietic necrosis virus (IHNV). Forsyth et al. (1997) documented induction of HSP70 in liver and head kidney tissues of coho salmon in response to a bacterial challenge of *Renibacterium salmoninarum*. Ackerman and Iwama (2001) reported augmentation of HSP70 in rainbow trout after acute *Vibrio anguillarum* challenge. Later in sea bream *Sparus sarba* Deane and Woo (2004) reported that hepatic HSP70 peaks 36 h post infection with live *V. alginolyticus*, although HSP60 and HSP90 are unchanged. Similarly, Dong et al., (2006) reported up-regulates the expression of three HSP40 genes in embryonic cell lines from the olive flounder *Paralichthys olivaceus* upon exposure to UV inactivated turbot rhabdovirus (SMRV). Recently, Chen et al. (2010) reported increase in HSP90 in orange-spotted grouper *Epinephelus coioides* exposed nodavirus. The underlying mechanisms that regulate HSP synthesis in fish during disease are unclear but are likely to be similar to those observed in response to other stressors wherein transcription is regulated by recognition of heat shock elements (HSEs) by heat shock factor (HSF), a process promoted by protein denaturation (Sung and McRae, 2011). The HSPs and the immune system are linked in several ways in organisms that are faced with bacterial challenges (Young, 1990), including fish. Perhaps the simplest explanation is that virulent pathogens may alter cellular homeostasis and inducing heat shock proteins by damaging components within a cell through the release of cytolytic substances. In fish, inflammatory responses caused due to pathogenic exposure may change the physiological processes at the cellular level, such as ion regulation and acid-base balance. Extracellular substances like reactive oxygen species, cationic peptides, lysozyme, and cytokines secreted by the host immune cells (phagocytes and granulocytes) are known to induce various heat shock proteins (Jacquier-Sarlin et al., 1994). Further studies on the relationship between the immune system and HSPs, are necessary to understand how their production assists fish immune system to defend against infectious challenge.

Thought cross-protection is well documented phenomenon in fish, but there is less information on the effect of a heat shock or any other stressor on subsequent resistance to pathogenic stressors and thus restricts our understanding on the role of HSPs in disease pathogenesis (Dalmo et al., 1997). Induction of HSPs requires exposure of an aquatic animal to some form of stressor, usually thermal shock because of the ease of application of such treatments to the cells, tissues or individual animals. However, recently novel methods for enhancing HSPs levels in the host have been developed either by supplying exogenous prokaryotic HSPs or by supplying exogenous HSP stimulation factor (Roberts et al., 2010). An increase in HSP70 following non-lethal heat shock (NLHS) fails to protect platyfish *Xiphophorus maculates* against *Yersinia ruckeri* infection, but protection is enhanced when NLHS is along with intracoelomal injection of GroEL and DnaK, bacterial HSPs equivalent to HSP60 and HSP70 (Ryckaert et al., 2010). Recently, a commercial product Pro-Tex® (which contains Tex-OE®, a patented extract of the skin of the prickly pear cactus, *Opuntia ficus indica*) has been reported to act as a non-stressful precursor for induction of high levels of endogenous or host-derived HSPs in animal tissues, has become available for use in fish and shellfish (Roberts et al., 2010; Sung et al., 2011). Studies of the effect of prestimulation of salmon and gilthead sea bream, *Sparus aurata* with Pro- Tex® enhanced their survival on subsequent exposure to *V. anguillarum* infection (El Fituri, 2009, Roberts et al., 2010).

Similar to those in higher animals, it has been demonstrated that HSPs derived from bacterial pathogens can be highly antigenic in fish. Wilhelm et al., (2006) demonstrated that recombinant HSP60 and HSP70 derived from the intracellular bacterium, *Piscirickettsia salmonis*, provided protection against the pathogen in Atlantic salmon *Salmo salar* compared with controls. Similarly, Plant et al., (2009) reported that HSP60 and HSP70 derived from the fish pathogen *Flavobacterium psychrophilum* are highly immunogenic, but vaccination with these proteins alone, or in combination, does not protect rainbow trout, *Oncorhychus mykiss* against infection. Marshall et al., (2007) the immunogenic potential of a novel immunogenic agent called ChaPs, a prokaryotic HSP, synthesized by *Piscirickettsia salmonis,* obtained from infected salmonid fish, for development of vaccines against salmonid rickettsial septicemia (SRS). Furthermore, vaccination with purified DnaJ, the prokaryotic homologue of HSP40, from *Edwardsiella tarda* could protect Japanese flounder *Paralichthys olivaceus* against this Gram negative pathogen compared non-immunized controls (Dang et al., 2011). The use of HSPs as vaccine appears to be an effective approach for control of disease with potential applications in many different commercially important aquatic organisms while reducing the environmental impact of aquaculture operations (Sung and MacRae, 2011).

CONCLUSION

The heat shock proteins are ubiquitously produced in all the organisms and their concentrations in the cells increase in response to various environmental stressors. HSPs therefore have potential as indicators for monitoring stress levels in fish in the nature and during aquaculture processes. However a thorough understanding of the influence of other environmental stressors, species specific HSP response, and response of a specific HSP family to a particular stressor or multiple stressors, is essential before using HSPs as bio-indicator molecules. HSPs are also involved in cross-protection, whereby their increased level due to one sub-lethal stressor or non-stressful exogenous compound may endow protection against another subsequent stressor. Therefore, increased expression of HSPs in fish via non-stressful methods may have application in aquaculture for enhancing tolerance to subsequent abiotic and biotic stressors. Since HSPs of pathogenic microorganisms can elicit a strong immune response in fishes, they have height potential for use as vaccine in aquaculture. However, this particular aspect of using HSPs for enhancing immunity and disease resistance in fish is still at the naive stage and needs further investigation.

REFERENCES

Ackerman, A. and G.K. Iwama (2001): Physiological and Cellular Response of Juvenile Rainbow Trout to Vibriosis. *Journal of Aquatic Animal Health*, 13: 173-180.

Airaksinen, S., C.M.I. Rabergh, A. Lahti, A. Kaatrasalo, L. Sistonen, and M. Nikinmaa (2003): Stressor-dependent Regulation of the Heat Shock Response in Zebrafish, Danio rerio. *Comparative Biochemistry and Physiology* (part- A), 134: 839-846.

Ashburner, M. and J.J. Bomer (1979): The Induction of Gene Activity in Drosophila by Heat shock. *Cell,* 17: 241-245.

Barton, B.A. (2002): Stress in Fishes: A Diversity of Responses with Particular Reference to Changes in Circulating Corticosteroids. *Integrative and Comparative Biology*, 42: 517-525.

Basu, N., T. Nakano, E.G. Grau and G.K. Iwama (2001): The Effects of Cortisol on Heat Shock Protein 70 Levels in Two Fish Species. *General and Comparative Endocrinology*, 124: 97-105.

Brett, J.R. (1958): Implications and Assessment of Environmental Stress. In: (Larkin P.A. Ed.), Investigations of Fish-power Problems, pp. 69-83.

Brown, M.A., R.P. Upender, L.E. Hightower and J.L. Renfro (1992): Thermoprotection of a Functional Epithelium: Heat Stress Effects on Transepithelial Transport by Flounder Renal Tubule in Primary Monolayer Culture. *Proceedings of the National Academy of Sciences USA,* 89: 3246-3250.

Bukau, B. and A.L. Horwich (1998): The HSP70 and HSP60 Chaperone Machines. *Cell,* 92: 351-366.

Chen, Y.M., C.E. Kuo, T.Y. Wang, P.S. Shie, W.C. Wang, S.L. Huang, T.J. Tsai, P.P. Chen, J.C. Chen and T.Y. Chen (2010): Cloning of an Orange-spotted Grouper *Epinephelus coioides* Heat Shock Protein 90AB (HSP90AB) and Characterization of its Expression in Response to Nodavirus. *Fish and Shellfish Immunology*, 28: 895-904.

Cho, W.J., S.J. Cha, J.W. Do, J.Y. Choi, J.Y. Lee, C.S. Jeong, K.J. Cho, W.S. Choi, H.S. Kang, H.D. Kim, J.W. Park (1997): A novel 90-kDa Stress Protein Induced in Fish Cells by Fish Rhabdovirus Infection. *Biochemical and Biophysical Research Communications,* 233: 316-319.

Chrousos, G.P. (1998): Stressors, Stress, and Neuroendocrine Integration of the Adaptive Response. *Annals of the New York Academy of Sciences,* 851: 311-335.

Chrousos, G.P. and P.W. Gold (1992): The Concept of Stress and the Stress System of Disorders: Overview of Physical and Behavioural Homeostasis. *Journal of the American Medical Association*, 267: 1244-1252.

Clegg, J.S., S.A. Jackson, N.V. Hoa, P. Sorgeloos (2000): Thermal Resistance, Developmental Rate and Heat Shock Proteins in Artemia Franciscana, from San Francisco Bay and Southern Vietnam. *Biochemical and Biophysical Research Communications,* 252: 85-96.

Dalmo, R.A., K. Ingebrigtsen and J. Bøgwald (1997): Non-specific Defence Mechanisms in Fish, with Particular Reference to the Reticuloendothelial System (RES). *Journal of Fish Diseases* 20, 241-273.

Dalvi, R.S., A.K. Pal, L.R. Tiwari and K. Baruah (2012): Influence of Acclimation Temperature on the Induction of Heat Shock Protein 70 in the Catfish *Horabagrus brachysoma* (Günther). *Fish Physiology and Biochemistry*, 38: 919-27.

Dang, W., M. Zhang and L. Sun (2011): *Edwardsiella tarda* DnaJ is a virulence Associated Molecular Chaperones with Immunoprotective Potential. *Fish and Shellfish Immunology,* 31: 182-188.

Das, P., G. Akhil and K.M. Sanjib (2005): Heat Shock Protein 70 Expression in Different Tissues of *Cirrhinus mrigala* (Ham.) Following Heat Stress. *Aquaculture Research,* 36(6): 525-529.

Das, T., A.K. Pal, S.K. Chakraborty, S.M. Manush, N. Chatterjee and S.K. Apte (2006): Metabolic Elasticity and induction of Heat Shock Protein 70 in *Labeo rohita* Acclimated to Three Temperatures. *Asian-Australasian Journal of Animal Science*, 19 (7): 1033-1039.

de Pomerai, D. (1996): Heat Shock Proteins as Biomarkers of Pollution. *Human and Experimental Toxicology*, 15: 279-285.

Deane, E.E., J. Li and N.Y.S. Woo (2004): Modulated Heat Shock Protein Expression during Pathogenic *Vibrio alginolyticus* Stress of Sea Bream. *Diseases of Aquatic Organisms*, 62: 205-215.

Del Razo, L.M., B. Quintanilla-Vega, E. Brambila-Colombres, E.S. Caldero´n-Aranda, M. Manno and A. Albores (2001): Stress Proteins Induced by Arsenic. *Toxicology and Applied Pharmacology*, 177, 132-148.

Demirovic, D. and S.I. Rattan (2013): Establishing Cellular Stress Response Profiles as Biomarkers of Homeodynamics, Health and Hormesis. *Experimental Gerontology,* 48: 94-98.

Dietz, T.J. and G.N. Somero (1992): The Threshold Induction Temperature of the 90-kDa Heat Shock Protein is Subject to Acclimatization in Eurythermal Goby Fishes (genus *Gillichthys*). *Proceedings of the National Academy of Science USA*, 89: 3389-3393.

Dietz, T.J. and G.N. Somero (1993): Species and Tissue-specific Synthesis Patterns for Heat-shock Proteins HSP70 and HSP90 in Several Marine Teleost Fishes. *Physiological Zoology*, 66: 863-880.

Dong, C.W., Y.B. Zhang, Q.Y. Zhang and J.F. Gui (2006): Differential Expression of Three *Paralichthys olivaceus* HSP40 Genes in Responses to Virus Infection and Heat Shock. *Fish and Shellfish Immunology*, 21: 146-158.

DuBeau, S.F., F. Pan, G.C. Tremblay and T.M. Bradley (1998): Thermal Shock of Salmon in vivo Induces the Heat Shock Protein HSP 70 and Confers Protection Against Osmotic Shock. *Aquaculture,* 168: 311-323.

Duffy, L.K., E. Scofield, T. Rodgers, M. Patton., R.T. Bowyer (1999): Comparative Baseline Levels of Mercury, HSP70 and HSP60 in Subsistence Fish from the Yukon-Kuskokwim Delta Region of Alaska. *Comparative Biochemistry and Physiology Part C*, 124: 181-186.

Dyer, S.D., K.L. Dickson and E.G. Zimmerman (1991): Tissue-specific Patterns for Heat-shock Proteins and Thermal Tolerance of the Fathead Minnow (*Pimephales prometas*). *Canadian Journal of Zoology*, 69: 2021-2027.

El Fituri, A.A. (2009): The Possible Role of TEX-OE in the Pathogenesis of Vibriosis. MSc thesis, University of Malta, 97.

Elliott, J.M. (1981): Some Aspects of Thermal Stress on Freshwater Teleosts. In: (Pickering A. D. Ed.), Stress and Fish, Academic Press, London, pp. 209-245.

Ellis, R.J. (1990): The Molecular Chaperone Concept. *Seminars in Cell Biology,* 1: 1-17.

Esch, G.W. and T.C. Hazen (1978): Thermal Ecology and Stress: A Case History for Red-sore Disease in Largemouth Bass. In (Thorp J.H. and Gibbon J.W. Eds.) Energy and Environmental Stress in Aquatic Ecosystems, Technical Information Center, U.S. Department of Energy, CONF, pp. 331-363.

Fader, S.C., Z. Yu and J.R. Spotila (1994): Seasonal Variation in Heat Shock Proteins (HSP70) in Stream Fish Under Natural Conditions. *Journal of Thermal Biology*, 19: 335-341.

Feder, M.E. and G.E Hofmann (1999): Heat-shock Proteins, Molecular Chaperones, and the Stress Response: Evolutionary and Ecological Physiology. *Annual Reviews in Physiology*, 61: 243-82.

Fink, A.L. (1999): Chaperone-Mediated Protein Folding. *Physiological Reviews*, 79 (2): 425-449.

Forsyth, R.B., E.P.M. Candido, S.L. Babich, G.K. Iwama (1997): Stress Protein Expression in coho salmon with Bacterial Kidney Disease. *Journal of Aquatic Animal Health*, 9: 18-25.

Gething, M. and J. Sambrook (1992): Protein Folding in the Cell. *Nature*, 355, 35-45.

Gupta, R.S. and G.B. Golding (1993): Evoluation of HSP70 Gene and its Implications Regarding Relationship Between Archaebacteria, Eubacteria, and Eukaryotes. *Journal of Molecular Evolution*, 37: 573-582.

Hassanein, H.M.A., M.A. Banhawy, F.M. Soliman, S.A. Abdel-Rehim, W.E.G. Muller and H.C. Schroder (1999): Induction of HSP70 by the Herbicide Oxyfluoren (goal) in the Egyptian Nile Fish, *Oreochromis niloticus. Archives of Environmental Contamination and Toxicology,* 37: 78-84.

Hightower, L.E. (1980): Cultured Animal Cells Exposed to Aminoacid Analogues or Puromycin Rapidly Synthesize Several Polypeptides. *Journal of Cellular Physiology*, 102: 407-427.

Hofmann, G.E., B.A. Buckley, S. Airaksinen, J.E. Keen and G.N. Somero (2000): Heat-shock Protein Expression is Absent in the Antarctic Fish *Trematomus bernacchii* (Family Nototheniidae). *Journal of Experimental Biology,* 203: 2331-2339.

Iwama, G.K., P.T. Thomas, R.B. Forsyth and M.M. Vijayan (1998): Heat Shock Protein Expression in Fish. *Reviews in Fish Biology and Fisheries*, 8: 35-56.

Iwama, G.K., M.M. Vijayan, R.B. Forsyth and P.A. Ackerman (1999): Heat Shock Proteins and Physiological Stress in Fish. *American Zoologist,* 39: 901-909.

Jacquier-Sarlin, M.R., K. Fuller, A.T. Dinh-Xuan, M.J. Richar and B.S. Polla (1994): Protective Effects of HSP70 in Inflammation. *Experientia* 50: 1031-1038.

Jobling, M. (1995): Human Impacts on Aquatic Environments. In: Environmental Biology of Fishes, Chapman and Hall Publication. pp. 416-436.

Kelley, P.M. and M.J. Schlesinger (1978): The Effect of Amino Acid Analogues and Heat Shock on Gene Expression in Chicken Embryo Fibroblasts. *Cell,* 15: 1277-1286.

Kikuchi, K., S. Watabe, Y. Suzuki, K. Aida and H. Nakajima (1993): The 65-kDa Cytisolic Protein Associated with Warm Temperature Acclimation in Goldfish, *Carassius auratus. Journal of Comparative Physiology* Part-B, 163: 349-354.

Koban, M., A.A. Yup, L.B Agellon and D.A. Powers (1991): Molecular Adaptation to Environmental Temperature: Heat-shock Response of Eurythermal Teleost *Fundulus Heteroclitus. Molecular Marine Biology and Biotechnology*, 1: 1-17.

Kregel, K.C. (2002): Invited Review: Heat Shock Proteins: Modifying Factors in Physiological Stress Responses and Acquired Thermotolerance. *Journal of Applied Physiology*, 92: 2177-2186.

Kulkarni, R., S. Behboudi and S. Sharif (2011): Insights into the Role of Toll-like Receptors in Modulation of T Cell Responses. *Cell and Tissue Research*, 343: 141-152.

Lele, Z., S. Engel and P.H. Krone (1997): HSP47 and HSP70 Gene Expression is Differentially Regulated in a Stress- and Tissue-specific Manner in Zebrafish Embryos. *Developmental Genetics*, 21: 123-133.

Lemaux, P.G., S.L. Herendeen, P.L. Bloch and F.C. Neidhardt (1978): Transient Rates of Synthesis of Individual Polypeptides in *E. coli* Following Temperature Shifts. *Cell,* 13: 427-434.

Lightner, D.V. and R.M. Redman (1998): Shrimp Diseases and Current Diagnostic Methods. *Aquaculture,* 164: 201-220.

Lindquist, S. (1992): Heat-shock Proteins and Stress Tolerance in Microorganisms. *Current Opininions on Genetics and Development*, 2: 748-755.

Lindquist, S. and E. A. Craig (1988): The Heat Shock Proteins. *Annual Review of Genetics,* 22: 631-677.

Marshall, S.H., P. Conejeros, M. Zahr, J. Olivares, F. Go´mez, P. Cataldo et al. (2007) Immunological Characterization of a Bacterial Protein Isolated from Salmonid Fish Naturally Infected with *Piscirickettsia salmonis. Vaccine,* 25: 2095-2102.

Martin, C.C., P. Tang, G. Barnardo and P.H. Krone (2001): Expression of the Chaperonin 10 Gene during Zebrafish Development. *Cell Stress and Chaperones,* 6: 38-43.

McAlister, L., and D.B. Finkelstein (1980): Heat Shock Proteins and Thermal Resistance in Yeast. *Biochemical and Biophysical Research Communications,* 93: 819-24.

Mommsen, T.P., M.M. Vijayan, and T.W. Moon (1999): Cortisol in Teleosts: Dynamics, Mechanisms of Action, and Metabolic Regulation. *Reviews in Fish Biology and Fisheries*, 9: 211-268.

Morimoto, R.I. and M.G. Santoro (1998): Stress-inducible Responses to Heat Shock Proteins: New Pharmacological Targets for Cytoprotection. *Nature- Biotechnology*. 16: 833-838.

Moseley, P. (2000): Stress Proteins and the Immune Response. *Immunopharmacology,* 48: 299-302.

Nakano, K. and G.K. Iwama (2002): The 70-kDa Heat Shock Protein Response in Two Intertidal Sculpins, *Oligocottus maculosus* and *O. snyderi*: Relationship of HSP70 and Thermal Tolerance. *Comparative Biochemistry and Physiology, Part-A*, 133: 79-94.

Pickering, A.D. (1981): Introduction: the Concept of Biological Stress. In: (Pickering, A.D., Ed.) Stress and Fish, London: Academic Press. pp. 1-9.

Plant, K.P., S.E. LaPatra and K.D. Cain (2009): Vaccination of Rainbow Trout, *Oncorhynchus mykiss* (Walbaum), with Recombinant and DNA Vaccines Produced to *Flavobacterium psychrophilum* Heat Shock Proteins 60 and 70. *Journal of Fish Diseases,* 32: 521-534.

Pockley, A.G. (2003): Heat Shock Proteins as Regulators of the Immune Response. *Lancet,* 362: 469-476.

Rabergh, C.M., S. Airaksinen, A. Soitamo, H.V. Bjorklund, T. Johansson, M. Nikinmaa, and L. Sistonen (2000): Tissue-specific Expression of Zebrafish *Danio rerio* Heat Shock Factor-1 mRNAs in Response to Heat Stress. *Journal of Experimental Biology*, 203: 1817-1824.

Rahman, M.M., M. Wille, R.O. Cavalli, P. Sorgeloos and J.S. Clegg (2004): Induced Thermotolerance and Stress Resistance in Larvae of the Freshwater Prawn, *Macrobrachium rosenbergii* (de Man, 1879). *Aquaculture,* 230: 569-579.

Ritossa, F. (1962): A New Puffing Pattern Induced by Heat Shock and DNP in *Drosophila. Experiementia,* 18: 571-573.

Roberts, R.J., C. Agius, P. Bossier, Y.Y. Sung (2010): Heat Shock Proteins (Chaperones) in Fish and Shellfish and Their Potential Role in Relation to Fish Health: A Review. *Journal of Fish Diseases,* 33: 789-801.

Ryckaert J., F. Pasmans, E. Tobback, L. Duchateau, E. Decostere, F. Haesebrouck, P. Sorgeloos and P. Bossier (2009): Heat Shock Proteins Protect Platyfish (Xiphophorus maculatus) from Yersinia ruckeri Induced Mortality. *Fish and Shellfish Immunology*, 28: 228-231.

Sanders, B.M. (1993): Stress Proteins in Aquatic Organisms: An Environmental Perspective. *Critical Reviews in Toxicology*, 23: 49-75.

Sanders, B.M., J. Nguyen, L.S. Martin, S.R. Howe and S. Coventry (1995): Induction and Subcellular Localization of Two Major Stress Proteins in Response to Copper in the Fathead Minnow *Pimephales promelas*. *Comparative Biochemistry and Physiology Part-C*, 112: 335-343.

Santacruz, H., S. Vriz and N. Angelier (1997): Molecular Characterization of a Heat Shock Cognate cDNA of zebrafish, hsc70, and Developmental Expression of the Corresponding Transcripts. *Developmental Genetics*, 21: 223-233.

Schlesinger, M.J. (1990): Minireview: Heat Shock Protein. *Journal of Biological Chemistry*, 265 (21). 12111-12114.

Schreck, C.B. (2000): Accumulation and Long-term Effects of Stress in Fish. In The Biology of Animal Stress: Basic Principles and Implications for Animal Welfare (ed. G.P. Moberg and J.A. Mench), pp. 147-158. Walingford, UK: CABI Publishing.

Selye, H. (1950): Stress and the General Adaptation Syndrome. *British Medical Journal,* 1: 1383-1392.

Smith, T.R., G.C. Tremblay and T.M. Bradley (1999): Characterization of the Heat Shock Protein Response of Atlantic Salmon (*Salmo salar*). *Fish Physiology and Biochemistry*, 20: 279-292.

Somero, G.N. (1995): Proteins and Temperature. *Annual Reviews in Physiology*, 57: 43-68.

Srivastava, P, (2002): Interaction of Heat Shock Proteins with Peptides and Antigen Presenting Cells: Chaperoning of the Innate and Adaptive Immune Responses. *Annual Reviews in Immunology,* 20: 395-425.

Sun, W.N., M. Van Montagu and N. Verbruggen (2002): Small Heat Shock Proteins and Stress Tolerance in Plants. *Biochimica et Biophysica Sinica Acta,* 1577: 1-9.

Sung, Y.Y. and MacRae T.H. (2011): Heat Shock Proteins and Disease Control in Aquatic Organisms. *Journal of Aquaculture Research and Development*, S2: 006. doi:10.4172/2155-9546. S2-006.

Sung, Y.Y., T.H. MacRae, P. Sorgeloos and P. Bossier (2011): Stress Response for Disease Control in Aquaculture. *Reviews in Aquaculture*, 3: 120-137.

Todgham, A.E., P.M. Schulte and G.K. Iwama (2005): Cross-tolerance in the Tidepool Sculpin: The Role of Heat Shock Proteins. *Physiological and Biochemical Zoology*, 78: 133-144.

Vijayan, M.M., C. Pereira and G.K. Iwama (1998): Sublethal Concentrations of Contaminant Induce the Expression of Hepatic Heat Shock Protein 70 in two Salmonids. *Aquatic Toxicology*, 40: 101-108.

Vijayan, M.M., C. Pereira, R.B. Forsyth, C.J. Kennedy and G.K. Iwama (1997): Handling Stress does not Affect the Expression of Hepatic Heat Shock Protein 70 and Conjugation Heat-shock-cognate hsc71 Gene from Rainbow Trout. *European Journal of Biochemistry*, 204: 893-900.

Washburn, B.S., J.J. Moreland, A.M. Slaughter, I. Werner, D.E. Hinton and B.M. Sanders (2002): Effects of Handling on Heat Shock Protein Expression in Rainbow Trout (*Oncorhynchus mykiss*). *Environmental Toxicology and Chemistry*, 21: 557-560.

Wedemeyer, G.A. and D.J. McLeay (1981): Methods for Determining the Tolerance of Fishes to Environmental Stressors. In Stress and Fish (Ed. A.D. Pickering), Academic Press, pp. 247-275.

Wendelaar Bonga, S.E. (1997): The Stress Response in Fish. *Physiological Reviews,* 77: 591-625.

Wilhelm V., A. Miquel, L.O. Burzio, M. Rosemblatt, E. Engel and P.D.T. Valenzuela (2006): A Vaccine Against the Salmonid Pathogen *Piscirickettsi salmonis* Based on Recombinant Proteins. *Vaccine,* 24: 5083-5091.

Williams, J.H., A.M. Farag, M.A. Stansbury, P.A. Young, H.L. Bergman and N.S. Petersen (1996): Accumulation of HSP70 in Juvenile and Adult Rainbow Trout Gill Exposed to Metal-contaminated Water and/or Diet. *Environmental Toxicology and Chemistry,* 15: 1324-1328.

Yamashita, M., T. Yabu, N. Ojima (2010): Stress Protein HSP70 in Fish. *Aqua-BioScience Monographs*, 3: 111-141.

Young, R.A. (1990): Stress Proteins and Immunology. *Annual Reviews in Immunology*, 8: 401-420.

Zarate, J. and T.M. Bradley (2003): Heat Shock Proteins are not Sensitive Indicators of Hatchery Stress in Salmon. *Aquaculture,* 223: 175-187.

3

Types and Mode of Action of Different Endocrine Disrupting Chemicals in Fish

Prem Kumar and P. Priya

ABSTRACT

Endocrine disrupting chemicals include a diverse group of synthetic industrial and agricultural chemicals and even some naturally occurring compounds that can affect endocrine system through mimicking the effects of endogenous hormones, antagonizing the effects of endogenous hormones, altering the pattern of synthesis and metabolism of normal hormones and modifying hormone receptor levels. Laboratory studies have shown a variety of synthetic and natural chemicals including certain industrial intermediates, pesticides, dioxins, trace elements and plant sterols can interfere with the endocrine system in fish. Overt endocrine disruption in fish does not appear to be a ubiquitous environmental phenomenon, but rather more likely to occur near sewage treatment plants, pulp and paper mills, and in areas of high organic chemical contamination. Partial- and full-life cycle tests with fish that are focused on key aspects of reproduction and development not only provide a basis for quantitative predictions of ecological risk of EDCs to fish populations but, through consideration of endpoints that are sensitive and diagnostic for different classes of EDCs, serve as effective generalized models for identifying chemicals that affect specific components of the vertebrate HPG axis.

Kewwords: endocrine, disrupting, chemicals, fish, reproduction, ecological.

INTRODUCTION

There have been several definitions of Endocrine Disrupting Chemicals (EDCs) from a mode of action (MOA) perspective, it is defined as "an exogenous agent that interferes with the production, release, transport, metabolism, binding, action, or elimination of natural hormones in the body responsible for the maintenance of homeostasis and the regulation of developmental processes" (Kavlock et al., 1996). From a regulatory perspective, EDCs encompasses agents that cause alterations in reproduction or development through direct effects on the vertebrate hypothalamic–pituitary–thyroidal or hypothalamic–pituitary–gonadal (HPG) axes (USEPA, 1998). In other words, EDCs, which are exogenous natural substances (e.g. phytoestrogens) or man-made chemical compounds (e.g., Synthetic steroids, alkylpheonols, phthalates, organochlorine pesticides, etc.), are well known to have similar properties to estrogenic hormone of wild animals including fish (Sumpter, 1995).

In 1996, the European Commission defined an endocrine disrupter as "an exogenous substance that causes adverse health effects in an intact organism, or its progeny, consequent to changes in endocrine function" (European Commission, 1996). As with Kavlock *et al.* (1996), this definition stresses that adverse health effects occur as a result of one or more changes in endocrine function. The National Research Council (NRC) adopted hormonally active agents as a more neutral mechanistic descriptor, and defined them broadly as substances that possess hormone like activity, regardless of structure (NRC, 1999).

EDCs include a diverse group of synthetic industrial and agricultural chemicals and even some naturally occurring compounds (Santodonato, 1997). Table 3.1 includes list of EDCs. As noted by Santodonato (1997), a number of estrogenic EDCs or their primary oxidative metabolites, share a common structural relationship with the phenolic-A ring in E2. More recently, however, the number of compounds identified as suspected or confirmed endocrine disrupters has increased substantially and includes industrial intermediates, such as 4-nonylphenol, bisphenol-A, and the phthalate ester plasticizers, as well as classic contaminants such as the polycyclic aromatic hydrocarbons (PAHs), polychlorinated biphenyls (PCBs), dioxins, certain pesticides, and even a number of trace elements (Knudsen and Pottinger, 1999). In plants, naturally occurring compounds termed phytoestrogens are also known to have hormonelike properties (Mitksicek, 1995).

Industrial Chemicals/Byproducts

Alkylphenols and alkylphenol polyethoxylates (APEs), are used as surfactants in many applications from soaps and detergents to pesticide formulations. Once in the environment, microbial degradation results in loss of the ethoxylates, eventually leaving the more persistent alkylphenol (e.g., 4- nonylphenol). Jobling *et al.* (1998) have shown that exposure to alkylphenolic compounds result in the synthesis of vitellogenin in male fish. APEs enter the aquatic environment via discharges from sewage treatment plant (STPs), textile, and pulp and paper mills (White *et al.* 1994; Field and Reed 1996).

Table 3.1: Confirmed or Suspected Endocrine Disrupting Compounds

Industrial Chemicals/Byproducts	
4-Nonylphenol	Surfactant intermediate/breakdown product
Octylphenol	Surfactant intermediate/breakdown product
Bisphenol-A (BPA)	Monomer of polycarbonate, plastic
4-tert-pentylphenol intermediate	
Benzo-*a*- pyrene	Fossil fuel combustion product
Phenanthrene	Fossil fuel combustion product
Polychlorinated biphenyls	Transformer oil
Dioxins	Industrial and waste incineration byproducts
Polybrominated diphenyl ethers	Flame retardants
Butyl benzyl	phthalate Plasticizer
Di-n-butyl	phthalate Plasticizer
Pesticides	
Atrazine	Herbicide
Carbofuran	Insecticide
Toxaphene	Insecticide
Endosulfan	Insecticide
Lindane	Insecticide
DDT	Insecticide
DDE	Degradation product of DDT
Metals	
Mercury	Industry (e.g., chloralkali plants)
Cadmium	Industry (e.g., metal plating, battery production)
Lead	Industry (e.g., battery production)
Natural Products	
b-Sitosterol	Pulp and paper industry by-product/plant sterol
Genistein	Plant sterol
Daidzein	Plant sterol
Enterodiol	Plant sterol
Pharmaceutical agents	
Diethylstilbestrol (DES) and synthetic estrogen ethinylestradiol	in Birth-control pills

Dioxins are not intentionally manufactured but are typically forme and released through industrial activities such as chlorine bleaching at pulp and paper mills, chlorination at waste and drinking water treatment plants, and from municipal solid waste and industrial incinerator emissions. Anderson *et al.* (1996a) have shown *in vitro* that both the dioxin TCDD (2, 3, 7, 8 tetrachlorodibenzo-p-dioxin) and the furan 2, 3, 4, 7, 8-pentachlorodibenzofuran are estrogen antagonists. One of the compounds that could be responsible is β sitosterol, a major byproduct of wood pulp delignification, which appears to be activated or produced in the presence of *Mycobacterium smegmatis* (Bortone and Cody, 1999; MacLatchy *et al.*, 1997).

Bisphenol-A is the monomer of the plastic polycarbonate. Bisphenol-A appears to be an estrogen mimic, with a demonstrated affinity for rat Estrogen receptor (ER) (Krishnan *et al.,* 1993).Polycyclic aromatic hydrocarbons (PAHs), are found in fossil fuels such as oil and coal and are released into the environment through combustion, surface runoff, oil spills, recreational boating and shipping, municipal waste effluents and atmospheric deposition (Kime, 1998). Santodonato (1997) noted that while PAHs may function as weak ER agonists, they are expected to bind preferentially to the Ah receptor, triggering the induction of Ahresponsive genes which can lead to an antiestrogenic effect. Polychlorinated biphenyls (PCBs) were manufactured and used widely as coolants and lubricants in transformers, capacitors, and other electrical equipment. There are no known natural sources of PCBs. PCBs generally appear to produce antiestrogenic and possibly antiandrogenic responses.

Phthalate esters are used in the manufacture of polyvinyl chloride as a softening agent and shown to be estrogenic. Compounds identified to date in descending order of potency include butylbenzyl phthalate (BBP), dibutyl phthalate, diisobutyl phthalate, and diethyl phthalate (Harris *et al.*, 1997).

Pesticides

Pesticides are used to control a wide variety of insect and plant pests. Pesticides are usually applied as a formulation containing the active ingredient, along with other materials, such as solvents, wetting agents or carriers (Pait *et al.*, 1992). Some active ingredients have the potential to impact the endocrine system, as do some of the surfactants used in the formulations. The carbamate and carbofuran insecticide has been shown to inhibit oocyte development in fish (Sukumar and Karpagaganapathy, 1992). Tennant *et al.* (1994), working with rats, concluded that while the chloro-s-triazine herbicides atrazine and simazine did not possess any intrinsic estrogenic activity, these two compounds were capable of weak inhibition of estrogen-stimulated responses in the rat uterus (i.e., effect on progesterone receptor binding, and thymidine incorporation into uterine DNA). More recently, Crain *et al.* (1997) showed that atrazine has the ability to stimulate production of the enzyme aromatase which converts androgens to estrogens, and presumably could interfere with sexual differentiation and development.

DDT, the pesticide has been shown to induce production of the egg protein vitellogenin in primary fish hepatocytes (Celius *et al.*, 1999). The metabolites of DDT also appear capable of impacting the endocrine system.

Natural Products

A number of phytoestrogens, including genistein, daidzein and enterodiol are known to affect the endocrine system. An infertility syndrome in sheep, known as clover disease, can be found in animals grazing on subterranean clover (Cheek *et al.*, 1998). Hughes (1988) has gone as far to suggest that phyoestrogens might actually be a defense strategy by plants to limit the fertility of grazing herbivores. Fungi are also known to produce several toxins which can affect the endocrine system (Celius *et al.* 1999). One of these is the mycotoxin zearalenone produced by *Fusarium*, a common contaminant in cereals and other plant products. One of the compounds that could be responsible is â sitosterol, a major byproduct of wood pulp delignification, which appears to be activated or produced in the presence of *Mycobacte rium smegmatis* (Bortone and Cody, 1999; MacLatchy *et al.*, 1997 . In addition to the compound types discussed above, there is growing acknowledgment that natural and synthetic estrogens, when present, are likely responsible for at least some of the endocrine-related effects seen in fish, particularly near sewage treatment plants) (STPs) (Harries *et al.*,1999; Purdom *et al.*, 1994; Larsson *et al.*, 1999). The synthetic estrogen 17α-ethinylestradiol used in oral contraceptives, has been found in STP effluents along with E2 and the E2 metabolites estrone and estriol. Industrial activities can be the source of a variety of endocrine disrupting compounds including surfactants and polycyclic aromatic hydrocarbons.

Trace Elements

Kime (1999) has pointed out that trace elements which induce the production of metallothioneins in the liver or gonads might disrupt gamete production by disturbing normal zinc homeostasis, essential for the development of both eggs and sperm. Cadmium, at aqueous concentrations of 50 ppm, has been shown to significantly decrease sperm motility (Kime *et al.*, 1996). Mercury has been shown to have a major impact on sperm motility at a concentration of only 1ppb (Rurangwa *et al.,* 1998), and to have a direct effect on the egg micropyle, preventing entry of sperm (Khan and Weis, 1993). In rainbow trout, exposure to lead resulted in smaller oocytes (eggs) (Ruby *et al.,* 2000).

Other Chemicals

Test chemicals used for the work include those that (could) impact HPG function relatively "high" in the axis, such as muscimol (a pharmaceutical) and fipronil (an insecticide) which act, respectively, as an agonist and antagonist of specific GABA (gamma amino butyric acid) receptors. The drugs apomorphine and haloperidol act as an agonist and antagonist, respectively, of dopamine receptors

(D2) involved in the release of gonadotrophic hormones from the pituitary. The fungicides ketoconazole and prochloraz, and the pharmaceuticals trilostane and fadrozole inhibit one or more enzymes involved in steroid biosynthesis in the gonad, including reactions catalyzed by 3-hydroxysteroid ehydrogenase (3-HSD) and different cytochromes P450 (CYPs). 17-ethinylestradiol and 17-trenbolone, potent synthetic steroidal agonists of the ER and androgen receptor (AR), respectively, and vinclozolin (a fungicide) and flutamide (a pharmaceutical), which antagonize the AR. The aquatic environment is the ultimate sink for the majority of these chemicals. Consequently, aquatic animals including fish are often exposed to these chemical compounds. The EEs in the sewage effluents induce a feminization in wild male fish due to disruption of the endocrine system, and interfere with the reproductive process of wild fish by mimicking the action of an endogenous hormone (Jobling and Tyler, 2003; Robinson et al., 2003). In wild animals, it is know that the EEs also have effects on induction of precursor protein synthesis and gene expression of yolk protein (vitellognenin, VTG) in male (Jobling et al 1998), alterations of sex steroid synthesis Folmar et al., 1996), and impediment of gonadal development and reproductive phenomena (Folmar et al., 1996).

MODE OF ACTION

Endocrine disrupting compounds are believed to exert their influence by: (*i*) mimicking the effects of endogenous hormones, such as the estrogens and androgens; (*ii*) antagonizing the effects of endogenous hormones; (*iii*) altering the pattern of synthesis and metabolism of normal hormones; and (*iv*) modifying hormone receptor levels (Soto *et al.*, 1995). EDCs may also interfere with the binding proteins that act to transport endogenous hormones to their destination.

The most frequently studied and best understood type of EDCs is those that mimic estrogens (Gillesby and Zacharewski, 1998; Kime, 1999). A current model for the binding and action of E2 is shown in Figure 1 . Estradiol produced by the ovaries and transported via the circulatory system is passively taken up by the cell (e.g., hepatocyte) and then crosses the nuclear membrane. The unliganded estrogen receptor (ER) is maintained in an inactive conformation through interactions with a number of proteins, primarily heat shock proteins Hsp 59, 70, and 90 (Gillesby and Zacharewski, 1998). Following the binding of estrogen to the receptor, the heat shock proteins dissociate allowing the ER to change its conformation to the active form. Once activated, the receptor forms a homodimer complex which seeks out specific DNA segments, in this case the estrogen response elements (EREs). Binding of the complex to the ERE results in a rearrangement of the chromatin and transcription of the gene, followed by production of the target protein. A compound able to bind to the estrogen receptor in the cell might very well result in transcription and pleiotropic responses potentially affecting numerous functions within the organism. While vitellogenin is normally associated with female fish, male fish also possess the hepatocyte ER and can synthesize vitellogenin when exposed to E2 or to estrogen mimics. The production of this egg protein in oviparous fish, particularly in males, has become an important biomarker in the investigation of EDCs, both in the laboratory and in the field. Normally, vitellogenin in males is either absent or at very low concentrations (Sumpter and Jobling, 1995; Panter *et al.*, 1998; Harries *et al.*, 1997). In females vitellogenin is taken up by the ovaries, in male fish vitellogenin produced as a result of exposure to estrogens or to estrogen mimics is only slowly metabolized, making it a valuable biomarker. Currently, however, the ecological significance of elevated levels of vitellogenin in fish, particularly in males, is unclear (Jobling *et al.*, 1998). Although the mode of action of estrogenic compounds on the production of vitellogenin in male fish is fairly well understood, there still remains much uncertainty as to how EDCs impact the overall development of aquatic organisms. In most cases, timing of exposure during development seems to be critical. It appears there is a labile period when fish are most susceptible to endocrine pertubation occurring just after hatching or at a juvenile stage, the time prior to morphological sex differentiation (Jobling *et al.*, 1998). Sex reversal in fish by treating eggs or larvae with E2 or testosterone has found widespread use in aquaculture (Yamaziki, 1983). There is also some evidence that adult gonadal organisation can be affected, but these changes appear to be reversible once the EDC is removed EDCs mimic our body's natural hormones, binding to cells and causing changes that our natural hormones would otherwise initiate. As a result, body responds as though our own hormones are sending signals for cells to grow, die, turn genes on or off, reproduce and so on. This can cause particularly devastating and lifelong health problems if the wrong signals are received by cells, starting at conception and going through adolescence when organs and tissues are developing. As a result, foetuses and children are at high risk of harm from exposures to EDCs, though adults can also be affected either from exposures early in life or from cumulative exposures over a lifetime.

CONCLUSION

Both from ecological effects and species extrapolation perspectives, fish tests are an important component of EDC screening and testing programmes. Partial- and full-life cycle tests with fish that are focused on key aspects of reproduction and development not only provide a basis for quantitative predictions of ecological risk of EDCs to fish populations but, through consideration of endpoints that are sensitive and diagnostic for different classes of EDCs, serve as effective generalized models for identifying chemicals that affect specific components of the vertebrate HPG axis.

Table 3.2: Overview of Reproductive Toxicity to the Fathead Minnow of Chemicals with Differing MOA in the Hypothalamic–pituitary–gonadal (HPG) axis

Test Chemical	Presumptive HPG Target(s)	References
Fipronil	GABA receptor antagonist	Kahl et al. (2007)
Muscimol	GABA receptor agonist	–
Apomorphine	D2 receptor agonist	–
Haloperidol	D2 receptor antagonist	
Trilostane	3 βHSD inhibitor, reduces egg production, inhibit of steroidogenesis, decreased Vtg concentrations in female fish due to a depression in synthesis of estradiol.	Villeneuve et al. (2008)
Ketoconazole	CYP11A/CYP17 inhibitor. Ketoconazole is a pharmaceutical that decreases fungal growth through inhibition of an ergosterol (cell wall component),biosynthesis step catalyzed by CYP51. However, ketoconazole is not particularly specific to CYP51, and can inhibit a variety of vertebrate CYPs involved in xenobiotic metabolism and steroid biosynthesis. In fact, the fungicide is considered amodel inhibitor of testosterone production in mammals and fish.	Ankley et al. (2007)
Fadrozole	CYP19 inhibitor, inhibit of steroidogenesis, decreased Vtg concentrations in female fish due to a depression in synthesis of estradiol . Fadrozole was developed to treat breast cancer as a relatively specific inhibitor of CYP19 aromatase, the enzyme that catalyzes conversion of estosterone to estradiol. decreased circulating concentration of Vtg in the females and, ultimately, decreased deposition of the lipoprotein in the developing oocytes This corresponds with significant reductions in fecundity of fadrozole-exposed fish, resulting in complete cessation of egg production at higher fadrozole exposure concentrations.	Ankley et al. (2002)
Prochloraz	CYP17/19 inhibitor, inhibit of steroidogenesis, decreased Vtg concentrations in female fish due to a depression in synthesis of estradiol.	Ankley et al. (2005)
Vinclozolin	AR antagonist, demasculinized males	Martinovi ´c et al. (2008)
Flutamide	AR antagonist	Jensen et al. (2004)
Trenbolone	AR agonist, reduces egg production, caused morphological masculinisation of female fathead minnows.	Ankley et al. (2003)
Ethinylestradiol	ER agonist, synhthetic estrogen used in birth control pills, bind to estrogen receptor more firmly than estrogen.	–

Abbreviations used: GABA: gamma-amino butyric acid; D2: dopamine; 3β-HSD: 3β-hydroxysteroid dehydrogenase; CYP11A: cytochrome P450scc (side-chain-cleavage); CYP17: cytochrome P450c17, 20-lyase; CYP19: cytochrome P450 aromatase; AR: androgen receptor; ER: estrogen receptor. LOEC: Lowest-observable effect concentration for egg production in 21-d tests. Values are nominal water concentrations provided in µg/L.

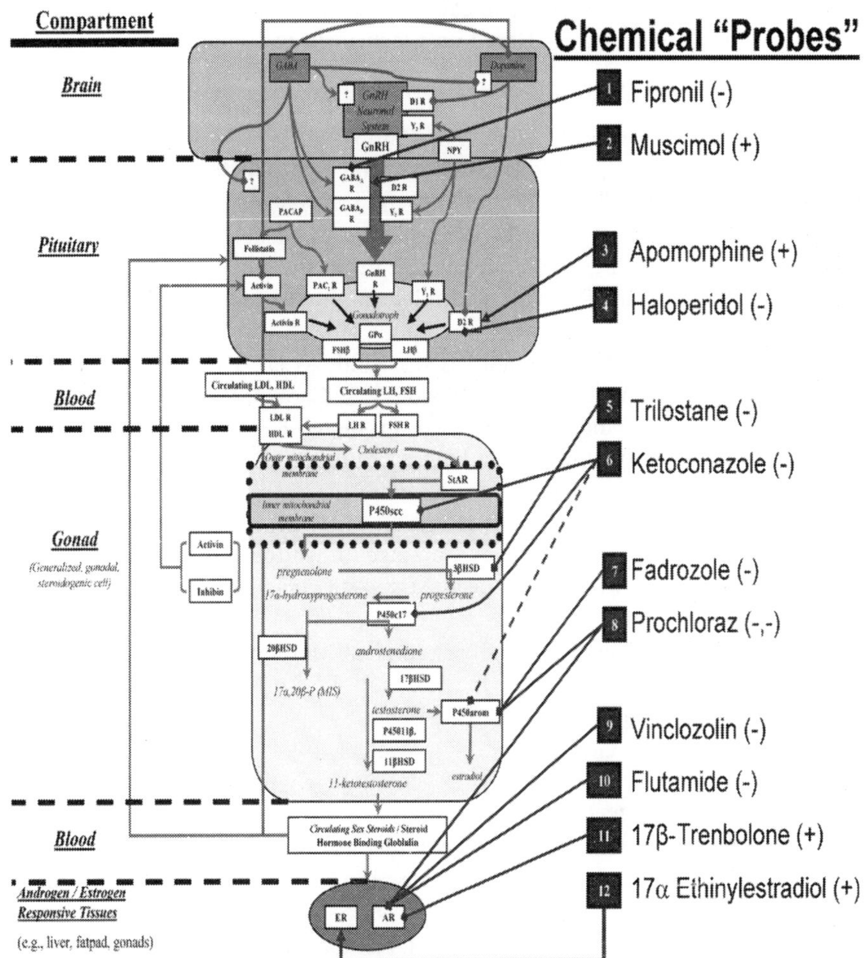

Fig. 3.1: Overview of the Fish Hypothalamic–pituitary–gonadal (HPG) Axis, and experimental chemical "probes" with different mechanisms of action. The "+" or "–" shown in parentheses indicate, respectively, stimulation or inhibition of a particular target (enzyme or receptor) by the test chemical (Ankley et al., 2009)

REFERENCES

Anderson, M.J., M.R. Miller, and D.E. Hinton. 1996a. *In vitro* Modulation of 17β-estradiol Induced Vitellogenin Synthesis: Effects of Cytochrome P4501A1 inducing Compounds on Rainbow Trout (*Oncorhynchus mykiss*) Liver Cells. Aquatic Toxicol. 34: 327-350.

Ankley Gerald T., David C. Bencic, Michael S. Breen, Timothy W. Collette, Rory B. Conolly, Nancy D. Denslow, StephenW. Edwards, Drew R. Ekman, Natalia Garcia-Reyero, Kathleen M. Jensen, James M. Lazorchak, Dalma Martinovi, David H. Miller, Edward J.

Perkins, Edward F. Orlando, Daniel L. Villeneuve, Rong-LinWang, Karen H.Watanabe, 2009. Endocrine Disrupting Chemicals in Fish: Developing Exposure Indicators and Predictive Models of Effects Based on Mechanism of Action. Aquatic Toxicology 92 (2009) 168-178.

Ankley, G.T., Jensen, K.M., Durhan, E.J., Makynen, E.A., Butterworth, B.C., Kahl, M.D., Villeneuve, D.L., Linnum, A., Gray, L.E., Cardon, M., Wilson, V.S., 2005. Effects of Two Fungicides with Multiple Modes of Action on Reproductive Endocrine Function in the Fathead Minnow (*Pimephales promelas*). Toxicol. Sci. 86, 300-308.

Ankley, G.T., Jensen, K.M., Kahl, M.D., Makynen, E.A., Blake, L.S., Greene, K.J., Johnson, R.D., Villeneuve, D.L., 2007. Ketoconazole in the Fathead Minnow (*Pimephales promelas*): Reproductive Toxicity and Biological Compensation. Environ. Toxicol. Chem. 26, 1214-1223.

Ankley, G.T., Jensen, K.M., Makynen, E.A., Kahl, M.D., Korte, J.J., Hornung,M.W., Henry,T.R., Denny, J.S., Leino, R.L., Wilson, V.S., Cardon, M.C., Hartig, P.C., Gray, L.E., 2003. Effects of the Androgenic Growth Promoter 17_-trenbolone on Fecundity and Reproductive Endocrinology of the Fathead Minnow (*Pimephales promelas*). Environ. Toxicol. Chem. 22, 1350-1360.

Ankley, G.T., Kahl, M.D., Jensen, K.M., Hornung, M.W., Korte, J.J., Makynen, E.A., Leino, R.L., 2002. Evaluation of the Aromatase Inhibitor Fadrozole in a Short-term Reproduction Assay with the Fathead Minnow (*Pimephales promelas*). Toxicol. Sci. 67, 121-130.

Bortone, S.A., and R.P. Cody. 1999. Morphological Masculinization in Poeciliid Females from a Papermill Effluent Receiving Tributary of the St. Johns River, Florida, USA. Bull. Environ. Contam. Toxicol. 63: 150-156.

Celius, T., T.B. Haugen, T. Grotmol, and B.T. Walther. 1999. A Sensitive Zonagenetic Assay for Rapid in vitro Assessment of Estrogenic Potency of Xenobiotics and Mycotoxins. Environ. Health Perspect. 107(1): 63-68.

Cheek, A.O., P.M. Vonier, E. Oberdorster, B.C. Burow, and J.A. McLachlan. 1998. Environmental Signaling: A Biological Context for Endocrine Disruption. Environ. Health Perspect. 106(Suppl): 5-10.

Crain, D.A., L.J. Guillette, A.A. Rooney, and D.B. Pickford. 1997. Alterations in Steroidogenesis in Alligators *(Alligator mississippiensis)* Exposed Naturally and Experimentally to Environmental Contaminants. Environ. Health Perspect. 105(5): 528-533.

Field, J.A., R.L. Reed. 1996. Nonylphenol Polyethoxy Carboxylate Metabolites of Nonionic Surfactants in U.S. Paper Mill Effluents, Municipal Effluents, Municipal Sewage Treatment Plant Effluents, and River Waters. Environ. Sci. Tech. 30: 3544-3550.

Folmar LC, Denslow ND, Rao V, Chow M, Crain DA, Enblom J, et al. 1996. Vitellogenin Induction and Reduced Serum Testosterone Concentrations in Feral Male Carp (*Cyprinus carpio*) Captured Near a Major Metropolitan Sewage Treatment Plant. Environ Health Perspect 104: 1096-1101.

Gillesby, B.E., and T.R. Zacharewski. 1998. Exoestrogens: Mechanisms of Action and Strategies for Identification and Assessment. Environ. Toxicol. Chem. 17(1): 3-14.

Harries, J.E., A. Janbakhsh, S. Jobling, P. Matthiessen, J.P. Sumpter, and C.R. Tyler. 1999. Estrogenic Potency of Effluent from Two Sewage Treatment Works in the United Kingdom. Environ. Toxicol. Chem. 18(5): 932-937.

Harris, C.A., P. Henttu, M.G. Parker, and J.P.Sumpter. 1997. The Estrogenic Activity of Phthalateesters in vitro. Environ. Health Perspect. 105(8): 802811.

Jensen, K.M., Kahl, M.D., Makynen, E.A., Korte, J.J., Leino, R.L., Butterworth, B.C., Ankley, G.T., 2004. Characterization of Responses to the Antiandrogen Flutamide in a Short-term Reproduction Assay with the Fathead Minnow. Aquat. Toxicol. 70, 99-110.

Jobling, S. and C.R. Tyler. 2003. Endocrine Disruption in Wild Freshwater Fish. *Pure and Applied Chemistry* 75: 2219-2234.

Jobling, S., M. Nolan, C.R. Tyler, G. Brightly, and J.P. Sumpter. 1998. Widespread Sexual Disruption in Wild Fish. Environ. Sci. Technol. 32:2498-2506.

Kahl, M.D., Bencic, D.C., Blake, L.S., Brodin, J.D., Durhan, E.J., Jensen, K.M., Ankley, G.T., 2007. Evaluation of a Novel Mechanism of Endocrine Disruption in the Fathead Minnow. In: Abstracts, 28th Annual Meeting of the Society of Environmental Toxicology and Chemistry, Milwaukee, WI.

Kavlock, R.J., Daston, G.P., DeRosa, C., Fenner-Crisp, P., Gray, L.E., Kaattari, S., et al.,1996. Research Needs for the Risk Assessment of Health and Environmental Effects of Endocrine Disruptors: A Report of the U.S. EPA-sponsored Workshop. Environ Health Perspect. 104 (Suppl. 4), 715-740.

Khan and Weis, 1993. Khan, A.T., and J.S. Weis. 1993. Differential Effects of Organic and Inorganic Mercury on the Micropyle of the Eggs of *Fundulus heteroclitus*. Environ. Biol. Fishes 37: 323-327.

Kime, D.E. 1998. Endocrine Disruption in Fish. Kluer Academic Publishers. Boston, MA 396 pp.

Kime, D.E., J.P. Nash and A.P. Scott. 1999. Vitellogenesis as a Biomarker of Reproductive Disruption by Xenobiotics. *Aquaculture* 177: 345-352.

Kime, D.E., M. Ebrahimi, and K. Nysten. 1996. Use of Computer Assisted Sperm Analysis (CASA) for Monitoring the Effects of Pollution on Sperm Quality of Fish; Application to Effects of Heavy Metals. Aqua. Toxicol. 36: 223-237.

Krishnan, R.V., P. Stathis, S.F. Permuth, L. Tokes, and D. Feldman. 1993. Bisphenol-A: and Estrogenic Substance is Released from Polycarbonate Flasks during Autoclaving. Endocrinology, 32(6): 2279-2286.

MacLatchy, D., L. Peters, J. Nickle, and G. Van Der Kraak. 1997. Exposure to β-sitosterol Alters the Endocrine Status of Goldfish Differently than 17βestradiol Environ. Toxicol. Chem. 16(9): 1895-1904.

Martinovi ´ c, D., Blake, L.S., Durhan, E.J., Greene, K.J., Kahl, M.D., Jensen, K.M., Makynen, E.A., Villeneuve, D.L., Ankley, G.T., 2008. Reproductive Toxicity of Vinclozolin in the Fathead Minnow: Confirming an Anti-androgenic Mode of Action. Environ. Toxicol. Chem. 27, 178 188.

Mitksicek, R.J. 1995. Estrogenic Flavonoids: Structural Requirements for Biological Activity. Proc. Exp. Biol.Med. 208:44-50.

Panter, G.H., R.S. Thompson, and J.P. Sumpter. 1998. Adverse Reproductive Effects in Male Fathead Minnows (*Pimphales promelas*) Exposed to Environmentally Relevant Concentrations of the Natural Oestrogens, Oestradiol and Oestrone. Aquat. Toxicol. 42: 243-253.

Purdom, C.E., P.A. Hardiman, V.J. Bye, N.C. Eno, C.R. Tyler, and J.P. Sumpter. 1994. Estrogenic Effects of Effluents from Sewage Treatment Works. ChemEcol. 8: 275-285.

Robinson, C.D., E. Brown, J.A. Craft, I.M. Davies, C.F. Moffat, D. Pirie, F. Rovertson, E.M. Stagg and S. Struthers. 2003. Effects of Sewage Effluent and Ethynyl Oestradiol Upon Molecular Markers of Oestrogenic Exposure, Maturation and Reproductive Success in the san goby (*Pomatoschistus minutus*, Pallas). *Aquatic Toxicology* 62: 119-134.

Ruby, S.M. R. Hull, and P. Anderson. 2000. Sublethal Lead Affects Pituitary Function of Rainbow Trout during Exogenous Vitellogenesis. Arch. Environ. Contam. Toxicol. 38: 46-51.

Rurangwa, E., I. Roelants, G. Huyskens, M. Ebrahimi,D.E. Kime, and F. Ollevier. 1998. The Minimum Effective Spermatozoa to Egg Ratio for Artificial insemination and the Effects of Mercury on Spermmotility and Fertilization Ability in *Clarias gariepinus*.J. Fish Biol. 53: 402-413.

Santodonato, J. 1997. Review of Estrogenic and Antiestrogenic Activity of Polycyclic Aromatic Hydrocarbons: Relationship to Carcinogenicity. Chemosphere. 34(4): 835-848.

Soto AM, Sonnenschein C, Chung KL, Fernandez MF, Olea N, Serrano FO (1995) Environ Sukumar, A. and P.R. Karpagaganapathy. 1992. Pesticide-induced Atresia in Ovary of a Fresh Water Fish, *Colisa lalia* (Hamilton-Buchanan). Bull. Environ. Contam. Toxicol. 48: 457-462.

Sukumar, A. and P.R. Karpagaganapathy. 1992. Pesticide-induced Atresia in Ovary of a Fresh Water Fish, *Colisa lalia* (Hamilton-Buchanan). Bull. Environ. Contam. Toxicol. 48: 457-462.

Sumpter, J.P. 1995. Feminized Responses in Fish to Environmental Estrogens. *Toxicology Letters*, 82/83: 737-742.

Sumpter, J.P., S. Jobling. 1995. Vitellogenesis as a Biomarker for Estrogenic Contamination.

Tennant, M.K., D.S. Hill, J.C. Eldridge, L.T. Wetzel, C.B. Breckenridge, and J.T. Stevens. 1994.

Possible Antiestrogenic Properties of Chloro-s-trianzines in Rat uterus. J. Toxicol. Environ. Health. 43: 183-196.

Villeneuve, D.L., Blake, L.S., Brodin, J.D., Cavallin, J.E., Durhan, E.J., Jensen, K.M., Kahl, M.D., Makynen, E.A., Martinovi ´ c, D., Mueller, N.D., Ankley, G.T., 2008. Effects of a 3_-hydroxysteroid Dehydrogenase Inhibitor, Trilostane, on the Fathead Minnow Reproductive Axis. Toxicol. Sci. 104, 113-123.

White, R., S. Jobling, S.A. Hoare, J.P. Sumpter, and M.G. Parker. 1994. Environmentally Persistent Alkylphenolic Compounds are Estrogenic. Endocrinology. 135/1: 175-182.

Yamazaki, F. 1983. Sex Control and Manipulation in Fish. Aquaculture. 33: 329-354.

4

Pearl Culture Technology in Freshwater Environment

Shailesh Saurabh; U.L. Mohanty; J.Mohanty and P. Jayasankar

ABSTRACT

Pearl culture is a billion dollar industry and one of the world's largest aquaculture activities in terms of value. The Vedas, the Bible and the Koran speak on pearls giving one of the highest places for it. In nature pearls are formed when an irritant like sand grain or parasite is swept into the pearl mollusks and is lodged within it and gets coated by micro layers of nacre, a shining substance made of 80-90% $CaCO_3$. *Realizing the scope and importance of freshwater pearl culture, the Central Institute of Freshwater Aquaculture (CIFA, ICAR), Kausalyaganga, Bhubaneswar, India has developed a base technology of growing pearls in freshwater environments. Indian pond mussel, Lamellidens marginalis is the major species used in pearl aquaculture. In this chapter an attempt has been made to briefly discuss about indigenously developed nucleus preparation technique, different surgical procedure used for implantation, pond culture, value addition etc. Apart from that biomineralization of pearl, pearl sac formation, difference between natural, cultured and artificial pearl, mechanism of pearl formation and current status of freshwater pearl culture is also dealt elsewhere. The Institute has also taken the lead to disseminate the technology of freshwater pearl culture to the fish farming communities, entrepreneurs, researchers and students of the country.*

Keywords: Pearl, *Lamellidens marginalis*, biocompatible nucleus, pond culture, value addition.

INTRODUCTION

The incomparable beauty of the pearl has beguiled human civilization since the dawn of time and it has been cherished by the all sections of peoples. Pearls are sources of wisdom, symbols of wealth, power, love, innocence, hope, femininity and prestige and have aesthetic values. The first pearls may have been found accidentally while searching for food. The Vedas, the Bible and the Koran speak on pearls giving one of the highest places for it. The Indian epics Ramayana and Mahabharata mention pearls and also indicate inclusion of pearl divers in the army units in times of war (Alagarswami, 1991). A Hindu legend recites that lord Krishna presented the first pearl to his daughter as a wedding gift and until today Indian brides traditionally wear pearls on their wedding days and other religious occasion. In Sanskrit pearls were named as "Mukta" which entails as much as purity or escape, alluding to the spirit of the mollusk that wants to escape and solidify as a pearl.Actuated by the high economic value and awesome beauty of natural pearls Japanese researchers-Tokichi Nishikawa, Tatsuhei Mise and Kokichi Mikimoto has developed technologies that brought pearl production under the control ofhuman (Gervis and Sims, 1992; Strack, 2008).

According to our Indian system of gemology, of nine *maharatnas*viz., Diamond, Ruby, Yellow sapphire, blue sapphire, Pearl, Red coral, Hessonite, Cat's eye, Emerald (Table 4.1) the pearl is positioned only next to diamond (Kumar *et al.,* 2012).

Table 4.1: Maharatna Gemstones and Their Planetary Representations

Sl. No.	Maharatna Gemstones		
	English Name	Hindi Name	Associated Planet
1.	Blue Sapphire	Neelam	Saturn or Shani
2.	Cat's Eye	Vaiduryam	Ketu
3.	Diamond	Heera or Vairam or Vajra	Venus or Shukra
4.	Emerald	Panna or Marakat	Mercury or Budh
5.	Hessonite	Gomed	Rahu
6.	Pearl	Moti or Mukta	Moon or Chandra
7.	Red Coral	Moonga	Mars or Kuja
8.	Ruby	Manikya or Manikkam	Sun or Surya
9.	Yellow Sapphire	Pukharaj	Jupiter or Guru

Each gemstone is related to one planet and considered auspicious and believed to give happiness, prosperity, peace of mind, and good health to those who wear it. Further, pearl was considered as an exclusive privilege of royalty and throughout history held presence within wealthy and powerful people. They are viewed as magic charms, symbols of purity and serenity.Moreover, pearl is the only gem that does not require the treatment by lapidary. Pearl culture is a billion dollar industry and one of the world's largest aquaculture activities in terms of value. Moreover, pearl cultivation is a lucrative venture because of the towering cost of the finished product. Realizing the scope and importance of freshwater pearl culture, the Central Institute of Freshwater Aquaculture (CIFA, ICAR), Kausalyaganga, Bhubaneswar, India has developed a base technology of growing pearls in freshwater environments.

NATURAL VS.CULTURED PEARLS VS. ARTIFICIAL PEARLS

Pearl also known as the queen of gems is an organic gem created by living mussels and oysters (Kumar *et al.,* 2009). As a response to a foreign irritant substance inside the shell of mollusks, the living organism creates a pearl to seal off the irritation. Natural pearls are formed when an irritant like sand grain or parasite is swept into the pearl mollusks and is lodged within it. As a self-defense reaction, the mollusks release a substance, popularly known as nacre, to coat the foreign irritant substance. Layer upon layer of this coating is accumulated on the irritant, resulting in a shimmering and iridescent creation of a pearly gem. On the other hand production of cultured pearl requires implantation ofprocessed mantle graft tissue from a donor mussel and a biocompatible nucleus into the mantle/gonadal region of the host organisms, which causes irritation inside the mollusks body followed by a secretion of nacreous substances on the foreign irritant substance. Pearls are then produced in a controlled aquaculture pondcondition over a long culture period of 8-18 months in Indian condition. Thus, the nature's hand is not completely eliminated;in factit is the animal that determines the character of the pearl produced. Thus both natural and cultured pearls are formed in a very similar process. The main difference is that whether the irritant that causes the creation process is invaded spontaneously by nature or inserted by technical experts (Saurabh, 2012, 2013).

Artificial pearl simply contain a rigid, round core or base and an outer pearly coating. The coating can vary from inexpensive shining paints to synthetic pearl essences to natural essences obtained from certain fish scales. Majority of imitation pearls givesa smooth feeling when rubbed against teeth and when a pin is pressed into the surface, it easily leaves a scratch or indent unlike genuine natural or cultured pearls (Kumar *et al.,* 2012). The difference between natural and cultured pearl as well as real verses artificial pearls are presented in the tables 4.2 and 4.3 respectively. The different steps in pearl process are depicted in figure 4.1.

Table 4.2: Natural vis-a-vis Cultured Pearl

Character	Natural Pearl	Cultured Pearl
Kernel	Sand or parasite	Graft tissue and or biocompatible nucleus
Nacre	Thick nacre	100% nacre or thin nacre
Shape	Irregular	Regular: Round, half round or Image
Transparency	More	Comparatively less
Texture	Fine and rough feeling	Rougher feeling
Growth time	Long	Short (1 to 1.6 years)

Table 4.3: Real vis-à-vis Artificial Pearl

Character	Real Pearl	Artificial Pearl
Materials	Nacre and Nucleus	Glass beads coated with fish scales powder or silvery powder
Luster	Beautiful, colourful and rainbow like shining	Monotonous shinning
Transparency	Welcome ray	Dull ray
Feelings	Smooth and cool	Warm
Cluster of pearl	No definite consistency of colour, shape, size etc.	Almost same colour, shape, size etc.
Visibility under magnifying glass	Growth texture visible	Only coating visible

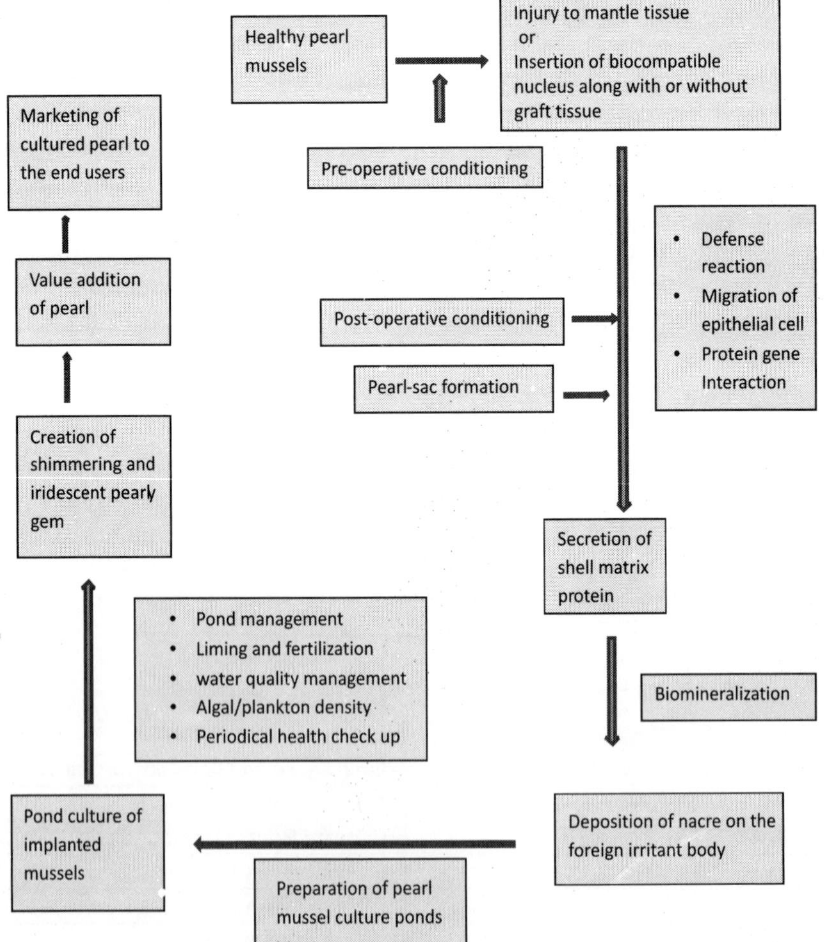

Fig. 4.1: Schematic Diagram of Different Steps in Pearl Production Process

COMPOSITION OF PEARL

Pearl is the most popular and precious type of mineralized carbonates, composed of several hundreds to thousands of alternating layers of aragonite crystals (one of the polymorphs of $CaCO_3$) and organic matter. It is both mystic and beautiful with its soft colour and cool luster. Scientifically a pearl can be defined in three ways. In simple chemical language, the composition of a pearl is about 82-86% aragonite crystals of calcium carbonate; 10 to 14% organic matrix, a scleroprotein termed as conchiolin; and 2-4% water, as described in Webster (1975). In physical terms, a pearl has 3.5 to 4.5 hardness on Moh's scale with a specific gravity of 2.7. Biologically, a pearl is more or less similar to the inner shining layer called 'mother of pearl layer' or nacre of shells which exhibits fracture toughness ~3,000 times greater than that of mineral alone (Shen *et al.,* 1997).It consists of layers of interlocking thin tablets of aragonite typically 400 nm thick and 5-10 μm wide surrounded on all sides by thin sheets of organic matrix approximately 30 nm thick (Nakahara, 1991). Organic matrix proteins are thought to be responsible for the toughness on the nacreous layer and to have some critical roles in calcification (Cariolou and Morse, 1988; Miyamoto *et al.,* 2005). Hence pearls are the biominerals of organic-inorganic composition with exceptional strength and hardness. The mechanical design of this biomaterial is intriguing and scientists have been exploring it for many years (Stephen, 2001).Similarly, Taylor and Strack (2008) reported that pearls are composed of calcium carbonate (91.50%) with traces of organic substances (3.83%), residual substances (0.01%) and water (3.97%). The residual substances include Na, Cl and K and traces of other elements such as Ba, Mg, P, Mn, Fe, Al, Cu, Zn, Ag, Hg, Li and Sr. The trace elements reflect the composition of the water at the location where a pearl was formed.

Identification of natural freshwater pearls is most reliably accomplished in the laboratory using a combination of X-radiography, which discloses the internal structural characteristics that show natural or cultured origin and X-ray fluorescence which usually establishes freshwater and saltwater origin (Sweaney and Latendresse, 1984). It is also reported that X-radiography has formed the backbone of pearl identification. In the field, distinctive characteristics of appearance are in many cases adequate to identify freshwater natural pearls. Important identifications should be confirmed by laboratory tests or by persons experienced in handling these goods.

BIOMINERALIZATION OF PEARLS

Biomineralization is the process of hard tissue formation in an organism and has been characterized as a highly controlled and functional process (Simkiss, 1989). It plays a vital role in pearl mussels shell formation. These processes construct a diversity of exo - and endo -skeletons by depositing biogenic solid minerals. The molluscan shell is a comprehensive product of biomineralization used to protect the soft body (Gong *et al.,* 2008),containing 94% calcium carbonate and about 6%

organic matrix. The minor organic composition includes proteins and polysaccharides; those influence the shell formation (Zhang and Zhang, 2006). Generally, the shell consists of three layers, namely an outer periostracum, the middle prismatic calcite and the inner nacreous or crystalline aragonite calcium carbonate layers. In the course of shell formation, the periostracum, which is not mineralized and covers the external surface of the shell, is formed first; subsequently, the prismatic layer is formed on the periostracum. Finally, the nacreous layer is formed on the prismatic layer. The mantle tissue is responsible for shell formation; it secretes organic matrix into the extrapallial fluid located between the tissue and the shell and regulates the ion composition of the body fluid for shell growth (Simkiss, 1989). When a part of the shell is damaged, a mantle starts to regenerate the shell in cooperation with the immune system (Mount *et al.,* 2004). Probably, cell to cell interactions may be also involved in these activities. In general, the outer surface of mantle is covered by a monolayer of epithelial cells, and these epithelial cells have principal roles in the production and regeneration of a shell (Awaji and Machii, 2011).

Shell matrix proteins secreted by the pearl sac have special effects on these different layers and play a vital role in pearl formation. Currently, more than twenty shell matrix proteins have been known at the molecular level. Further, it has been reported that nacrein, lustrin A, MSI60, mucoperlin, perlusin, N16/pearlin, P10, N19, pfi80 and pif97 are involved in the nacreous layer, while MSI31, MSI7, prismalin-14, aspein, KRMP family, prisilkin-39 and the prismin family are involved in the prismatic layer of pearl oyster, *Pinctada fucata*(Suzuki *et al.,* 2004; Takeuchi and Endo, 2006; Fang *et al.,* 2011). In addition, the shematrin family of proteins is involved in the formation of both nacreous and prismatic layers (Fang *et al.,* 2011). During the biomineralization process, calcium is an indispensable element in shell formation. Rousseau *et al.* (2003, 2005) reported that the circulating calcium concentration of 12.3 mM in 48-month old *Pinctada margaritifera* is 0.8mM higher than the calcium concentration of 11.5 mM in 24-month old animals; this indicates that the calcium requirement increases during the growth of animal and during shell growth. Recently Gong *et al.* (2008) developed ELISA assay for quantification of nacrein and of other matrix proteins. ELISA method should have extensive applications in both *in vivo* and *in vitros* studies of biomineralization.

PEARL SAC THEORY

Theoretically any shelled mollusks can produce some sort of a pearl. However, only those mollusks which have a pearl lining or pearl nacre on the interior of the shell surface can produce lustrous pearls. It is an abnormal process in the normal biological system of the animal. The mantle with its outer epithelial cells is the tissue responsible for producing mother of pearl layer or nacre. When an external stimulus such as accidental trapping of a hard foreign body or a parasite or a lesion occurs in the outer epithelium of the mantle tissue, it leads to deposition of micro-layers of pearl nacre around the source of stimulus or foreign body resulting in a pearl.

In designer pearl production, biocompatible nucleus is directly inserted inside the mantle cavity of mussel whereas in round cultured pearl production,a pallial tissue obtained from a donor mussel along with or without biocompatible nucleus is surgically inserted into the mantle tissue and or gonadal region of recipient mussels. The recipient mussel recognizes the mantle graft tissue and the nucleus as a foreign body. They are encapsulated by haemocytes of the recipient. The haemocytes phagocytose the tissue debris and also secretes extracellular matrices (Suzuki and Funakoshi, 1992). During this process the recipient mussel starts to heal the wound. In the course of wound healing processes, the outer epithelial cells of the mantle allograft become squamousand emigrate into the space between the nucleus and the surrounding haemocyte sheets. Finally, the outer epithelial cells of the mantle form a pearl-sac surrounding the irritant foreign body or nucleus forming the cellular basis for crystallization of calcium carbonate. This process of pearl formation is well known to the scientific community as 'Pearl sac Theory'. After completion of the pearl sac formation, pearl-sac epithelial cells start to secrete materials for pearl formation. The pearl formation activities, however, vary greatly from a sac to another sac, and it is quite common to observe the difference in the secretive activities among pearl sac epithelial cells even in a single pearl sac (Awaji and Machii, 2011). Thus this abnormal response to a foreign irritant body in the normal biological processes that build up the shell in certain mollusks constituted the base for pearl culture operations. The shape and size of the pearl are governed by that of the irritant foreign body and its quality by the nature of the secretions of the pearl sac. Thus, the outer epithelium of the mantle tissue is the 'key-note' in the 'orchestra' of biomineralization of a pearl.

Generally, the outer epithelium in the pallial zone of the mantle synthesizes the matrix proteins involved in the inner aragonitic layer of the shell and the edge of the outer epithelium are always related to the outer prismatic layer (Sudo *et al.,* 1997). The mRNA of many shell matrix proteins are specifically expressed in the outer mantle epithelium bordering upon the shell (Takeuchi and Endo, 2006). Moreover, the behaviour of the outer epithelial cells in the course of pearl sac formation provides interesting and important information on the cell-to-cell interactions involved in the wound healing and cell proliferation in mollusks (Awaji and Suzuki, 1998). However, the mechanism by which the outer epithelium regulates the shell formation and matrix synthesis, ion transport etc.is poorly understood. Knowledge of this process is essential for revealing the cellular mechanisms of shell biomineralization (Gong *et al.,* 2008).

INDIAN FRESHWATER PEARL MUSSELS

The genus *Lamellidens* and *Parreysia* are vital for freshwater pearl culture technology in India. There are more than fifty two species of these genera distributed throughout the country (Subba Rao, 1989). Of these, the most common species viz., *L. marginalis* (Fig. 4.2), *L. corrianus* and *P. corrugata*are being employed for freshwater pearl culture technology (Janakiram, 2003). The genus *Lamellidens* is represented by nine species and two sub-species, while the genus *Parreysia* is represented by 35 species and 6 sub-species under two sub-genera.Other species also possess nacreous layer, but their potentialities in culture pearl production are yet to be realized. A list of important candidate species of pearl mussels found in different countries is given in table 4.4.

Fig. 4.2: Indian Freshwater Pearl Mussel *Lamellidens marginalis* (a) Surface view, (b) Internal view

Table 4.4: Freshwater Pearl Producing Mussels

Country	Scientific Name	Remarks
1	2	3
Australia	*Cucumerunio novaehollandiae*	
Bangladesh	*Lamellidens marginalis*	
	Parreysia daccaensis	
China	*Cristaria plicata*	First cultured pearl produced in the shape of Lord Buddha in this species
	Hyriopsis cumingii	Principal pearl producing species
	Hyriopsis cumingii X Hyriopsis schlegelii (Hybrid species)	Producing Superior quality pearl as compared to either species
	Lamprotula mansuyi	
India	*Lamellidens marginalis*	Main pearl producing species; easily available
	Lamellidens corrianus	Available near paddy field
	Parreysia corrugata	Riverine species
Japan	*Cristaria plicata*	
	Hyriopsis schlegelii	Lake Biwa; Biwa pearl
	Hyriopsis schlegelii X Hyriopsis cumingii (Hybrid)	Lake Kasumigaura and lake Biwa

(Contd...)

1	2	3
Korea	*Cristaria plicata*	
Philippines	*Anodonta sp.*	
	Cristaria plicata	
Taiwan	*Anodonta woodiana*	
Thailand	*Chamberlainia hainesiana*	Giving superior pearl quality
	Hyriopsis bialatus	
	Hyriopsis dezowitzi	Giving superior pearl quality
	Hyriopsis myersiana	Giving superior pearl quality, *In vitro* culture of glochidia larvae also developed in this species
	Pseudodon inoscularis cumingi	
	Pseudodon vondembuschianus ellipticus	
	Pseudodon sp.	Giving superior pearl quality
USA	*Potamilus alatus*	Produces purple pearl
	Quadrulaebena	
	Quadrula undulata	
	Unio sp.	
	Pleurobemaoesopus	
	Tritogoniaverrucosa	
	Margaritiferamargaritifera	Endangered species
Vietnam	*Anodonta elliptica*	
	Anodonta jourdyi	
	Cristaria bialata	
	Cristaria plicata	
	Sinohyriopsis cumingii	

STATE OF ART TECHNOLOGY OF FRESHWATER PEARL PRODUCTION

The Central Institute of Freshwater Aquaculture has developed the state of art technology for freshwater pearl production from freshwater mussels. The basic steps in freshwater pearl production are given below:

- Preparation of biocompatible nucleus beads
- Collection of mussels
- Pre-operative conditioning
- Surgical implantation of graft tissue and biocompatible nuclei
- Post-operative care of mussels

- Pond culture of implanted mussels
- Harvest of mussels and pearls
- Value addition of pearls

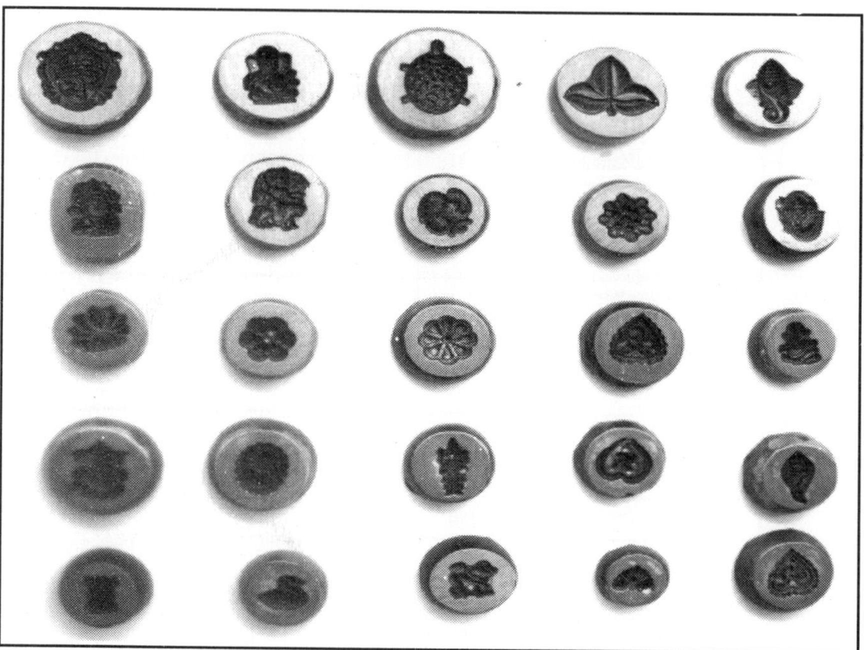

Fig. 4.3: Designer Die

Preparation of Biocompatible Nucleus Beads

The Central Institute of Freshwater Aquaculture has developed the technology of nucleus preparation from indigenous raw materials which was found to be at par with the imported shell-made nuclear bead. The indigenous nuclei developed are made from inexpensive and locally available ingredient like mussel shell powder, acrylic material and egg-shell powder. The procedure for the preparation of these nuclei is fairly simple and most importantly it is found to be accepted by the mussels resulting best quality pearls. For the preparation of the biocompatible nucleus, dead shells of freshwater mussels are collected and washed thoroughly in tap water in order to remove mud and sand particles. The dry flesh materials, if present are scraped out. The shells are then dipped in 5000 ppm of chlorine solution for 5 days. The completely lye-peeled shells are sorted out and are then thoroughly washed in tap water. They are then kept in an oven maintained at 60°C, for more than two hours or can even be sun dried for 2-3 days to ensure the complete removal of chlorine from the treated shells. The dried shells are made into small pieces by using a mortar and pestle and are then finely powdered by means of an electric grinder. The shell powderis then processed through a sieve of 0.01-0.05 mm mesh size. The commercial glue Araldite hardener and resin (acts as a binder) are mixed in a ratio of 1:1 to prepare a paste. To this paste the sieved shell powder is added gradually to prepare dough of thick consistency. The ratio of the shell powder to the binder paste should be 5:1. Immediately, nuclei of desired shape and size are prepared using designer die (Fig. 4.3) or round nucleus are prepared manuallyand then air dried till they become hard (Fig. 4.4). The prepared nuclei are stored in airtight containers. Prior to implantation, the nuclei are boiled in the water and cooled (Kumar, 2012)

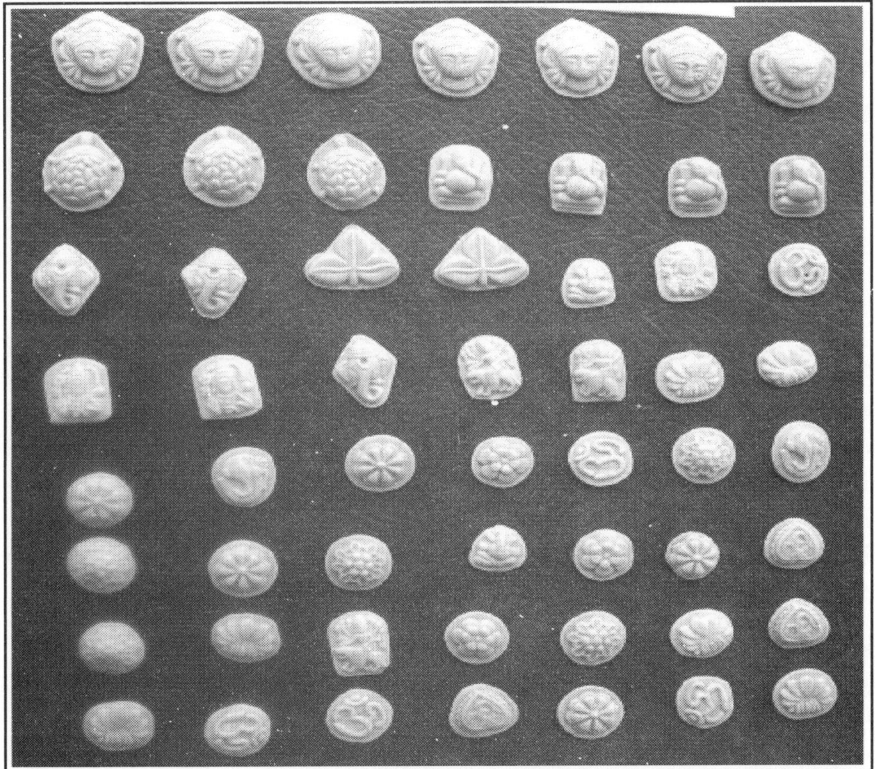

Fig. 4.4: Image Nuclei

Collection of Mussels

Mussels are hand-picked and collected from the natural resources with water for short distance transportation, preferably in the early hours of the morning by skilled workers. The size criteria of the mussels are to be taken care of during collection. It has been observed that the pearl mussels of the size 8-12 cm in shell length and weight of 50 g and above are suitable for pearl culture operations (Fig. 4.5).

Fig. 4.5: Haul of Freshwater Mussel, *L. marginalis*

Pre-operative Conditioning

Pre-operative conditioning ensures proper relaxation of adductor muscles and keeps metabolic rate of animal in reduced state to get the best possible result during the surgical implantation process. Prior to surgery the indigenous pearl musselscollected from the freshwater bodies are subjected to pre-operative conditioning for 24 to 48 hours. The mussels are stocked in aged tap water at a density of one mussel L^{-1} of water. Supplementation of algal feed is restricted during this period. This aspect is important in view of the limited application of narcotizing procedures as followed in marine pearl culture operation.

Surgical Implantations

Depending on the variety of pearl products targeted the surgery is performed in the internal structure of pearl mussel. For production of designer pearl or half round pearl mantle cavity insertion techniques is usually used to do. Unattached non-nucleated small rice pearls and small nucleated round pearls are produced by using the mantle tissue implantation method whereas unattached regular round pearl is produced by the gonadal implantation method. Details of these techniques are discussed below.

Mantle Cavity Implantation

Mantle cavity insertion method is a simple surgical technique, involving less risk and monitoring is easy. Prior to surgery, the indigenous freshwater mussel of 8-12 cm shell length is collected. They are carefully opened by using speculum and nucleus of desired size and shape is inserted into the mantle cavity and is further pushed deep to avoid rejection. Care should be taken that the implanted nuclei do not interfere with the opening and closing of the pearl mussel's shell and haveenough space to allow the coating of nacreous substances. Apart from that the size of the nucleus should be compatible to the mussel so that it can stay inside the mussel body throughout the culture period. Two implantations can be made per mussel targeting two half-round or designer shell attached pearl internationally popular as the mabe pearls. Designer pearl in the form of pendant or half round pearl in the form of ring has become increasing fashionable, in recent years, particularly among young generation.

Mantle Tissue Implantation

In mantle tissue method the mussels before surgery are segregated into two groups, the mussels to be operated upon the 'operations mussels' or 'recipient mussels' and those to be sacrificed, the 'cell mussels' or the 'donor mussels'. The live donor mussel is sacrificed and the pallial mantle ribbon of approximately 0.5 cm wide and 7.0 cm long is collected on a pre-cleaned moist wooden board. The strip is then cut into appropriate sized graft pieces (~2 mm x 2 mm) and implanted alone or along with a small nucleus (~2 mm dia.) into the mantle tissue of the recipient mussel. Grafting is done on both the sides of the mantle lobes. It is worth to mention that mantle tissue used in the grafting process is a vital factor in determining the appearance and quality of the cultured pearl production. Apart from that water quality, soil characteristic, availability of minerals in the water body, pond management and surgical implantation process also affectsthe quality of pearl production. The number of implantations can vary between 2-8 depending upon the size and mantle thickness of the recipient mussel. Small 2 to 3 mm sized pearls of round (nucleated) oval and baroque (non-nucleated) shaped are harvested at the end of the culture period.

Fig. 4.6: Placement of Nucleus in Mantle Tissue

Gonadal Method of Implantation

In the gonadal method of implantation, the recipient mussels are carefully opened once the live graft tissues (~2 to 3 mm^2) are processed for implantation (Fig. 7). A small incision is made by means of a special knife placed at the other end of the graft needle, under the outer membrane of the gonad and a live graft piece along with the nucleus (3 mm to 6 mm) is pushed into it. The critical factor is ensuring that the outer surface of the graft tissue must be in contact with the nucleus. If the graft is not in contact with the nucleus, the pearl-sac will not form around it and only a non-nucleated irregular shape pearl may result. Further, care should also be taken not to cut deep into the gonadal tissue. Single implantation is ideal per mussels and at the end of the culture period regular round pearls are harvested. It is a cumbersome procedure and hence requires special skill,attention and patience.

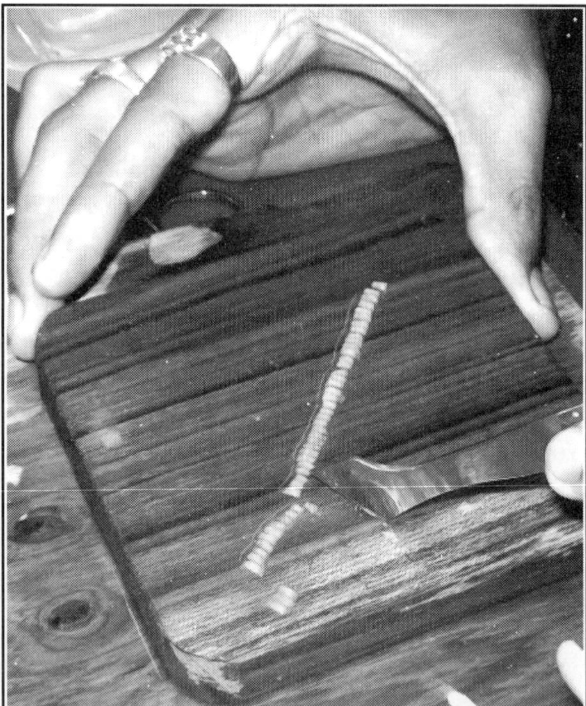

Fig. 4.7: Processing of Pallial Graft Tissue

POST-OPERATIVE CARE

Pearl mussels are kept in the post-operative care unit after surgery for different observations. It is a vital step in freshwater pearl culture operation, which is required for the implanted mussels to recoup. Immediately after surgery restricted movement of the mussel is essential for the retention of the implanted graft and nucleus. Thus, after implantation, the mussels are kept in post operation care units. The implanted mussels are placed at the rate of 2 mussels per bag (30 cm × 13 cm; mesh size 1.5 – 3.0 cm) with the ventral side up position (Fig. 4.8).They are subjected to careful observations for a period of 5-10 days. Sufficient care is taken to allow free opening and closing of the shell valves for respiration. Treatment of the water in post-operative care units with broad spectrum antibiotic, Chloramphenicol, at the rate of 1-2 ppm as a prophylactic measure is beneficial for the survival and wound healing of the implanted mussels(Kumar *et al.,* 2013). The mussels under post-operative care are not fed initially, however on the second or third day onwards they are supplemented with cultured green algae. If there is any mortality occurs during intensive care in implanted mussels then it should be removed immediately from the system.

Fig. 4.8: Implanted Mussels in Post-operative Care Unit

MECHANISM OF PEARL FORMATION IN FRESHWATER MUSSELS

The process of pearl formation is identical to that of shell formation (Farn, 1986). The pearl sac encircled the implanted mantle graft within 15 days after implantation due to the rapid proliferation of epithelial cells of implanted mantle graft in freshwater mussel *L. marginalis* (Janakiram and Mishra, 1997). Similarly, Chatchavalvanich *et al.* (2010) reported that Thai freshwater mussels completed pearl sac formation by 7 days, which is close to the time taken by the freshwater mussel *Hyriopsis scheleglii* (Machii, 1962). On the other hand, in *H.cumingii* pearl sac formation occurs in 30 days (Shi *et al.,* 1985).Panha and Kosavititkul (1997) studied mantle transplantations in three species of freshwater pearl mussel,

H. myersiana, H. desowitzi and *Chamberlainia hainesiana,* and reported that the pearl sac formation was done within 15 days after an allograft. After 60 days, calcium deposition found in the pearl sacs of cultured Thai freshwater mussels (Chatchavalvanich *et al.,* 2010).

In *L. marginalis* pearl sac epithelium layer comprises small radially-elongated cells (4 to 6 μm lengths) with centrally placed nuclei has microvilli extending into the pearl sac fluid and are likely epitactile in nature involved in the secretion and active transport of calcium into the pearl sac fluid and then on to the embedded nucleus bead or a foreign body. The pearl sac fluid is translucent containing free-floating actively secreting cells and various stages of crystals of calcium carbonate or nacre and their interphases. In the pearl sac fluid rectangular brick work like arrangement of aragonite crystals and sheet like round crystal of calcite crystals are visible (Janakiram and Mishra, 1997). Generally, a quality pearl contains more number of aragonite crystals and these pearls are termed as nacreous pearls (Alagarswami, 1991). Thus the outer epithelium all along the pallial line is the important tissue in pearl formation in *L. marginalis.* This mantle epithelium leads to enveloping the entrapped foreign body in the form of a pearl sac and the microvilli of the pearl sac constitute the cellular basis in crystallization of calcium carbonate, the first step in the formation of a pearl.

POND CULTURE OF IMPLANTED MUSSELS

In India freshwater mussel implantation is carried out throughout the year, except during the peak summer months (May to June) to minimize post-operative mussel mortality and rejection of graft and biocompatible nucleus beads. Traditional carp culture ponds (2.5 m deep) with clay-soil base and slightly alkaline waters are suitable for pearl culture operations (Janakiram, 1997). Ponds without aquatic macrophytes and algal blooms such as *Microcystis*and *Euglena* are ideal for pearl culture farming. The ponds are provided with bamboo poles as rafts for hanging the implanted pearl mussels. The implanted mussels at a density of 50,000 to 75,000/ ha are placed in nylon bags (30 cm × 13 cm; mesh size 1.5 – 3.0 cm) @ 2 mussels per bag and reared (Fig. 4.9 & 4.11).

Careful pond management particularly in terms of natural food production and management of water quality through liming or fertilization is utmost important during the culture period as it affects the quality and quantity of pearl production.Periodic addition of green water (*Chlorella* sp., *Chlorococcum* sp. and *Scenedesmus* sp.) at regular intervals into the pearl culture ponds as direct mussel feed is observed to be an ideal practice for proper up-keep of the pearl bearing mussel standing crop. The green algae can be developed by 'open culture method' in ferro-cement tanks (200 litres) kept all along the pond dyke (Fig. 4.10). The water in the tanks is fertilized with cattle manure (10,000 kg/ha/yr), urea (100 kg/ha/yr) and single super phosphate (100 kg/ha/yr) in equal monthly installments.

Fig. 4.9: Implanted Mussels Ready for Transfer to Pond

Fig. 4.10: Green Algae Developed on Pond Dyke

Fig. 4.11: Pond Culture of Freshwater Mussels

When the fertilizers degrade in 10 to 15 days and green water develops, the enriched water is channeled into the pearl culture ponds. It is reported that some species of algae belonging to Chlorophyceae (green algae), Bacillariophyceae (diatoms) and Cyanophyceae (blue green algae) are normally used as feed by the freshwater mussels (Mandal *et al.*, 2007). The commonly preferred algal species by the freshwater mussel, *L. marginalis* are diatoms, green algae (*Chlorella, Chlorococcum, Scenedesmus* etc.) and blue-green algae (*Spirulina*). The mussels by virtue of being mucoid filter feeders can accept a variety of particulate organic materials as feed (Misra*et al.*, 1998). A regular health checkup of the cultured mussels must be done at fortnight intervals as there are many chances of mortality of operated mussels due to internal incision, less availability of food and parasitic infection.

Hence the quality as well as quantity of the pearl is also lost in time. So the mussels should be taken off from the net bags, checked and cleaned before replacing. Sometimes due to heavy nutrient loads, algal growth is observed on the mussels as they are sedentary and static inside the enclosures. The physico-chemical parameters and water level of the ponds are monitored throughout the culture period. The optimum temperature ranges from 25 to 30 °C. Some of the desirable water and soil parameters for pearl culture are given in table 4.5.

Table 4.5: Water and Soil Parameters for Pearl Culture Pond

	Parameters		Range
Water Characteristics	pH	:	7.5-8.5
	Dissolved oxygen	:	4-6 ppm
	Total alkalinity	:	75-150 ppm
	Total hardness	:	40-75 ppm
	Dissolved calcium	:	25-50 ppm
	Ammonia	:	less than 0.004 ppm
	Nitrite	:	less than 0.005 ppm
	Transparency	:	40-60 cm
Soil Characteristics	pH	:	6.5-7.5
	Organic carbon	:	0.5-1.0%
	Available nitrogen	:	30-40 mg/100 g soil
	Available phosphorus	:	0.4-0.8 mg/100 g

HARVEST OF PEARLS

The pond culture of operated mussels varies from eight months or more depending upon the size and number of nuclei implanted, the health of the mussels and the condition of the pond environment. At the end of the culture period, harvesting is done. The mussels are either crushed followed by sieving to extract pearls or the mussel is individually sacrificed, or individually pearls are taken out from the pearl sac of the live mussels without sacrificing. The latter method, though difficult, is desirable to prevent depletion of stocks of mussels in the natural environment.

The success rate of pearl formation has been recorded at 60-70% in mantle cavity and in mantle tissue implantations and at 25-30% in gonadal implantation of the mussels (Janakiram, 2003). The colour of the half-round and designer pearls produced through mantle cavity insertion generally followed the colour of the shell interior of the mussels employed. In case of mantle tissue and gonadal implantations, colour of pearls varied among silvery white, golden yellow to pink. It has been demonstrated that homogenic mantle grafts collected from smaller donor mussels (shell length d" 6.0 cm; wet weight d" 20 g) and xenogenicmantle grafts collected from a different genus, *Parreysia* when implanted in recipient mussels *L. marginalis* have yielded poor quality pearls and deep pink pearls respectively (Janakiram *et al.,* 1994). This study has tremendous practical application potential in freshwater pearl culture opening a new line of thinking and approach in view of the country's rich mussel fauna comprising more than fifty species belonging to different genera.

VALUE ADDITION OF FRESHWATER PEARL

The value of a pearl is decided by its quality: shape, size, colour, luster, surface clarity, lack of flaws and orientation. Being a product of biological origin, an individual variation is bound to occur in each and every cultured pearl. Even under the highest possible man management, the quality of cultured pearls cannot be controlled absolutely, but can be considerably improved by selecting healthy mussels and appropriate care in handling, implantation, pond management and by following physical, chemical and biological means of quality improvements.

To maintain uniformity in colouration and quality, pearls after harvest are subjected to value addition through surface cleaning or bleaching and dyeing or both cleaning or bleaching which may also enhance their shine and luster. In physical method, ultrasonication (22 kHz) is practiced. However, the traditional cleaning agents like Sikakai (*Acacia sinuata*) and Ritha Phal (*Sapindus trifoliatus*) extract is used which can be adopted by the farming communities (Misra, 2005). Chemically the reflectivity of pearl can be increased by exposing the pearl to EDTA solution, 1-4% of Sodium hypochlorite solution and 0.2-2% chlorine solution along with hydrogen peroxide (Maharathy, 2000).

The colouration of pearls can be manipulated by exposing pearls to 5.423% 10^{-2}M rad of gamma radiation for 48 h, 1.2% solution of eosin for 24 h, 20% solution of iodine for 48 h and 0.2% solution of $AgNO_3$ for 24 h have indicated distinct changes in colour of the pearl from white to black, pink, yellow and metallic brown or metallic black, respectively (Maharathy, 2000). Out of these four colours, colouration due to gamma radiation and silver nitrate was found to be permanent. Biologically the colour of pearl can be manipulated by xenogenic mantle graft transplantation to the recipient mussels (Janakiram *et al.,* 1994).

ADVANCES IN FRESHWATER PEARL CULTURE TECHNOLOGY

The idea of culturing pearls in the laboratory and thus abandoning the vagaries of farming has been an attractive idea for many in the pearling industry (Taylor and Strack, 2008). It is an established fact in pearl culture operation that the quality of nacre deposition in terms of luster and colour is primarily due to the nature of secretion of implanted grafts. Janakiram *et al.* (1994) grafted mantle tissue of the riverine mussel *P. corrugata*on to the freshwater pearl mussel *L. marginalis* to obtain lustrous light yellow to deep pink pearls instead of conventional hue. Success has also been achieved in producing quality pearls by using xenografts of the Indian pearl mussel *L. marginalis* and the Chinese freshwater mussel *Hyriopsis cumingii* (Janakiram and Mishra, 2003).

In recent timeslots of literatures are available on the production of nacre using *in vitro* culturing of mantle cells (Awaji and Suzuki, 1998; Barik *et al.,* 2004; Suja and Dharmaraj, 2005; Suja *et al.,* 2007and Phuc *et al.* 2011). *In vitro* mussel culture and the induction of nacre secretion may open doors to new screening methods of mussel quality and *in vitro* pearl production (Phuc *et al.,* 2011). Itmay overcome many disadvantages of traditional methods of pearl farming. Naturally nacre is secreted by mussel epithelial cells as a self-defense reaction against some foreign irritant agents like sand or parasites. Nacre is produced by the mixture of calcium carbonate and secretory protein like conchiolin that are produced by mantle epithelial cells. However, under *in vitro* conditions, induction of nacre in the mussel body was carried out by utilizing stress causing agents in the culture medium. *In vitro* nacre was formed from matrix protein that mantle epithelial cells expressed (Mayumi and Yasushi, 2006) and calcium carbonate as a component of culture medium. Recently Phuc *et al.* (2011) shown *in vitro* culture and inducing nacre crystal formation of freshwater pearl mussel mantle epithelial cell *Sinohyriopsis cumingii.*However, yet there is no report of the production of commercial pearl by utilizing this technology.

In recent years report is also found on *in vitro* culture of freshwater pearl mussel *H. myersiana* from glochidia to adult in artificial media (Uthaiwan *et al.,* 2001; Kovitvadhi *et al.,* 2007). Similarly, larvae of the freshwater mussel *Anodonta cygnea* could be cultured in artificial media at the controlled temperature of 23±2 °C, with successful metamorphosis. In this artificial medium, the glochidial larvae could be developed into juveniles within 11 days with a hook likes shell and foot (Lima *et al.,* 2006). This artificial media could be useful to bypass the parasitic stage of larvae on fish. Literatures are also available on immune response of freshwater pearl mussel *H. cumingii* against foreign nucleus as well as quality of pearl production. Li *et al.* (2010) reported that the insertion of pearl nucleus enhanced the immune response of mussel. Xu *et al.* (2011) reported that the quality of the cultured pearl was related to the immunological activities of haemocytes or plasma in freshwater pearl mussels. In recent years China has also started genomic research on freshwater mussels (Bai *et al.,* 2009).Suzuki *et al.* (2009) have developed RNAi technology to clarify the function of a nacre-specific matrix protein and reported that the knockdown of the gene of acidic matrix protein Pif *in vivo* affects the crystal structure of nacre. Recently in India, Mohanty *et al.* (2011) has generated and annotated few transcripts from cDNA libraries of the Indian freshwater pearl mussel, *L. marginalis* related to nacre formation.

CURRENT STATUS OF FRESHWATER PEARL PRODUCTION

Pearls are precious gem and also have aesthetic importance and their market pricewill be influenced by consumer demands. Pearl markets and prices are also influenced by levels of production and supply, quality control and market perceptions of particular products (Torry and Sheung, 2008). At present freshwater pearl production is mainly dominated by China which has not only a very long history of pearl culture, but is also the largest freshwater pearl producer in the world, with a total culture area of over 57,000 ha (Liu*et al.,* 2009). The annual output of freshwater pearl production is over 1800 tonnes, which accounts for 95% of world production (Li *et al.,* 2009; Liu *et al.,* 2013).

China has more than hundred forty mussel species, however; only *H. cumingii* and *Cristaria plicata* have been successfully utilized for freshwater pearl production (Yan *et al.,* 2009). This is due to better pearl production qualityand well developed hatchery technology for this species. Moreover, the Chinese freshwater pearl production has significantly improved in shape, size and surface quality with substantive advancement in grafting and culture techniques.They are available in a variety of sizes ranging from 2 mm to over 10 mm and in an interesting variety of shapes such as round, oval, drop button and baroque and in rich colours such as orange and purple, often with a metallic luster (Akamatsu *et al.,*2001). Hua and Neves (2007) reported that purple, pink and lavender colour pearl are most desirable and fetches high prices in the international market.

The low price of Chinese freshwater pearl has gained them an important advantage in the mass market and international gem shows are often awash in them (Torry and Sheung, 2008). Chinese freshwater pearl is generally made up of 100% nacre because they are mostly practicing non-nucleated implantation using a tiny pieceof mantle tissue. In recent years, Chinese also useanother species of mussel, *H. schlegelii*, introduced from Japan and Coin-bead nucleation techniques. This nucleation method involves implanting a coin-shaped bead and tissue piece at first generation and often only a spherical bead at the second generation. The process produces the pearls called fireballs, other baroque shapes, keshis, coin pearls and rounds and near rounds (Fiske and Shepherd, 2007).They are also utilizing hybrid mussel (*H. cumingii* X *H. schlegelii*) for producing superior quality of freshwater pearl (Xie *et al.,* 2006).

In India commercial production of freshwater pearls is very meager. However, the Central Institute of Freshwater Aquaculture regularly organizes training programmes for the farmers, entrepreneurs and researchers on various aspects of pearl farming. Some of the farmers from different parts of the country after getting training have also started their pearl farming venture but the production is not very much significant. A farmer near Surat has produced a 48 carat pink pearl weighing 15 grams.In his Bhargav Freshwater Aquaculture Farm,he also produced pearls of different sizes and shapes including Ganesha, Jesus Christ and Sai Baba. A Hyderabad-based businessman owning his Swathi pearl farm is also involved in pearl farming activities and has adopted the technology since 2000 (Kumar *et al.,* 2009).At present in India the major demand is for the larger round pearl and designer pearl of different shapes such as goddess Laxmi, Holy cross, Ganesha and different fancy shapes etc (Fig. 4.12).

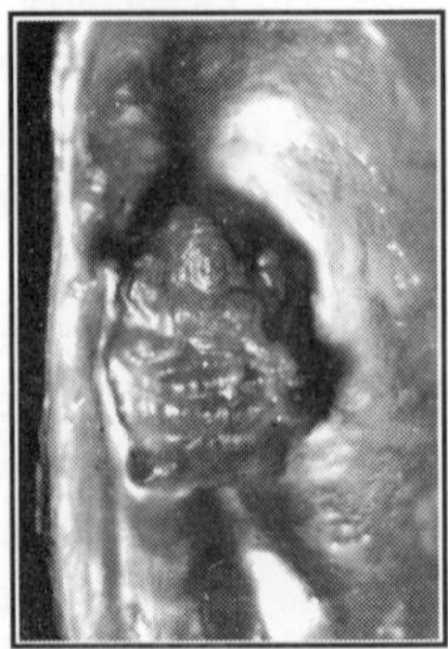

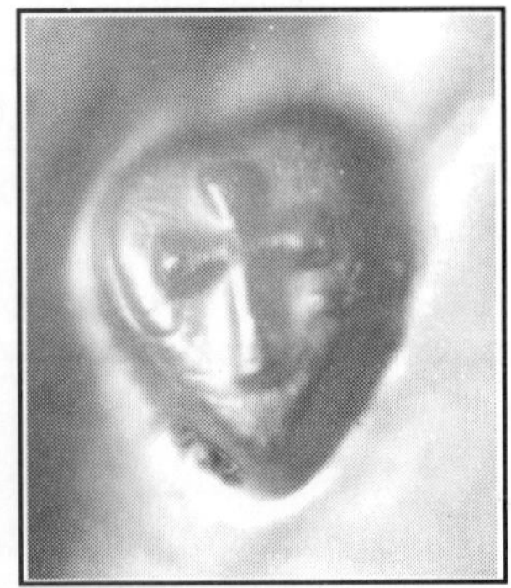

Fig. 4.12 (a, b,): Designer Pearls

Fig. 4.13: Value Addition to Designer Pearl

CONCLUSION

At present, the Central Institute of Freshwater Aquaculture has made significant progress in areas such as identification of newer biocompatible nucleus, surgical implantation technique, pre and post-operative care of mussels, minimizing graft and nucleus rejection, pond culture of implanted mussels and value addition of pearl (Fig. 4.13). Efforts are also being taken to develop low cost technology for the farmers by utilizing simple handy instruments in pearl farming. Research work has also been initiated to find the gene responsible for nacre secretion, glochidial larvae culture in artificial medium as well as some cell line development from epithelial explants of *L. marginalis.* Concerted attention is also being paid to disseminate the technology of freshwater pearl culture by regularly conducting training programme to the farmers, entrepreneurs, researchers and students of the country in order to develop technical expertise and popularization of freshwater pearl culture technology to the newer height (Fig. 4.14).

Fig. 4.14 (a, b): Hands on Training on Freshwater Pearl Culture

REFERENCES

Akamatsu, S., L.T. Zansheng, T.M. Moses and K. Scarratt (2001): The Current Status of Chinese Freshwater Cultured Pearls. *Gems and Gemology,* 37 (2): 96-113.

Alagarswami, K. (1991): Production of Cultured Pearls. Indian Council of Agricultural Research, New Delhi, pp. 112.

Awaji, M. and T. Suzuki (1998): Monolayer Formation and DNA Synthesis of the Outer Epithelial Cells from Pearl Oyster Mantle in Coculture with Amoebocytes. *In Vitro Cellular and Developmental Biology-Animal,* 34: 486-491.

Awaji, M. and A. Machii (2011): Fundamental Studies on *in vivo* and *in vitro* Pearl Formation-Contribution of Outer Epithelial Cells of Pearl Oyster Mantle and Pearl sacs. *Aqua-BioScience Monographs,* 4(1): 1-39.

Bai, Z., Y. Yin, S. Hu, G. Wang, X. Zhang and J. Li (2009): Identification of Genes Involved in Immune Response, Microsatellite and SNP Markers from Expressed Sequence Tags Generated from Haemocytes of Freshwater Pearl Mussel (*Hyriopsis cumingii*). *Marine Biotechnology*, 11: 520-530.

Barik, S.K., J.K. Jena and K. Janakiram (2004): $CaCO_3$ Crystallization in Primary Culture of Mantle Epithelial Cells of Freshwater Pearl Mussel. *Current Science,* 86 (5): 730-734.

Cariolou, M.A. and D.E. Morse (1988): Purification and Characterization of Calcium Binding Conchiolin Shell Peptides from the Mollusc, *Haliotis rufescens,* as a Function of Development. *Journal of Comparative Physiology B,* 157: 717-729.

Chatchavalvanich, K., A. Nagachinda, U. Kovitvadhi, S. Kovitvadhi, A. Thongpan and O. Meejui (2010): Histological Development of Pearl-sac Formation in Thai Freshwater Mussels. *Kasetsart Journal (Natural Science),* 44: 202-209.

Fang, D., G. Xu; Y. Hu; C. Pan; L. Xie and R. Zhang (2011): Identification of Genes Directly Involved in Shell Formation and Their Functions in Pearl Oyster, *Pinctada fucata.* PloS ONE 6 (7): e21860.

Farn, A.E. (1986): Pearls Natural, Cultured and Imitation. *Butterworth Gem Books, London,* pp. 150.

Fiske D. and J. Shepherd (2007): Continuity and Change in Chinese Freshwater Pearl Culture. *Gems and Gemology,* 43 (2): 138-145.

Gervis, M.H. and N.A. Sims (1992): The Biology and Culture of Pearl Oysters (Bivalvia: Pteriidae). *ICLARM Stud. Rev. 21, ODA (Pub.), London,* pp. 49.

Gong, N., Q. Li, J. Huang, Z. Fang, G. Zhang, L. Xie and R. Zhang (2008): Culture of Outer Epithelial Cells from Mantle Tissue to Study Shell Matrix Protein Secretion for Biomineralization. *Cell and Tissue Research,* 333: 493-501.

Hua, D. and R.J. Neves (2007): Captive Survival and Pearl Culture Potential of the Pink Heelsplitter *Potamilus alatus.North American Journal of Aquaculture,* 69: 147-158.

Janakiram K. and G. Misra (2003): Homogenic and Xenogenic Implantation in Pearl Mussel Surgery. *Current Science,* 85 (6): 727-729.

Janakiram, K. (1997): Freshwater Pearl Culture in India. NAGA, The International Center for Living Aquatic Resources Management (ICLARM), Philippines, 20 (3, 4): 12-17.

Janakiram, K. (2003): Freshwater Pearl Culture Technology Development in India. *Journal of Applied Aquaculture,* 13 (3-4): 341-349.

Janakiram, K. and G. Misra (1997): Preliminary Studies on Histology of Pallial Mantle and Pearl sac of Indian Freshwater Pearl Mussel, *Lamellidens marginalis* (L.). *Journal of Aquaculture* 5: 95-98.

Janakiram, K., K. Kumar and G. Misra (1994): Possible Use of Different Graft Donors in Freshwater Pearl Mussel Surgery. *Indian Journal of Experimental Biology*, 32: 366-368.

Kovitvadhi, S., U. Kovitvadhi, P. Sawangwong and J. Machado (2007): Morphological Development of the Juvenile Through to the Adult in the Freshwater Pearl Mussel, *Hyriopsis (Limnoscapha) myersiana,* Under Artificial Culture. *Invertebrate Reproduction and Development,* 50(4): 207-218.

Kumar, K., G. Misra and S. Saurabh (2013). Designer Pearl: A Profitable Product for Cottage Industry. In: Aquaculture: New Possibilities and Concerns (V.R.P. Sinha and P. Jayasankar, eds.). *Narendra Publishing House, New Delhi,* pp: 213-219 (In Press).

Kumar, K., G. Misra, U.L. Mohanty and J.K. Jena (2009): Freshwater Pearl Farming. In: New Frontiers of Zoology (B. N. Pandey and P.N. Pandeyeds.). *Narendra Publishing House, New Delhi,* pp. 97-109.

Kumar, K., S. Saurabh, R. Kumar and U.L. Mohanty (2012): Freshwater Pearl Culture. Training Manual, Central Institute of Freshwater Aquaculture, Bhubaneswar, India. 49 pp.

Li, J.L., G.L. Wang and Z.Y. Bai (2009): Genetic Diversity of Freshwater Pearl Mussel (*Hyriopsis cumingii*) in Populations from the Five Largest Lakes in China Revealed by Inter-simple Sequence Repeat (ISSR). *Aquaculture International,* 17: 323-330.

Li, W., Z. Shi and X. He (2010): Study on Immune Regulation in *Hyriopsis cumingiiLea*: Effect of Pearl-nucleus Insertion in the Visceral Mass on Immune Factors Present in the Hemolymph. *Fish and Shellfish Immunology,* 28: 789-794.

Lima, P., U. Kovitvadhi, S. Kovitvadhi and J. Machado (2006): *In vitro* Culture of Glochidia from the Freshwater Mussel *Anodontacygnea.Invertebrate Biology,* 125 (1): 34-44.

Liu, C., H. Zhou, Y.C. Su, Y. Li and J. Li (2009): Chemical Compositions and Functional Properties of Protein Isolated from By-product of Triangular Shell Pearl Mussel *Hyriopsis cumingii. Journal of Aquatic Food Product Technology,* 18: 193-208.

Liu, Y., Z. Bai, Q. Li, Y. Zhao and J. Li (2013): Healing and Regeneration of the Freshwater Pearl Mussel *Hyriopsis cumingii* Lea after Donating Mantle Saibos. *Aquaculture,* 392-395: 34-43.

Machii, A. (1962): Studies on the Histology of Pearl sac VIII. On the Formation of Epithelium Derived from the Inner Epithelium of the Mantle Piece. *Bulletin of the Natural Pearl Research Laboratory*, 8: 884-890.

Maharathy, C. (2000): Hydrochemical Materials Beneficiation of Freshwater Culture Pearls. Ph.D. Thesis, Bhanja Bihar, Orissa.

Mandal, R.N., K. Kumar, U.L. Mohanty and P.K. Meher (2007): Estimation of gut Contents of the Freshwater Mussel *Lamellidens marginalis* L. *Aquaculture Research,* 38 (3): 1364-1369.

Mayumi, E. and H. Yasushi (2006): Culture of Mantle Epithelial Cells Expressing Shell Matrix Proteins from Scallop *Patinopecten yessoensis. Fisheries Science,* 72: 1277-1285.

Misra, G. (2005): Pearl Farming-Avenue for Women Entrepreneurship. In: Women Empowerment in Fisheries (A.S. Ninawe and A.D. Diwan, eds.). *Narendra Publishing House, New Delhi,* pp. 201-211.

Misra, G., K. Kumar and K. Janakiram (1998): Role of Selected Feeds in Captive Culture of Indian Pearl Mussel *Lamellidens marginalis* (Lamarck). In: Current and Emerging Trends in Aquaculture. *Daya Publishing House, New Delhi,* pp. 241-243.

Miyamoto H., F. Miyoshi and J. Kohno (2005): The Carbonic Anhydrase Domain Protein Nacrein is Expressed in the Epithelial Cells of the Mantle and Acts as a Negative Regulator in Calcification in the Mollusk *Pinctada fucata. Zoological Science,* 22: 311-315.

Mohanty, U.L., D.K. Sahu, S. Nandi, K. Kumar, D.R. Sahoo, H.K. Barman, A. Saha, M. Panda, R.P. Panda, G. Misra, C. Mohapatra, R. Kumar, R.K. Hazra and J. K. Jena (2011): Generation and Annotation of a Few Transcripts from cDNA Libraries of the Indian Freshwater Pearl Mussel, *Lamellidens marginalis*, with Reference to Nacre Formation. In: Book of Abstract, 9th Indian Fisheries Forum, 19-23 December, 2011, Chennai, pp: 230.

Mount, A.S., A.P. Wheeler, R.P. Paradkar and D. Snider (2004): Haemocyte-mediated Shell Mineralization in the Eastern Oyster. *Science,* 304: 297-300.

Nakahara, H. (1991): Mechanisms and Phylogeny of Mineralization in Biological Systems (S. Suga and H. Nakahara, eds.). *Springer-Verlag, New York,* pp. 343-350.

Panha, S. and P. Kosavititkul (1997): Mantle Transplantations in Freshwater Mussels in Thailand. *Aquaculture International,* 5: 267-276.

Phuc, P.V., P.Q. Viet, N.M. Hoang, N.T. Tam and P.K. Ngoc (2011): Research on *in vitro* Culture and Inducing Nacre Crystal Formation of Freshwater Pearl Mussel Mantle Epithelial Cell *Sinohyriopsiscumingii. International Journal of Fisheries and Aquaculture,* 3 (6): 105-113.

Rousseau, M., E. Lopez, P. Stempfle, M. Brendle, L. Franke, A. Guette, R. Naslain and X Bourrat (2005): Multiscale Structure of Sheet Nacre. *Biomaterials*, 26: 6254-6262.

Rousseau, M., E. Plouguerne, G. Wan, R. Wan, E. Lopez and M.F. Peron (2003): Biomineralisation Marker during a Phase of Active Growth in *Pinctada margaritifera. Comparative Biochemistry and Physiology (A)*, 135: 271-278.

Saurabh, S. (2013): Freshwater Pearl Culture Technology In: Course Manual: Techniques in Marine Designer Pearl Production (M.K. Anil, ed.). Central Marine Fisheries Research Institute, Vizhinzam, March 19-23, 2013, pp. 47-51.

Saurabh, S., K. Kumar and U.L. Mohanty (2012): Freshwater Pearl Culture: A Novel Technology for Entrepreneurship Development. In: International Training on Fisheries Administration and Seed Production of Freshwater Fishes, 11-17 Nov. 2012, Training Manual, CIFA, Bhubaneswar.

Shen, X., A.M. Belcher, P.K. Hansma, G.D. Stucky and D.E. Morse (1997): Molecular Cloning and Characterization of Lustrin A, a Matrix Protein from Shell and Pearl Nacre of *Haliotis rufescens. The Journal of Biological Chemistry,* 272 (51): 32472-32481.

Shi, A.T., M. Zhang, Z.W. Wu and X.F. Peng (1985): On the Formation of Pearl Sac in Freshwater Mussel. *Journal of Fisheries of China Shui Chan Xue Bao,* 9 (3): 247-253.

Simkiss, K. (1989): Biomineralization: Mollusks, Epithelial Control of Matrix and Minerals. Academic Press, San Diego, pp: 230-232.

Stephen, M. (2001): Biomineralization: Principles and Concepts in Bioinorganic Material Chemistry Oxford University Press.

Strack, E. (2008): The Pearl Oyster (P. Southgate and J.S. Lucas, eds.). *Elsevier BV, The Netherlands,* pp. 1-21.

Subba Rao, N.V. (1989): Handbook of Freshwater Molluscs of India. *Zoological Survey of India, Calcutta,* pp: 289.

Sudo, S., T. Fujikawa, T. Nagakura, T. Ohkubo, K. Sakaguchi, M. Tanaka, K. Nakashima and T. Takahashi (1997): Structure of Mollusk Shell Framework Proteins. *Nature,* 387: 563-564.

Suja, C.P. and S. Dharmaraj (2005): *In vitro* Culture of Mantle Tissue of the Abalone *Haliotis varia* Linnaeus. *Tissue and Cell,* 37: 1-10.

Suja, C.P., N. Sukumaran and S. Dharmaraj (2007): Effect of Culture Media and Tissue Extracts in the Mantle Explant Culture of Abalone, *Haliotis varia* Linnaeus. *Aquaculture,* 271: 516-522.

Suzuki, M., E. Murayama, H. Inoue, N. Ozaki, H. Tohse, T. Kogure and H. Nagasawa (2004): Characterization of Prismalin-14, a Novel Matrix Protein from the Prismatic Layer of the Japanese Pearl Oyster (*Pinctada fucata*). *Biochemical Journal,* 382: 205-213.

Suzuki, M., K. Saruwatari, T. Kogure, Y. Yamamoto, T. Nishimura, T. Kato and H. Nagasawa (2009): An Acidic Matrix Protein, Pif, is a Key Macromolecule for nacre Formation. *Science,* 325: 1388-1390.

Suzuki, T. and S. Funakoshi (1992): Isolation and a Fibronectin-like Molecule from a Marine Bivalve, *Pinctada fucata,* and its Secretion by Amoebocytes. *Zoological Science,* 9: 541-550.

Sweaney J.L. and J.R. Latendresse (1984): Freshwater Pearls of North America. *Gems and Gemology,* 125-139.

Takeuchi, T. and K. Endo (2006): Biphasic and Dually Coordinated Expression of the Genes Encoding Major Shell Matrix Proteins in the Pearl Oyster *Pinctada fucata.Marine Biotechnology,* 8: 52-61.

Taylor, J. and E. Strack (2008): Pearl Production. In: The Pearl Oyster (P. Southgate and J.S. Lucas, eds.). *Elsevier BV, The Netherlands,* pp. 273-301.

Torrey, R.D. and B. Sheung (2008): The Pearl Market In: The Pearl Oyster (P. Southgate and J.S. Lucas, eds.). *Elsevier BV, The Netherlands,* pp. 357-365.

Uthaiwan, K., N. Noparatnaraporn and J. Machado (2001): Culture of Glochidia of the Freshwater Pearl Mussel *Hyriopsis myersiana* (Lea, 1856) in Artificial media. *Aquaculture,* 195: 61-69.

Webster, R. (1975): Gems. *3rd ed. Arehon Books, Hamden, CT.*

Xie N., Y. Li, H. Zheng, G. Wang, J. Li, N. Oi and W. Yuan (2006): Comparison of Culture and Pearl Performances Among *Hyriopsisschlegelii, Hyriopsiscumingii* and Their Reciprocal Hybrids. *Journal of Shanghai Fisheries University,* 15 (3): 264-269.

Xu, Q.Q., L.G. Guo, J. Xie and C. Zhao (2011): Relationship Between Quality of Pearl Cultured in the Triangle Mussel *Hyriopsis cumingii* of Different Ages and its Immune Mechanism. *Aquaculture,* 315: 196-200.

Yan, L.I., G.F. Zhang, Q.G. Liu and J.L. Li (2009): Optimization of Culturing the Freshwater Pearl Mussels, *Hyriopsis cumingii* with Filter Feeding Chinese Carps (bighead carp and silver carp) by Orthogonal Array Design. *Aquaculture,* 292: 60-66.

Zhang, C. and R. Zhang (2006): Matrix Proteins in the Outer Shells of Molluscs. *Marine Biotechnology,* 8:572-586.

5

Management of Problematic Red Soil Based Upland Aquaculture System in NE India

Mrinal Kanti Datta and Chandra Prakash

ABSTRACT

Pond bottom soil plays a key role in determining pond productivity and yield. Red-lateritic soils comprising about 91.0 mha, forms around 28% of total land area in India while NE India has about 90% red-lateritic soils of its total area, majority of acid soils had pH below 5.6 and remaining between 5.5 and 6.5. These soils were generally poor in nitrogen, phosphorus, calcium and humus. Iron and aluminium phosphate predominate in acid soils and thus reflected in pond water. As most of the land profile of North East India is undulating, red in colour, acidic in nature, poor in productivity and deficient in organic matter, these limiting factors are quite responsible for poor fish production. Other tan leaching processes both chemical and organic fertilizers may eventually make the soil more acidic. Management of this problematic red soil based upland aquaculture system is of paramount importance. Reclamation of acidic soil and water with large scale fish production through the use of medium dose organic fertilizers for restoration of the pH from acidic to alkaline along with medium dose of lime is found suitable apart from the methodology developed and described for ameliorating the acidic pond soil and water. The study contributed the need of soil specific fertilization specially for acidic soils to enhance aquaculture productivity.

Keywords: North Eastern state of India, Red acidic soil, Cation Exchange Capacity (CEC), Productivity, Leaching process.

INTRODUCTION

The properties of pond soil are of greater significance than is generally realized. When soil conditions are not favourable, the production will be limited. Occurrence of important nutrients like nitrogen, carbon, phosphorus, potash etc. in pond water and maintenance of their relevant chemical condition depends largely on the nature and properties of the bottom soil wherein a series of chemical and biochemical reactions continuously take place resulting in release of different nutrients in overlaying water and also their absorption in the soil mass. The colloidal content of the soil, especially of the muddy layer on the top, is of importance in its capacity to fix or chemically bind nutrients. The productive capacity of the pond bottom has to be preserved by alternate periods of mud formation and mineralization – the practice of regularly draining fish pond.

Pond bottom soils are the storehouse for many substances that accumulate in pond ecosystem. Chemical and biological processes occurring in surface layers of pond soils, influence water quality and in turn aquaculture production. Same way, substances may also enter the solid phase of the soil from the aqueous phase through the ion- exchange adsorption and precipitation. Bacteria, fungi, algae, higher aquatic plants, small invertebrates and other aquatic organisms known as benthos live in and on the bottom soil which serves as food for some culturable species. It is also involved in gas exchange, primary and secondary productivity, decomposition, and nutrients recycling. The four most important soil features for aquacultural production are texture, pH, organic matter content and presence or absence of particular soluble compounds. That may be beneficial or harmful to water quality. When soils in the ponds are flooded, the most marked change in their composition is less air in the pore space enhancing particle density and the gradual accumulation of organic matters (Boyd, 1995).

Importance of Soil in Aquaculture

Pond soils do not differ from terrestrial soils in their major physical, chemical and mineralogical features. When soil conditions are not favourable, the production will be limited. Productivity of fishponds depends on the occurrence of suitable environmental conditions and abundance of fish food organisms. The first step in the food chain of a fish pond is constituted by primary food organisms e.g. phyto-planktons, which derive their nutrients from the pond environment with the help of solar radiation, undergo photosynthetic activities.

Important Nutrients in Fish Pond

The two most important nutrients in pond aquaculture are nitrogen and phosphorus because these two nutrients often are present in short supply and limit phytoplankton growth. These two nutrients are added to ponds through fertilizers, manures, and feeds. The two most important nutrients in pond aquaculture are nitrogen and phosphorus because these two nutrients often are present in short supply and limit phytoplankton growth.

Fertilizer nitrogen usually is in the form of urea or ammo-nium, and urea quickly hydrolyzes to ammonium in pond water. Ammonium may be absorbed by phytoplankton, converted to organic nitrogen, and eventually transformed into nitrogen of fish protein via the food web. Ammonium may be oxidized to nitrate by nitrifying bacteria, and nitrate may be used by phytoplankton or denitrified by anaerobic microorganisms in the sediment. Nitrogen gas formed by denitrification diffuses from sediment to pond water to the atmosphere. Ammonium is in equilibrium with ammonia, and ammonia also can diffuse from pond waters to the atmosphere. A small amount of ammonium may be ad-sorbed on cation exchange sites in pond bottom soils. Organic nitrogen in plankton and in aquatic animal excreta may settle to the bottom to become soil organic nitrogen. Nitrogen in soil organic matter may be mineralized to ammonia and recycled to the pond water. Recent studies suggest that decomposition in bottoms of aquaculture ponds usually does not result in mineralization of significant amounts of nitrogen.

Phosphorus usually is present in fertilizer as calcium or ammonium phosphate. Phytoplankton can rapidly remove phosphate from water, and phosphorus in phytoplankton may enter the food web culminating in fish or shrimp. Pond soil strongly adsorbs phosphorus, and the capacity of pond soil to adsorb phosphorus increases as a function of increasing clay content.

Acidic Soils in India and Abroad

Egna and Boyd, (1996) studied extensively on the acidic soils and concluded that these soils were generally poor in nitrogen, phosphorus, calcium and humus with the predominance of the mineral kaolinite. Red soils possess little capacity for absorption of moisture. Their capacity for retention of bases by exchange is also limited. Phosphorus gets more readily fixed in these soils and thus iron and aluminium phosphate predominate in acid soils. The predominance of iron and aluminum phosphate in acid soils was also reported by Chang and Jackson, 1958; Chang and Chu, 1961 and Bapat *et al.,* 1965. Study of Sehgal, (1993) revealed that among various kinds of soil groups available in India, red- laterite soils comprised an important soil groups occupying about 70 million of the total land area of the country. Dhanajaya & Ananthanrayana, (2006) and Hegde *et al.,* (1991) studied on soil acidity in Karnataka and found that the soil in general, is acidic with poor base saturation and low exchange capacity. Addition of acid forming fertilizers, intensive cultivation and heavy irrigation also resulted in the development of acidity of these soils. Jhingran, (1991) cited that old alluvium soils are acidic, but new alluvium are lesser acidic in Northeast region.

North East India and Resources

The north eastern states contribute 8% of India's territory and 4% of its population. The region is characterized by diverse and distinct agro-climatic and geographical areas in regards to parameters like topography, temperature, rainfall and soil types. The region is land-locked and thus possesses only fresh water resources. The fish production during 2000-01 and 2001-02 was 2.21 and 2.23 lakh tones respectively (Munilkumar & Nandeesha, 2007). It contributes about 7% of the total inland fish production in the country and almost 6 kg per capita of fish to its present population. The region needs about 4.0 lakh tonnes of fish per annum. The average production from ponds aquaculture during 2002 was about 1500 kg ha^{-1} yr^{-1} (Chauhan, 2004).The north east region has a vast untapped potential for fish yield through enhancement from rivers, streams, flood plain wetlands, reservoirs, lakes, ponds and paddy fields. The region has rich and diverse aquatic resources indifferent topographical and climatic conditions in the plains of the Brahmaputra and Barak valleys in Assam, from upland plain lands of the Imphal valley in Manipur to the predominantly hilly regions of Meghalaya, Mizoram, Nagaland, Tripura, and Sikkim with elevations ranging from 200-900 m above mean sea level (MSL). The annual rainfall in the region exceeds 2,000 mm and more than 60% of the area is covered by forest. The soils are mostly acidic in nature, having pH in the range 4.5-5.0.

Status of NE Aquaculture

Fig. 5.1: Red Soil based Water Body of NE India

In the past rural households obtained their fish in take mostly from subsistence fishing in open access aquatic resources. However, with the reduction in fish catches from open waters as a result of increased fishing pressure, and other natural causes and human interventions, the availability and consequently per capita intake of fish has declined. Most of the household water bodies in this region is smaller in nature and has multipurpose use. On the other hand Northeast is best wasted with vast bioresearches with flora and fauna. It has tradition on live stock rearing and agriculture.

Table 5.1: Resources of NE India

State	Total Geographical Area (000'ha)	Cultivable Land (000'ha)	% of Geographical Area	Total Crop Area (000'ha)	Area Sown More Than Once (000'ha)	Net Sown Area (000'ha)	% of Cultivable Area Used	Gross Irrigated Area (000'ha)	% of Gross Cropped Area
Arunachal Pradesh	8374.3	293	3.50	244	59	185	63.14	36	14.75
Assam	7843.8	3387	43.18	3938	1158	2780	82.08	572	14.53
Manipur	2232.7	164	7.35	182	42	140	85.37	75	41.21
Meghalaya	2242.9	1074	47.88	247	41	206	19.18	45	18.22
Mizoram	2108.1	445	21.11	109	0	109	24.49	9	8.26
Nagaland	1657.9	626	37.76	228	17	211	33.71	72	31.58
Tripura	1048.6	310	29.56	426	149	277	89.35	60	14.08
All NE	25508.3	6299	24.69	5374	1466	3908	62.04	869	16.17
All India	328726.3	194680	59.22	186561	44346	142215	73.05	71510	38.33

Table 5.2: Aquatic Resources of NE Region of India

States	Rivers (km)	Reservoir (ha)	Beels, lakes etc. (ha)	Pond/tanks (ha)	Paddy cum fish (ha)
Arunachal Pradesh	2000	160	2500	150	575
Assam	5050	10730	100,000	22,800	–
Manipur	2000	100	19150	5000	–
Meghalaya	5600	8430	375	500	85
Mizoram	1700	32	–	1752	120
Nagaland	1600	–	275	500	2000
Tripura	1200	4500	500	10264	–
Total	19150	23792	1,43,740	40,809	2780

Economically most of the farmers are weak and feeds needed in aquaculture, fetches about 50-60% of the total in put cost when as productivity level is lower than national level. The water is slightly acidic is nature where as demand of fish is many high and supplemented by importing from other states. Integration of aquaculture with other farming's may be a welcome addition to the farmers for better utilization of the bio resources and to cut down the ever-increasing expenses towards the feed in aquaculture. The region is importing fish to the tune of 38,340 tons per annum in addition to unaccounted import from the neighboring countries of Bangladesh and Myanmar.

Productivity

All the states in the region have reported productivity levels of around 1000-2500 kg $ha^{-1}year^{-1}$with an average of 1500 kg $ha^{-1}Year^{-1}$, compared to the national average of more than 2000 kg $ha^{-1}year^{-1}$. However, in integrated farming systems, productivity was better in Assam and Tripura, while in Arunachal Pradesh, Nagaland and Mizoram, the productivity was less than 1500 kg $ha^{-1}year^{-1}$.Rice–fish culture is an important activity prevalent in some areas of the region and the reported production ranges from 250 to 1200 kg ha^{-1}. Arunachal Pradesh has the traditional farming of rice–fish, yielding around 500 kg $ha^{-1}year^{-1}$ (Munilkumar. & Nandeesha, 2007).

Soil Properties of NE India

Red -lateritic soils comprising about 91.0 mha, forms around 28% of total land area in India while NE India has about 90% red-lateritic soils of its total area 10486 Km^2 (Sehgal,1993). Agricultural productivity of such soils is usually of low order owing to light texture, poor organic matter, low water holding capacity, acidic pH, poor NPK status and also inadequate as well as toxic occurrence of some trace elements. Highly weathered soil especially in the tropics and subtropics contains iron and aluminum oxide such as $Al(OH)_2$ (Gibbsite) and FeOOH (goethite), which exist as fine particles and considered part of the clay fraction (Too and Boyd, 1994).

Table 5.3: Fish Production of NE State

States Production	Fish Production				Fish Seed
	Total Production (Tons)	Contribution from Culture Ponds (%)	Perha Productivity of Culture Ponds (kg)	Per capita Availability (kg)	(Million fry)
Arunachal Pradesh	2,770	67	845	2.17	26.50
Assam	1,81,480 (1,90,000)	57	1820	6.79 (6.99)	2,100 (3,200)
Manipur	18,610 (18,652)	60	1198	7.75 (7.64)	118
Meghalaya	5,490	NA	NA	2.00	0.74
Mizoram	3,760	NA	NA	3.61	18
Nagaland	5,800	NA	NA	2.10	45
Sikkim					
Tripura	28,630 (32,383)	94	1859 (1931)	8.90 (9.90)	240.7 (253.3)

Source: Handbook of Fisheries Statistics, 2007, Government of India, Ministry of Agriculture, Department of Animal Husbandry, Dairying and Fisheries, Krishi Bhavan, New Delhi, and State Directorates of Fisheries–Personal Communication.

Some iron and aluminum oxides have definite crystalline substances and others are amorphous. They have no strong electrical charges and do not expand when wet. In many tropical soils, iron and aluminium oxides dominate the clay fraction. These characteristics are wide spread in the soils of NE states, referred as red acidic soil (Panda, 1988). Meticulous studies were carried out by Banerjea and Mandal, (1965); Singh *et al*., (1989); Singh *et al*., (1991), Banerjee and Ghosh, (1970) and Bhattacharyya *et al*., (1996), Sharma *et al.,* (2006) and Laskar *et al*., (1983) and Datta *et, al*.(2011) with the soils of fish ponds from Tripura, Manipur and Assam etc. Prasad *et al.,* (1985) found that more than 80% of soils in NE states are acidic in reaction covering 34.8% of total area of the country. Panda, (1988) reported that in North-East, majority of acid soils had pH below 5.6 and remaining between 5.5 and 6.5.

Dhruva Narayana & Ram, (1983); Dhruva Narayana & Patnaik, (1990) and Dhruva Narayana, (2002) studied on high sheet erosion in red soil and reported that there was high soil loss of an area of 69 million hectares due to rolling, undulating topography as well as high rain fall.

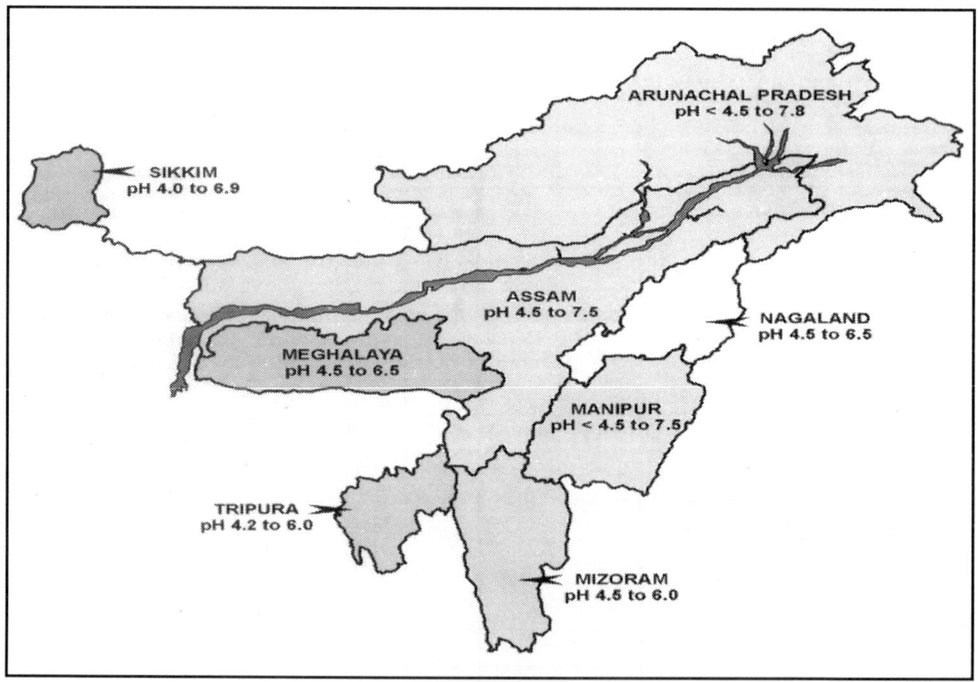

Fig. 5.2: pH Profile of NE Soils

Process of Formation of Acidic Soil

The leaching of bases is the prerequisite for the formation of acid soils which are dominantly found to occur in regions with high rainfall. The mean annual temperature, type of vegetation, parent materials and hydrological conditions also govern the extent of acid soils and the degree of acidity. The major process involved in the formation of acid soil is laterization of varying degrees, polzolization of areas in the sub- temperate to temperate climate, intense leaching of light alluvial soils and marshy conditions coupled with significant amount of partly decomposed organic matter.

Fig. 5.3: Red Acidic Soil of NE State

How Leaching Process Affects in Acidic Soil Formation

Rainfall also affects soil pH. Water passing through the soil leaches basic cations such as calcium (Ca^{2+}), magnesium (Mg^{2+}), and potassium (K^{+}) into drainage water. These basic cations are replaced by acidic cations such as aluminum (Al^{3+}) and hydrogen (H^{+}). For this reason, soils formed under high rainfall conditions are comparatively more acidic.

Coleman and Thomas (1967) identified soil acidity in terms of KCl extractable and pH dependent acidity. The first type of acidity is ascribed to the isomorphous substitution while the second type of polymers of Fe and Al, the Kaolinitic clays and soil organic matter. The proportion of these two types of acidities determines the production potential as well as lime requirement of these acid soils for amelioration.

Properties of Acidic Soils

Low pH coupled with high proportion of exchangeable hydrogen and aluminium is the main characteristics of acid soils. Kaolitic and illitic types of clay minerals are dominant in these soils. These soils have low CEC and high base unsaturation. The adverse effect of acid soils on aquatic productivity is mainly related to the presence of aluminium, manganese and iron in higher concentrations, deficiency of calcium and magnesium nutrients and microbial imbalance. They are generally low in available phosphorus and have high phosphate fixation capacity. Soil acidity inhibits biological nitrogen fixation. The non-availability of the nutrients for aquatic productivity caused due to lower pH is the main factor responsible to make the acid soil infertile.

Role of Fertilizers in Soil Acidity

Both chemical and organic fertilizers may eventually make the soil more acidic. Hydrogen is added in the form of ammonium-based fertilizers (NH_4^+), urea-based fertilizers [$CO\ (NH_2)_2$] and as proteins (amino acids) in organic fertilizers. Transformations of these sources of N into nitrate (NO_3^-) release H^+ to create soil acidity. Therefore, fertilization with fertilizers containing ammonium or even adding large quantities of organic matter to a soil will ultimately increase the soil acidity and in turn the decrease in pH level.

Concerns About Soil Acidity

Soil acidity is a management concern because both total alkalinity and total hardness of pond water are closely related to bottom soil acidity. Total alkalinity and total hardness should be above 20 mgl^{-1} in aquaculture ponds to provide enough buffering capacity to maintain pH of 6.0- 9.5 and sufficient dissolved inorganic carbon to support good phytoplankton growth (Boyd, 1990).

Role of Cation Exchange Capacity (CEC) in Soil Acidity

Boyd, (1970) studied the cation exchange capacity of bottom soil from 28 public fishing impoundments in Alabama which had CEC values of 0.5 - 26 $meq100g^{-1}$. The CEC of pond soils also varied with location in the pond and with depth below the soil surface. The CEC of soils depends on the quantity and type of colloids in the soil. Soils vary greatly in cation exchange capacity; lowest values are <1 $meq100g^{-1}$ and highest values are > 100 $meq100g^{-1}$. Boyd, (1995) further studied on the CEC at Alabama and found out that a soil containing 10 % kaolinite, 20% iron and aluminium oxide clay and 1% organic matter had CEC of 3-4 meq $100g^{-1}$.Landau and Scarpa, (2001) studied the soil and water interaction in pond and found that soil may also affect the aquatic chemistry because of their cation exchange capacity. Soils that are high in organics usually have a high exchange capacity, soil with expanding clay materials are intermediate, while those soils dominated by nonexpanding minerals have a very small cation exchange capacity. Nath, (1985) studied ponds of West Bengal, India in different soil conditions. From his study he revealed that the ponds having acidic soil reaction and CEC lower than 13 $meq100g^{-1}$ were poorly productive due to low retention of important nutrients coupled with poor cation exchange capacity, resulting in high seepage and leaching losses of nutrients. However, highly productive ponds reported with high cation exchange capacity (15-22 meq100g^{-1}) and optimum release of essential nutrients have the minimum loses due to leaching. Datta *et. al.* (2011) studied the CEC of NE pond soils and found a low range of CEC responsible for soil and water acidity.

Ion Adsorption

The soil particles due to the presence of charges adsorb and exchange ions in solution. When fertilizers are added to agricultural soils or ponds, most of the nutrients in the fertilizer (cations as well as anions) are adsorbed on the negatively and positively charged sites of the soil or pond mud and released slowly to the soil water or pond water over a long period of time. This explains why fertilizers added to a pond may remain active for many years. In the case of phosphorus fertilizer, not much of the original fertilizer applied is washed out of the pond at each draining. The pond mud acts as a buffer system for many elements which could control the concentrations in the overlying waters because of the large concentrations of some elements present in the mud sediments. The effects of this buffer system could be to keep the concentrations in the overlying waters relatively constant even though the concentrations of the element in the water are altered. The large quantity of lime required to increase the pH of ponds is often due to the neutratization of the potential or exchange acidity resulting from adsorbed hydrogen and aluminium ions.

In a soil, charges arise from all the above 3 sources. Negative charges increase with increase in pH of the water surrounding the soil particles and positive charges increase with decrease in pH. At very low pH, the soil or pond mud adsorbs anions and acts as an anioh exchanger. At higher pH, it adsorbs cations and acts as a cation exchanger.

As the pH of most agricultural soils and pond muds are generally higher than 4, the soil or mud is principally a cation exchanger, though it has some anion exchange properties. On the negatively charged sites or cation exchange sites, exchangeable cations are adsorbed and on the positively charged sites or anion exchange sites, exchangeable anions are adsorbed. Exchangeable cations can be acidic or basic cations. Acidic cations are those which produce acidity in soil. Common exchangeable cations and anions in soils are given below:

Exchangeable

$$\left(\frac{Al^{3+}, H^{+}, Fe^{3+}}{\text{Acidic cations}}\right) \left(\frac{Ca^{2+}, Mg^{2+}, K^{+}, Na^{+}, Zn^{2+}}{\text{Basic cations}}\right) \text{etc.}$$

cations:

Exchangeable anions: SO^{2-}_{4}, BO^{2-}_{3}, CO^{2-}_{3}, HCO_3^-, OH^-, $H_2PO_4^-$, HPO^{2-}_{4}, PO^{3-}_{4}, etc.

The quantity of cations which are adsorbed on the muds is expressed as milliequivalents of cations per 100 g (meq/100 g) of dry mud and is termed the cation exchange capacity (CEC). CEC is a measure of the total negative charges in the soil. CEC increase with increase in pH, % clay and % organic matter content in the soil. The fraction of CEC occupied by basic cations is called base saturation and the fraction of CEC occupied by acidic cations is base unsaturation.

Pond Water and its Properties

Wetzel, (1983) extensively studied on the relationship between carbon dioxide, alkalinity and pH in aquaculture. Boyd, (1990) found that alkalinity is a measure of the total titratable bases in water, which includes carbonates and bicarbonates, ammonia, hydroxide, phosphate, silicate and some organic acids. The source of alkalinity in water is due to the salts of weak acids getting dissociated in water. Most of the alkalinity in fresh water is composed of carbon ions ($CO_3^{--2}$and HCO_3^{-1}) which are interrelated. At a pH of about 4, most inorganic carbon in water is in the form of CO_2. As pH is increased, bicarbonate becomes more common, until pH reaches 8.3 when most inorganic carbon is present as HCO_3^-. Finally, as pH continues to rise, CO_3^{-2} becomes more common. Total alkalinity is often considered as an indicator of the organic carbon content of water. Since, the desirable pH in aquaculture ponds is often 7-8, most of the inorganic carbon is in the form of bicarbonate. Alkalinity potentially limits primary production and fish yield since inorganic carbon is necessary for photosynthesis.

Study of Hillary *et al*., (1997) showed that since pH, CO_2 and alkalinity are interrelated, diel change in CO_2, resulting from photosynthetic and respiratory processes can result in diel changes in pH more particularly in low alkalinity ponds. Crecco and Suvoy, (1985) found that the age and growth of any fish are dependent on environmental conditions. A given species can grow faster or slower in response to numerous biotic and abiotic variables, including nutrients, prey availability, competition, predators and water flow.

Yew-Hu Chien and Whay- Ming Roy, (1990) reported that water quality was inversely related to stocking density. Sediment had significant role in buffering capacity of water quality and reduction of total nitrogen, nitrite, and ammonia and sulfide concentration. Pond sediment plays important role on the balance of aquacultural systems and concomitantly on the growth and survival of aquatic organisms. It serves as biological filter through the absorption of the organic residues of food, fish excretions and algal metabolites. According to Roule, (1930) the largest fish crops are usually produced in water, which is just on the alkaline side of neutrality between pH 7.0 and 8.0. Ohle, (1938) found out that the limit above or below which pH has a harmful effect is given as 4.8 and 10.8. Neess, (1946) found out that a weak alkaline reaction (pH 7.0 to 8.0) has been found in most productive fishponds and on the other hand the very acidic waters are distinctly undesirable.

Acidic Soil and Water

Brinkman, (1982) explained that the source of acid condition in water is from organic acid of peaty wetlands, acid soils in pond mud or source water. Whereas Egna and Boyd, (1996) described that acid soils also contain high concentrations of iron and aluminium ions which are toxic to fish and other aquatic organisms and precipitate phosphate, making the fertilizer unavailable to organisms in the environment.

Reclamation of Acid Soil

Reclamation and utilization of acid sulfate soils in the coastal regions for aquaculture are well documented (Hickling, 1962; Brinkman & Singh, 1982 and Singh,1985). Avault, (1998) observed that high dose of organic manure may cause oxygen depletion in pond water as manures consume oxygen when getting decomposed in soil profile. But Egna and Boyd, (1996) demonstrated reclamation of acidic soil and water with large scale fish production through integration with livestock rearing and use of organic fertilizers for restoration of the pH from acidic to alkaline. The constant deposition and active decomposition of the organic matter at pond bottom in this system might have created anaerobic conditions in superficial sediments and thus effectively prevented acidification in deeper soils.

Conventional Methodology for Rectification of Acidity in Soil and Water

Lime reduces soil acidity in turn increases pH by changing sum of the hydrogen ions into water and further strengthening buffering capacity. A Ca^{++} ion from the lime replaces two H^+ ions on the cation exchange complex. The buffering capacity is related to the cation exchange capacity (CEC). The higher the CEC, the more exchangeable acidity (hydrogen and aluminum) is held by the soil colloids. As with CEC, buffering capacity increases with the amounts of clay and organic matter in the soil. The carbonate (CO_3^-) reacts with water to form bicarbonate (HCO_3^-). They further react with H^+ to form H_2O and CO_2. The pH increases due to reduced H^+ concentration and thus improves survival, reproduction and growth rate of culturable organisms (Boyd, 1974). Comparatively application of lime alone is not cost effective as its action is not long lasting in pond ecosystem and its high dose was also found to be detrimental to the pond productivity (Millar ,2004).Even application of wood ash (oxide of phosphorus and potassium) in water neutralizes acidity which has neutralizing values of 20-40%.

Role of Lime in Soil Amelioration

Boyd, (1974) reported that the favourable influence of liming on aquatic animal production in soft acidic waters has been attributed to several of the effects of liming on water quality. In extremely acidic waters, liming will increase the pH of the water and improve survival, reproduction and growth of aquatic life. Lime application increases the pH of bottom mud and thus enhancing availability of phosphorus. Arce and Boyd, (1975) studied the influence of liming on mud and the rise of pH as well as alkalinity of water coupled with the availability of CO_2 for photosynthesis.

Haster *et al.,* (1951) reported that by lime treatment, water may be cleared of humic stains of vegetative origin which restrict light penetration. The net effect of changes in water quality following liming is to increase phytoplankton productivity which in turn leads to increase fish production. Boyd and Tucker, (1998) stressed on liming in fish pond and reported that the purpose of liming is to neutralize acidity in pond soil and water and further to enhance total alkalinity and total hardness.

Use of lime in ponds and their requirements were studied by Silapajarn *et al.*, (2005). They observed that there were strong correlations between soil pH and pH of water and total alkalinity. Moreover, water pH and total alkalinity were highly correlated. Although soil carbonate concentration was not correlated with total alkalinity, there was a correlation between the product of soil carbonate and soil organic carbon and total alkalinity. Other soil properties like exchange acidity, cation exchange capacity, base saturation and total sulfur were either not correlated or weakly correlated with total alkalinity. It did not exceed 20 mgl^{-1} except in systems with soils containing free carbonate. A lime requirement method that estimates the amount of liming material needed to completely base saturate bottom soils and provides an excess of carbonate.

Deka and Yasmin, (2006) studied on the utilization of lime sludge waste from paper mills for fish culture in Assam and found that fishes cultured in lime sludge(66% $CaCO_3$) waste mixed water showed normal fish growth. There was no adverse impact on growth of fish and this can be used as alternative to lime in fish farming.

Chatterjee and Saha, (1986) observed the effect of lime like calcium oxide, calcium hydroxide and calcium carbonate at three rates(250., 500 and 1000 kg ha^{-1}) on silty acidic fish pond soil (pH 6.0) in enhancing soil pH and mineralization of nutrients. The soil reaction, available nitrogen and available phosphorus increased with the three forms of lime according to the enhanced rate of application with corresponding decrease in carbon. Identical results were also obtained in the water quality with regards to pH, total alkalinity and dissolved inorganic phosphate. While the maximum increase was recorded with the highest rate of each forms of calcium, the effect of calcium carbonate appeared superior as compared to the other two forms.

Observation of Sibrell *et al.,* (2006) on limestone fluidized bed treatment of acid-impacted water at the Craig Brook National Fish Hatchery, Maine, USA. Decades of atmospheric acid deposition had resulted in widespread lake and river acidification in the northeastern U.S. Biological effects of acidification include increased mortality of sensitive aquatic species such as the endangered Atlantic salmon (*Salmo salar*). The purpose was to describe the development of a limestone-based fluidized bed system for the treatment of acid-impacted waters. The treatment system was tested at the Craig Brook National Fish Hatchery in East Orland, Maine over a period of 3 years. The product water from the treatment system was diluted with hatchery water to make water supplies with three different levels of alkalinity for testing of fish health and survival. Based on the positive results from a prototype system used in the first year of the study, a larger demonstration system was introduced in the second and third years with the objective of decreasing operating costs. Carbon dioxide was used to accelerate limestone dissolution and it was the major factor in system performance, as evidenced by the model result: $Alk = 72.84 \times P(CO_2)^{1/2}$; $R^2 = 0.975$. No significant acidic incursions were noted for the control water over the course of the study. Had these incursions occurred, survival in the untreated water would likely have been much more severely affected.

Lime Requirements to Ameliorate Pond Soil

Kamprath, (1970) studied on soil acidity and found that soil acidity could be calculated as tonnes of $CaCO_3$ ha^{-1} = 1.65x Exchangeable Al^{3+}. Prasad *et al.,* (1978) found that besides aluminium, other acidity producing factors play dominant role in ascertaining lime requirement of soils

Alternative Methodology for Neutralization of Acidity

As an alternative methodology for effective neutralization of acidity, use of organic manure in combination with lime also advocated and found with varied success. The amounts and kinds of fertilizers that need to be applied to the pond depend on the natural fertility of the soil. High doses of fertilizers had negative impact on improvement of acidity of soil and water of ponds. In order to continue the high production of the pond, fertilizers containing the nutrients need to be applied frequently to the ponds as per their budgetary requirement. A good fraction of the fertilizers applied does not act directly on the organisms or water but often gets adsorbed on to the soil which releases the nutrients little at a time for a longer period. As a result, the fertilizers had prolonged action. Use of organic fertilizers in pond for restoration of the pH from acidic to alkaline had demonstrated success and exhibited high yield (Egna and Boyd, 1996 and Lin, 1986).

Study Conducted the Role of Acidic Soil in Relation to Nutrients Budget in Pond Ecosystems in NE Region

Elaborate studies of Datta *et.al.* (2010, 2011) revealed that the physico-chemical observations of the soil profile of the red acidic ponds of Tripura had shown its poor status in respect of neutrality with high H^+, Al as well as Fe contents. The high availability of sand coupled with low clay and calcium contents elucidated the need of liming to the pond soil. The low capacity of cation exchange was also experienced, showing the need of higher organic input to sustain the minimum basic nutrients availability for aquaculture productivity enhancement. The other important observation was the availability of comparatively higher phosphorus and potassium contents unlike other red soils around the country. These phenomenons attributed the need of addition of organic substances into the system moderately.

Evaluated the Role of C: N Ratio on Primary Productivity Enhancement in Acidic Soil Based Natural Ponds

The study of Datta *et.al.* (2010a, 2010b, 2011) also revealed that the pond soils had wide range of carbon nitrogen ratio (C: N) showing poor availability of both, carbon and nitrogen. Hence, overall productivity of the ponds was noticed low and positively correlated with the pervious findings. However, treatment to acidic ponds by using moderate doses of lime and organic manures in fish culture practices recovered soil profile from its poor unsaturated exchange capacity coupled with desirable carbon and nitrogen ratio (>12).

Growth and survival of fish stages in acidic soil specific aqua- farming: Experiments (Datta, 2009) were also conducted in red soil base ponds pertaining to culture of several fish stages after making necessary corrections of the soil and water parameters though leaching, seepage, acidity and poor productivity were major hurdles faced. But through effective trials suitable methodology was developed for the problematic soil base ponds in both seed rearing as well as grow out practices. The survival in rearing of common carp was excellent with encouraging growth of Indian major carps compared to medium survival at spawn stage. The outcome of carp culture into yield in such acidic ponds with moderate manures and supplementary feed was positively higher.

Overall four major experiments were conducted for achieving the above goal namely, soil and water analysis; quantification of lime, manure and fertilizer for ameliorate the acidic pond soil and water for aquaculture practices ; seed rearing as well as grow out practices of carps in red acidic soil based ponds. The analysis of pond soils and water revealed the nature of their vital parameters as soil pH 5.77, water pH 6.62, sand 80.86%, organic carbon 0.369% , nitrogen 0.020%, CEC 2.75 meq100g^{-1}, C:N ratio 20.49 with Fe 3.43 mg100g^{-1} and Al 5.92 mg100g^{-1}. Lime was used to counteract the acidity of the water. The soils of surveyed ponds were analysed to ascertain the actual need of lime and it was found 346.371 kg ha^{-1}yr^{-1} as CaO contradicting the conventional rate (622.461 kg).

Instead of depending on costly lime (almost two times more costlier than rest of the country) as remover of water and soil acidity, quantification and application of manure partly with medium dose of lime (260 kg ha^{-1}yr^{-1}) was selected as an alternative methodology for taming the soil acidity in fish farming. Therefore, the experiment was conducted for 120 days duration and the outcome revealed that organic manures *viz*., RCD @10,000 kg ha^{-1} yr^{-1} or poultry manure @ 5,000 kg ha^{-1} yr^{-1} would improve the red acidic soil nature in respect of their physico-chemical properties (soil pH 7.07; C:N ratio 4.25) as well as biological productivity for aquaculture.

Table 5.4: Physico-chemical Parameter of Acidic Soil in NE India

Parameter	Minimum	Maximum	Mean ± SE	Std. deviation	CV
Sand (%)	69	91	80.86 ± 1.11	5.97	7.38
Silt (%)	3	10	5.72 ± 0.36	1.93	33.63
Clay (%)	6	22	13.31 ± 0.86	4.64	34.84
Redox potential (mv)	26	128	53.55 ± 4.62	24.89	46.49
EC(Scm^{-1})	7	20	10.10 ± 0.43	2.32	22.96
pH	4.33	6.4	5.77 ± 0.11	0.57	9.82
OC (%)	0.03	0.85	0.37 ± 0.04	0.23	61.42
Nitrogen (%)	0.01	0.05	.02 ± 0.002	0.01	49.24
C:N ratio	3.80	50.8	20.49 ± 2.27	12.24	59.71
P ($mg100g^{-1}$)	0.41	27.13	7.39 ± 0.97	5.24	70.88
K ($mg100g^{-1}$)	1.06	14.94	4.09 ± 0.55	2.97	4.10
Iron ($mg100g^{-1}$)	1.08	3.84	3.43 ± 0.27	0.19	5.49
Calcium ($mg100g^{-1}$)	1.87	39.04	14.52 ± 1.71	9.19	14.52
C.E.C($meq100g^{-1}$)	1.19	8.23	2.75 ± 0.32	1.72	2.75
Al($mg100g^{-1}$)	0.34	12.67	5.92 ± 0.58	3.11	5.92

Table 5.5: Lime Requirement of NE Acidic Pond Soil

Type	Size(ha)	Soil pH	SoilTexture	$CaCO_3$ Required Based on pH (CIFRI Method)*	Lime Required as CaO*	$CaCO_3$ Required Based on Chemical Analysis*	Lime Required as CaO Based on Chemical Analysis*	Actual Rate of Lime Applied (CaO)*	Water pH	Recommended Rate*
Perennialal & old	0.08	6.4	Sandy-loam	500	280	227	127.12	300	7.1	
-Do-	0.24	4.5	Sandy	2000	1120	907	507.92	400	7.4	
-Do-	0.10	6.3	Sandy	500	280	680	300.80	200	6.8	
-Do-	0.12	6.3	Sandy	500	280	1020.6	576.53	200	6.7	
-Do-	0.08	6.0	Sandy-loam	1200	672	1360	761.60	300	6.4	
-Do-	0.04	5.8	Sandy	1200	672	227	127.12	200	7.2	
-Do-	0.04	5.8	Sandy-loam	1200	672	1020.6	571.2	200	6.8	
-Do-	0.08	5.9	Sandy-loam	1200	672	567	317.52	250	6.9	
-Do-	0.04	4.8	Sandy	2000	1120	567	317.52	250	7.1	
-Do-	0.04	6.3	Loamy-sand	500	280	567	318.00	250	7.2	
-Do-	0.067	6.1	Sandy-loam	1200	672	567	317.52	500	6.8	
-Do-	0.067	5.8	Sandy-loam	1200	672	680	317.52	500	6.9	
-Do-& new	0.03	6.2	Sandy	1000	560	680	317.52	500	6.6	
-Do-	0.03	6.1	Sandy-loam	1000	560	907	317.52	500	6.4	
-Do-	0.03	6.1	-Do-	1200	672	567	317.52	500	6.6	
-Do-	0.03	6.2	-Do-	1000	560	567	317.52	500	6.43	

(Contd...)

1	2	3	4	5	6	7	8	9	10	11
-Do-	0.03	6.2	-Do-	1000	560	227	317.52	500	6.4	
-Do-	0.03	6.1	-Do-	1200	672	680	317.52	500	7.1	
-Do-	0.03	5.5	-Do-	1200	672	454	317.52	500	6.3	260
-Do-	0.03	6.1	Sandy	1000	560	567	317.52	500	6.4	
-Do-	0.1	5.8	-Do-	1200	672	1134	317.52	500	7.1	
-Do-	0.1	5.6	-Do-	1200	672	454	317.52	500	7.8	
-Do-	0.17	5.4	-Do-	1200	672	454	317.52	500	6.0	
-Do-	0.25	4.9	-Do-	2000	1120	1020	317.52	500	6.0	
-Do-	0.25	5.4	-Do-	1200	672	794	317.52	500	6.5	
-Do-	0.17	4.3	-Do-	2000	1120	1020	317.52	500	7.1	
Average	**0.0874**	**5.8**		**1176.92**	**672.0**	**689.00**	**346.37**	**405.77**	**6.77**	

Performance of these manuring schedules in aquaculture practices in selected acidic soils were tested initially in seed rearing and subsequently in grow out practices. The results indicated positive impact and elucidated high rate of survival of common carp (97.5-98.0%) and rohu (65.65 -72.05%) fingerlings and that of moderate in fry of rohu (29.05-31.50%) with major improvement in soil and water profile enhancing water pH (7.13 to 7.78), total alkalinity (30 to 101 mgl-^{1}) and reducing the Fe(from 0.892 to 0.064 mgl-^{1}) and Al (from 0.985 to 0.200 mgl-^{1}) contents in both the treatments. Same trend was noticed in grow out practices of carps with raw cow dung and a production of 2,703.195 to 4,320.32 kg ha^{-1}yr^{-1} was obtained with a rate of the survival of 75.0 to 91.2%. There was substantial improvement in major physico-chemical properties responsible for aquaculture practices in acidic soil base ponds. The study would be immensely useful and applicable in productivity and yield enhancement in North East region of the country.

Methodology developed for ameliorating the acidic pond soil and water

(a) Correction of red acidic soil

- The soil should not be allowed to get fully dried under sunlight to avoid the oxidation process of the iron and aluminium as it may lead to acute acidity and phosphate binding.
- While excavating the ponds in red soil, it needs to be damp.
- The pond should not be totally dewatered and dried.
- Catchment rain water should not be allowed to get direct entry into the pond. This phenomenon controls the acidity by checking intense leaching and in turn removal of minerals.
- Minimizing free board area by water filling to reduce iron oxidation. The replacement of basic cations by acidic cations such as aluminum (Al^{3+}) and hydrogen (H^{+}) could be controlled even in high rain fall areas.
- High altitude ponds need to have polythene lining to check intensive seepage.
- The acidic nature of pond soil and water with low to medium pH could be corrected by using quick lime (CaO) @ 250-350 kg of kg ha^{-1} y^{-1} in splitted doses. Subsequently organic manure can be applied for long lasting amendment process.
- Either raw cow dung @ 10,000 kg ha^{-1} y^{-1} or poultry manure@ 5,000 kg ha^{-1} y^{-1} in splitted doses may be applied preferably fortnightly.
- The next alternate is the application of organic manure in medium doses along with molasses (50kg ha^{-1} y^{-1}).
- The above processes can elevate the soil and water pH to desirable alkaline level and in turn will enhance the productivity coupled with high productive C: N ratio (8-14).
- The amendments need continuity.

CONCLUSION

The study on management of problematic red acidic soil based fish culture hopefully may help in understanding the correlation among the prime nutrients pattern like low C: N ratio, CEC, calcium, low to medium phosphorus and potassium with high Fe and Al contents and their regulatory factors like redox potential, electrical conductivity coupled with high sand and low clay percentage in relation to release of the nutrients for better productivity and fish yield. Based on this study, the farmers can be encouraged on the suggested lines as the technology is simple, easy to adopt, ecologically sustainable and cost effective too. Such problematic soil base ponds which are generally not exploited for aquafarming can very well attract the attention of both farmers and extension workers for their commercial use and rural economic development; thus it can pave the way to provide nutritional security to the food basket of North Eastern region.

REFERENCES

Arce, R.C. and Boyd, C.E., 1975. Effects of Agricultural Lime Stone on Water Chemistry, Phytoplankton Productivity and Fish Production in Soft Water Ponds, *Transactions of the American Fisheries Society*. 104: 308-312.

Avault, J.W., 1998. Fundamentals of Aquaculture. AVA Publishing Company. USA. 346 pp.

Banerjea, S.M. and Ghosh, S.R.,1970. Studies on the Correlation Between Soil Relation and Different forms Bound Phosphorus in Pond Soils. *J.Inland Fish.Soc.India*, pp. 113-120.

Banerjea, S.M. and Mandal, L.N.,1965. Inorganic Transformation of Water Soluble Phosphate Added in Fish Ponds as Influenced by the Nature of the Pond Soils. *J. Indian Soc. Soil.*13: 167-73.

Bhattacharyya, T.; Sehagal, J. and Sarkar, D., 1996. Soils of Tripura: Their Kinds, Distribution and Suitability for Major Field Crops and Rubber for Optimizing Land Use. *NBSS Publication.* 65, National Bureau of Soil Survey and Land Use Planning, Nagpur.

Bapat, M. V.; Padole, G.C.; Toky, N.G. and Bedakar, V.G.,1965. Forms of Phosphorus in Vidarbha Soils. *J. Indian Soc. Soil.,* 13: 31-36.

Boyd, C.E., 1970. Influence of Organic Matter on Some Characteristics of Aquatic Soils. *Hydrobiologi*a. 36: 17-21.

Boyd, C.E., 1974. Lime Requirements of Alabama Fish Ponds. Alabama Agricultural Experiment Station Bulletin 459, Auburn University, Auburn, AL, 20 pp.

Boyd, C.E., 1990. Water Quality in Ponds for Aquaculture, Alabama Agricultural Experiment Station, Auburn University, Auburn, USA.

Boyd, C.E., 1995. Bottom Soils Sediment and Pond Aquaculture. Chapman & Hall, New York, USA, pp. 66-67.

Boyd, C.E. and Tucker, C.S., 1998. Pond Aquaculture Water Quality Management, Kluwer Academic Publishers, London, 187 pp.

Brinkman, R and Singh, V.P., 1982. Rapid Reclamation of Brackish Water Ponds in Acid Sulfate Soils, in *Proc. Of Int. symp. on Acid Sulfate Soils* Publ. No. 31, Wageningen, Natherlands, 318 pp.

Chang, S.C. and Jackson, M.L, 1958. Soil Phosphate Fractions in Some Representative Soils. . *J. Soil. Sci.,* 9: 109-19.

Chang, S.C. and Chu, W.K., 1961. The Fate of Soluble Phosphate Applied to Soils. *J. Soil. Sci.*

Chatterjee, D.K. and Saha, G.N.,1986. Effect of Lime on Fish Pond Soils. *J. Inland Fish Soc. India.* 18(1): 41-44.

Chauhan, D.P.S., 2004. Fisheries and Aquaculture Development in North Eastern States: A Review. *Fishing Chimes*, 23 (10 & 11): 45-48.

Coleman, N.T. and Thomas, G.W. 1967. The Basic Chemistry of Soil Acidity. *In:* Soil Acidity and Liming (ed. Peterson, R.W and Adams, F): 1-41.

Crecco, V.A. and Savoy, T.F., 1985. Effects of Biotic and Abiotic Factors on Growth and Relative Survival of Young American Shed; *Slosa Sapidissima*, in the Connecticut River, *Canadian Journal of Fisheries and aquatic Societies*, 42: 1640-1648.

Datta, M.K, 2009. Standardization of Aquaculture Practices in Acidic Soils of Tripura Ph.D., Dissertation at CIFE, Mumbai, 2006-09.

Datta, M.K.; Ratan K. Saha, J. R. Dhanze, Chandra Prakash, M. P. Singh Kohli and N. Saharan, 2010a, Nutrient Profile of Pond Water in Northeastern State of Tripura and Impact of Water Acidity on Aquaculture Productivity, *Journal of Indian Fisheries Association*, CIFE, ICAR Mumbai. Vol. 35: 11-20.

Datta, M.K.; Ratan K. Saha, J.R. Dhanze, Chandra Prakash, M.P. Singh Kohli and N. Saharan, 2010b. Role of cation Exchange Capacity (CEC) in Pond Soil Acidity and Primary Productivity for Yield Enhancement, *J. Aqua Trop.* Vol. 25. No. 1-2 (2010) pp. 67-74.

Datta, M.K., Ratan K. Saha, , Chandra Prakash, 2011. Nutrient Profile of Pond Soils in Northeast Indian State of Tripura and Impact of Soil Acidity on Aquaculture Productivity, *Inland Fisheries Society of India*, Barrack pore, Kolkata - 700 120, West Bengal, India, Vol. 43(2): 97-102.

Deka, S. and Yasmin, S., 2006. Utilization of Lime Sludge Waste from Paper Mills for Fish Culture. *Current Science*, 90(8): 1125-1130.

Dhanajaya, B.C. and Ananthanrayana. R., 2006. Forms of Acidity in Some Acid Soils of Karnataka. *Envirnment and Ecology*. 24S (3A): 778-790.64:286.

Dhruva Narayana, V.V. and Patnaik, U.S., 1990.Water Shed Management. ICAR, New Delhi.

Dhruva Narayana, V.V. and Ram, B., 1983. Estimation of Soil Erosion in India. *J. Irrig. Drain. Engg*. 109 (4): 419-34.

Dhruva Narayana, V.V. 2002. Soil and Water Conservation Research in India, ICAR, New Delhi, pp. 107-15.

Egna, H.S. and. Boyd, C.E., 1996. Dynamics of Pond Aquaculture.CRC Press. New York.

Haster, A.D.; Brynildson, O.M. and Helm, W.T., 1951. Improving Condition of Fish in Brown-water Bog Lakes by Alkalinazation. *Journal of Wild life Management*., 15: 347- 352.

Hegde, B.R.; Chanappa, T.C. and Ananda Ram, B.K., 1991. Water Harvesting and Recycling in the Red Soils of Karnataka. Indian, *J .Soil .Conserv*, 9(2 & 3): 107-15.

Hickling, C.F., 1962, Fish Culture, *Faber and Faber,* London, 225, pp.

Hillary, S.; Egna, H.S. and Boyd C.E., 1997. *In:* Dynamics of Pond Aquaculture, CRC Press, New York, pp. 56-57.

Jhingran, V.G.,1991. Fish and Fisheries of India. *Hindustan Publ. Corp*. New Delhi. 954 pp.

Kamprath, E.J., 1970. Proceeding of Soil Science Society of America. 34:252.

Landau, M. and Scarpa, J., 2001. Demonstrations and Laboratory Exercises in Aquaculture. I. Pond Soil. *World Aquaculture*, 32(.2): 10-13.

Laskar, S.; Dadhwal, K.S. and Prasad, R.N., 1983. *Bulletin*, ICAR Research Complex for NEH Region, Meghalaya.

Lin, C.K., 1986. Acidification and Reclamation of Acid Sulfate Soil Fish Ponds in Thailand, *In:* Proc. of the First Asian Fisheries Forum, (ed. Mclean, J., Dizon, L.B., and Hosilos, L.V.) *Asian Fisheries Society*, Manila, 71 pp.

Millar, C.E., 2004. Soil fertility. *Biotech Book*. N.D.

Munilkumar. S & Nandeesha, M. C.(2007). Aquaculture Practices in Northeast India: Current Status and Future Directions. Fish Physiol Biochem. 33: 399-412.

Nath, D., 1985. Role of cation Exchange Capacity on Productivity of Freshwater Ponds. *J. Inland Fish Soc. India.* 17(1&2): 71-73.

Neess, J.C., 1946. Development and Status of Pond Fertilization in Central Europe. *Trans. Amer. Fish. Soc.* No. 76: 335-358.

Ohle, W., 1938. Teichwirtschaftliche kalkkontrolle und die pH- SBV- Tasche (Control of Liming in Ponds with an Outfit for pH and Alkalinity Determination). *Z. fish.* 36: 185-191.

Panda, N., 1988. Acid Soils of Eastern India, Their Chemistry and Management. *Journal of Indian Society of Soil Science.* 35: 568.

Prasad, R.N.; Patiram and Munna, R., 1985. *Journal of Research, Assam Agricultural University*. 3: 131.

Roule, l., 1930. pH Determination in the Evaluation of Carp Ponds. *C.R. Acad. Agri. France*, 16: 1056-1060.

Sehgal, J.L., 1993. Red and Laterite Soils of India: An Overview. *In*: Red and Lateritie Soils of India. NBSS and LUP. Nagpur, India.

Sibrell, P. L.; Wattena, B. J.; Haines, T. A. and Spauldingc, B. W., 2006. Limestone Fluidized Bed Treatment of Acid-impacted Water at the Craig Brook National Fish Hatchery, Maine, USA. *Aquaculture engineering*. 34(2): 61-71

Silapajarn, K.; Orawan, S. and Boyd, C. E., 2005. Evaluation of Lime Requirement Procedures and Liming Materials for Aquaculture Ponds in Thailand. *Journal of Applied Aquaculture*, 17(3): 77-88.

Singh, V.P., 1985. Management and Utilization of Acid Sulfate Soils for Aquaculture: A Monograph, University of the Philippines, Visya.

Singh, B.; Das, P.; Madhumita; Munna, R.; Dwivedi, B.S. and Prasad, R.N., 1989. *Journal of Indian society of Soil Science* 37: 591.

Singh, R.S.; Verma, T.P.; Dubey, P.N. and Maji, A.K.,1991. *Annual Report, NBSS & LUP*, Nagpur, India.

Sharma, U.C.; Datta, M. and Shamra J.S., 2006. Soils and Their Management in NE India. ICAR Research Complex for NEH Region, Meghalaya.

Too, K.H. and Boyd, C.E., 1994. Hydrobiology and Water Supply for Aquaculture. Chapman & Hall, New York.

Wetzel, R.G.,1983. *Limnology*, 2nd ed. Saunders College Publishing, Philadelphia, Pa.

6

Ecological Requirements of Sustainable Fisheries in Lower Stretch of the River Brahmaputra of North East India

Bhaskar J. Saud* and **Mitali Chetia**

ABSTRACT

The Brahmaputra River is the fourth largest river in the world in terms of average flow discharge, finds its origin in the Chema Yungdung glacier of Tibet and flow through the Assam of North-east India furnishing huge ichthyofaunal diversity to the region. The present study was carried out to assess the ecological requirements (water quality) of the lower stretch of the Brahmaputra River for the survival and growth of fish fauna. Water samples were collected from 6 stations located in three districts of Assam in 4 different seasons (pre-monsoon, monsoon, post monsoon and winter) in the lower stretch of the river during 2006-2008. Parameters for the water quality study included pH, temperature, Dissolved Oxygen (DO), Free Carbon di-oxide (FCO$_2$), Total alkalinity and hardness. Salient water quality variables of the studied stretch of the river found more or less within the optimal range for fish production and can be considered as the suitable ecological criteria for the fishes found in the lower stretch of the River Brahmaputra. Altogether 84 fish species (e.g. Chitala chitala, Tenulosa ilisha, Labeo rohita, L. pangusia, Catla catla, Cirhhinus mrigala, Sperata seenghala, Tor putitora,) were recorded from the study area.

Keywords: Brahmaputra River, Physico-chemical parameter, Ecology, Ichthyofaunal diversity.

INTRODUCTION

Fisheries in the Brahmaputra River are very complex, both in terms of eco-biology and management systems. The largest fish species like *Bagarius yarrelli* to fresh water river dolphins (*Platanista gangetica*) have been recorded from this river system. Apart from large species, there are also medium and small pieces that support more than 50% of the total catch in entire Brahmaputra valley, which provide the main source of food and additional income for the rural poor. The river has a unique diversity of fish throughout its flowing stretch. However, the fish species available in a particular stretch of the river are not totally similar to those of the other stretch. As the species are aquatic habitat oriented, it is the quality of water in a riverine stretch that determines their distribution. Different fish species need particular physico-chemical characteristics of water in which they survive, grow and reproduce. It is the water quality parameter which influences in the density of fishery forming species, abundance and richness of the fish species and in the maturation and spawning of fishes in the riverine environment (Whiteside and McNatt, 1972; Donaldson, 1975; Reash and Jimmie, 1990; Sabo *et.al.*, 1991; Woiwode, 1996; Braaten and guy 1999). Matthews (1998) postulated that the local fish assemblage and dynamics in a river are dependent on environmental stress as well as capability of the fish species to cope up with the water quality changes. Major fishes like *Chitala chitala, Tenulosa ilisha, Labeo rohita, Catla catla, Cirhhinus mrigala, Sperata seenghala, S. aor, Wallago attu, Silonia silondia, Rita rita* are more abundant in the lower stretch of the river from Dhubri, Goalpara to Kamrup districts. The diversity of fish is found to be more numerous in lower reaches of Brahmaputra basin up to Bangladesh. In the present chapter the basic water quality database-suitable ecological requirements for the survival and growth of sustainable fishery of the lower stretch of the Brahmaputra River is highlighted.

Fig. 6.1: Commercial Fishers Fishing in the Brahmaputra River

Fig. 6.2: Commercial Fishers Fishing in the Brahmaputra River

The study was carried out in the stretches passing through the districts of Dhubri, Goalpara and Kamrup district of Assam. The whole stretch was divided in to six sampling sites for water quality analysis. Seasonal estimation of seven physico-chemical parameters (pH, water temperature, Dissolved Oxygen, Free Carbon di oxide, alkalinity, hardness and chloride) of water were done for each site following APHA (1992). The water temperatures of the studied areas were measured with the help of Mercury in glass thermometer graduated from 0° C to 100° C × 1/10 °C and recorded. The monthly average atmospheric temperature, rainfall and the humidity data were collected from the Indian Meteorological Station, Borjhar, Guwahati.The fish catch composition was recorded on-spot randomly from craft and gear operated by fishermen.

Study Area

The Brahmaputra is a trans-boundary river and one of the major rivers of Asia which originates in the Chema Yundung glacier of Tibet approximately at 31° 30/N and 82° 0/E. From its origin in southwestern Tibet at the Yarlung Tsangpo River, it flows across southern Tibet where it is known as Dihang to break through the Himalayas in great gorges. It bisects Assam valley as Brahmaputra which flowthrough Bangladesh as the Yamuna. The Brahmaputra traverses a total distance of 2880 km and comprises an easterly course of 1625 in Tibet, a south and westerly course of 918 km in India and a course of 337 km in Bangladesh. In India the Brahmaputra flows through the state of Arunachal Pradesh for 278 km mostly across the Himalayas, where it is called Dihang or Siang River. The Dihang emerges onto the plains at Passighat near Kobo in Assam, which at 52 km down stream from the Pasighat, it is joined by two large rivers Lohit and Dibang and from this point the river is known as Brahmaputra. The Brahmaputra River flows for about 670 km through the state of Assam along the Assam valley. And within Assam valley the Brahmaputra receives 103 tributaries (including sub tributaries), 65 on the north bank and 38 on the south bank. The slop of the river becomes steep as soon as it crosses the Himalayas at Tibet. Thereafter the river slope variations are recorded to be 1.63 m/km in Tibet, 4.3 m/km to 16.8 m/km across the Himalayas, 0.62 m/km in plains upto Kobo to Dibrugarh district.0.17m/km from Dibrugarh to Nimatighat, 0.15 m/km Nimatighat to Tezpur, 0.14 m/km from Tezpur district to Pandu, Guwahati, Kamrup district 0.11 m/km from Pandu to Jogighopa, Goalpara district 0.094 m/km from Jogighopa to Dhubri district (Goswami, 1985). The Brahmaputra River is the fourth largest river in the world in terms of average flow discharge at its mouth with a flow of 19830 m^3 s^{-1} (Goswami, 1985).

The present ecological survey is conducted in the lower reaches of the Brahmaputra River basin. For the comprehensive brevity of the studies maneuvered in the present investigation three principle survey stations have been selected representing the lower zone, middle zone and the upper zone (Fig. 6.2). The lower zone lies in the stretch of the Brahmaputra River in Dhubri district, the middle zone lies in the stretch of Brahmaputra River in Goalpara district and the upper zone lies in the Kamrup district.

ZONE – 1: Lower zone (Stretch of the Brahmaputra River in Dhubri District)

The lower reaches of the Brahmaputra River in the Dhubri district is one of the most productive and important zone of fish diversity. The stretches from the Dhubri town to the boarder of the Assam and Bangladesh is rich in the catching of fishes (26°11/16// N, 90° 23/23//E to 26°2/36//N, 90° 7/41//E)

ZONE – 2: Middle zone (Stretch of the Brahmaputra River in Goalpara district)

The stretches of the Goalpara district near the Goalpara town (26°12/09//N, 90° 33/10//E to 26°11/30//N, 90° 38/30//E)

ZONE – 3: Upper zone (Stretch of the Brahmaputra River in Kamrup district)

The stretches of Brahmaputra near the Palashbarı and Amingaon are last two sampling site in Kamrup district. (26°10/13//N, 91° 18/17// E to 26°8/47// N, 91° 32/ 83//E)

INFORMATION ON ECOLOGICAL REQUIREMENTS

The main objective of the study was to find out the ecological requirements of the available fish fauna in the lower stretch of the Brahmaputra River.

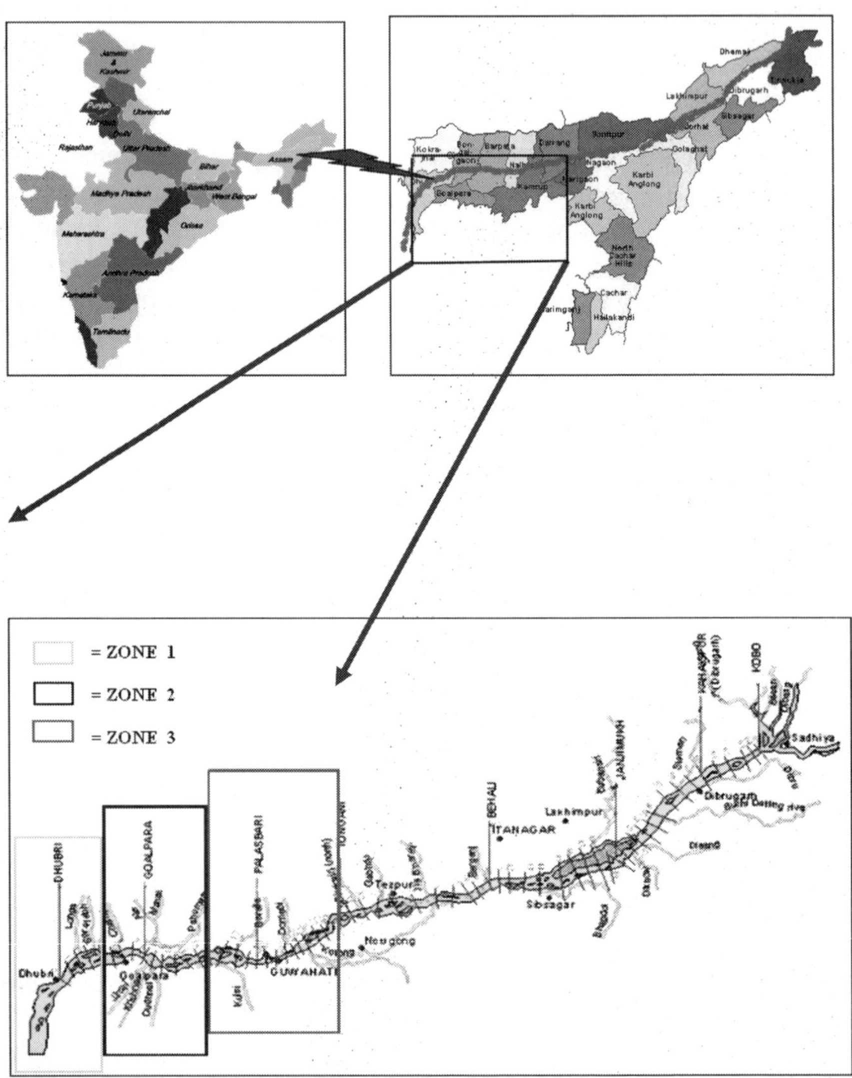

Fig. 6.3: Location Map of the Study Area

In this context seven most significant water quality parameters like Temperature, pH, Dissolved oxygen (DO), Free carbon dioxide as FCO_2, alkalinity and total hardness were considered. Further, the climatological parameters like humidity, rainfall and air temperature of the region were secondarily collected to see their influence in the seasonal variation of the studied river water quality.

CLIMATOLOGICAL PARAMETERS

Among the climatic factors air temperature, relative humidity and rainfall were collected from the meteorological centre during the study period from June, 2006 to

July, 2008, since these parameters have enormous impact on the agro climatic condition of Assam in general and the Brahmaputra River in particular. It is also directly associated with the seasonal changes to the physico-chemical attributes of the studied river stretch.

Air Temperature

The atmospheric temperature during the study period June 2006 to May 2007 and June 2007 to May 2008 were collected monthly and the monthly average value was calculated. The highest air temperature was found to be 34.1°C during the month of August, 2006, and the minimum monthly average temperature was recorded as 9.9°C in the month of January, 2007. Similarly during the study period from March, 2007 to June, 2008 the highest average air temperature was recorded as 34° C in August, 2007 and the minimum average air temperature was recorded as 11.1° C in February, 2008 (Table 6.1). The data indicates that the air temperature attains to the highest during the month of May to August and lowest during the winter in the month of January and February in the study areas.

Rainfall

Monthly average rainfall in the studied area was found to be 1192.51 mm with a fluctuation between 0.29 mm in the month of February to maximum 550.80 mm in the month of June during the period June, 2006 to May, 2007. Similarly during the period of June, 2007 to July, 2008, the mean rainfall was recorded 129.34 mm with a range of minimum 0.6 mm in the month of January, 2008 and maximum 399.39 mm in the month of July, 2007. During both the study period it was observed that the heavy rainfall occurs from April to September and relatively dry period was recorded from the month of October to March.

Relative Humidity

The monthly average value of maximum relative humidity at morning time had been recorded as 82.76 ± 4.65 with a fluctuation from 93.6% (December 2006 and January, 2007) to 75% (May, 2007). Similarly the humidity at evening time had been recorded 78.88 ± 7.45 with a fluctuation from maximum 87% (September 2006) to minimum 46% (March, 2007).

Similarly during June, 2007 to July, 2008 the fluctuation of maximum humidity was recorded from 87% (December 2007 and January, 2008) to 75% (March, 2008) at morning time with the mean level 82.34 ± 3.74. On the other hand the fluctuation of humidity at evening time was recorded of 53% (February, 2008) and maximum 83% (July, 2007) with a mean value of 72.23 ± 3.75.

PHYSICO-CHEMICAL PARAMETERS

Four seasons were demarcated namely; Premonsoon, Monsoon, Post monsoon and winter and accordingly the eco-habitat studies of the fishes were oriented in the river. The seasonal fluctuation in physico-chemical properties of the water parameters in different zones of the study area throughout April, 2006 – March, 2008 were given in the tabular form (Table 6.3 - 6.8). Following were the changes in the physico-chemical characteristics of the water in different survey stations of the study area.

Dissolved Oxygen (DO_2)

The dissolved oxygen concentration fluctuation in the study areas had been recorded seasonally and depicted in the table (6.3-6.8). During the investigation dissolved oxygen was found maximum (10.2 mg/l) in the Jogomaya station, Dhubri in winter season of 2006 than all other stations of observation along the course of the study stretch. Where as minimum (7.8 mg/ l) was found in Amingaon station in monsoon period of 2006.

Free Carbon dioxide (FCO_2)

Carbon-di-oxide content was found maximum (3.5 mg/ l) in Birshing ghat station, Dhubri in post monsoon period of 2007 and minimum (2.2 mg/l) in Amingaon station of Kamrup in monsoon period of 2006.

Alkalinity

Alkalinity was found maximum (44.4 mg/ l) in Amingaon station, Kamrup district in monsoon of 2006 during the investigation. The minimum value of alkalinity (26.1 mg/l) was found in winter at Jogighopa station, Goalpara district in 2007.

Hardness

Hardness was found maximum (23.3 mg/l) in winter season of 2006 at Jogighopa station and the minimum hardness (11.2 mg/l) was recorded from Amingaon station of Kamrup district in 2006.

Chloride

Chloride was recorded maximum of 17.5 mg/l from Birshing station, Dhubri in monsoon season of 2006. The minimum value of chloride 10.5 mg/l was recorded from Jogomaya station in winter season of 2007.

P^{H}

pH was found maximum (8.1) in Jogomaya station in the pre monsoon season of 2006 and in Amingaon station in post monsoon period of 2006. The minimum value of pH (6.5) was found in pre monsoon season of Jogighopa station in 2006.

Temperature

Temperature was found maximum (22.8° C) in Jogighopa station, Goalpara district in post monsoon in 2006 and the minimum temperature (10.8° C) was recorded from Kachari station, Goalpara district in winter season in 2006.

Table 6.1: Summary of Air Temperature (°C) Recorded during the Study Period from June, 2006 to June, 2008

Study Period	Maximum Temperature °C	Minimum Temperature °C
June, 2006 to May, 2007	34.1 (August, 2006)	9.9 (January, 2007)
June, 2007 to May, 2008	34 (August, 2007)	11.1 (February, 2008)

Source: Indian Meteorological Station, Borjhar, Guwahati, Assam.

Table 6.2: Summary of Relative Humidity (%) and Average Rainfall (mm) during the Study Period from June, 2006 to June, 2008

	Relative Humidity (%)		Rainfall (mm)
	June, 2006 to May, 2007		
	8.30 am	17.30 pm	Average
Maximum	89 (Dec., 06 and Jan., 07)	79 (Sep., 06)	286.6 (Apr., 07)
Minimum	67 (March, 07)	46 (March, 07)	0.0 (Jan., 07)
Mean	81.08	70.5	108.58
SD	6.20	9.08	92.30
	June, 2007 to May, 2008		
Maximum	87 (Dec., 07 and Jan., 08)	83 (Jul., 06)	315.9 (Sep., 07)
Minimum	75 (March, 07)	53 (Feb., 08)	0.0 (Dec., 2007)
Mean	81.58	71	135.95
SD	4.05	9.24	111.95

Source: Indian Meteorological Station, Borjhar, Guwahati, Assam.

INFORMATION ON ICHTHYOFAUNAL DIVERSITY

Altogether 81 fish species (Table 6.9) were recorded in the studied area of Kamrup and Goalpara disttrict belonging to 58 genera under 26 families. On the other hand 84 fish species were recorded from the stretches of the Brahmaputra River in the Dhubri diastrict belonging to 60 genera under 26 families. The ichthyofaunal diversity of the Dhubri district is depicted in (Table 6.10). It is found that some of the cold water fishes like *Tor putitora, Labeo pungusia, Cyprinion semiloptum* are also seen in the catches of the fishermen. This is due to the tributary Manas river originating at an altitude of 4900 m, which travers a distance of 270 km in hills posses diversified rheophilic fauna in its bed and the source of hill steam fishes in this stretch.

Table 6.3: Seasonal Variation in Physico-chemical Characteristics of Water of Jogomaya Ghat in Dhubri District (2006-2008)

Sl.No.	Pysico-chemical Parameter	Survey Station	Year	Pre Monsoon		Monsoon		Post Monsoon		Winter	
				Range	Mean	Range	Mean	Range	Mean	Range	Mean
1.	Dissolved oxygen (mg/l)	Dhubri (Jogomaya Ghat)	2006-07	8.2-9.7	9.4	7.9-[illegible].1	8.5	8.1-9.7	9.3	8.9-10.5	10.2
			2007-08	7.8-10.1	9.9	8.2-[illegible].4	8.4	9.1-9.8	9.4	9.5-10.3	10.1
2.	Dissolved free carbon-di- oxide (mg/l)		2006-07	2.3-3.4	2.8	2.1-[illegible].5	2.3	3.1-3.3	3.1	2.5-2.9	2.6
			2007-08	3.1-3.8	3.3	1.8-[illegible].7	2.5	2.9-3.2	3.0	2.4-3.1	2.8
3.	Alkalinity (mg/l)		2006-07	38-41	39.7	40-[illegible]2	40.8	43-46	43.6	35-37	36.2
			2007-08	38-43	41.3	39-[illegible]2	40.5	40-45	42.9	35-38	36.5
4.	Hardness (mg/l)		2006-07	16-20	18	13-[illegible]4	13.5	15-20	17.8	18-22	20.0
			2007-08	17-22	19.8	12-[illegible]5	13.2	16-19	17.4	19-22	20.4
5.	Chloride		2006-07	12.5-12.6	12.5	16.5-[illegible]7.7	17	14.2-14.9	14.6	10.6-10.8	10.6
			2007-08	11.7-12.5	12.2	17.1-[illegible]7.5	17.2	14.5-15.0	14.5	10.5-11.0	10.5
6.	pH		2006-07	6.8-7.2	7	7.5-[illegible].8	7.6	7.9-8.4	8.1	6.7-7.1	6.9
			2007-08	6.6-7.2	7.1	7.4-[illegible].7	7.5	7.9-8.1	7.9	6.8-7.4	7.1
7.	Temperature		2006-07	18-19	18.5	21-[illegible]3	22	16-19	17.3	9-14	11.5
			2007-08	19-20	19.5	21-[illegible]3	22.1	18-20	19	10.5-13	11.7

Table 6.4: Seasonal Variation in Physico-chemical Characteristics of Water of Birising Ghat in Dhubri District (2006-2008)

Sl.No.	Pysico-chemical Parameter	Survey Station	Year	Pre Monsoon		Monsoon		Post Monsoon		Winter	
				Range	Mean	Range	Mean	Range	Mean	Range	Mean
1.	Dissolved oxygen (mg/l)	Dhubri (Birising Ghat)	2006-07	8.5-9.8	8.7	9.4-9.9	9.6	9.5-9.7	9.2	9.1-10.5	9.6
			2007-08	8.8-9.7	9.1	8.7-9.7	9.0	8.7-9.5	9.0	9.2-10.8	9.4
2.	Dissolved free carbon-di-oxide (mg/ l)		2006-07	2.3-3.0	2.6	2.5-2.9	2.6	2.8-3.2	2.9	2.5-3.1	2.8
			2007-08	2.1-3.1	2.7	2.8-3.5	3.0	3.2-3.9	3.5	2.8-3.1	2.9
3.	Alkalinity (mg/l)		2006-07	35-39	36.6	38-42	40	35-37	35.8	43-46	44.0
			2007-08	37-41	41.3	39-42	40.2	35-38	36.2	40-45	42.2
4.	Hardness (mg/l)		2006-07	18-24	20.6	13-15	13.9	15-20	17.5	20-24	22.2
			2007-08	20-23	21.8	12-17	14.6	17-18	17.6	22-24	22.5
5.	Chloride		2006-07	11.5-12.4	11.9	17.0-17.9	17.5	14.5-15.0	14.8	11.2-11.8	11.5
			2007-08	11.5-12.5	11.9	16.9-17.5	17.2	14.5-15.0	14.6	10.5-11.0	10.7
6.	pH		2006-07	7-7.2	7.0	7.1-7.5	7.3	7.2-7.4	7.3	7.0-7.2	7.1
			2007-08	6.9-7.2	7.0	7.4-7.5	7.4	7.1-7.3	7.2	6.8-7.2	7.0
7.	Temperature		2006-07	18.5-19	18.7	22-23	22.5	18-19	18.5	10-13	11.7
			2007-08	18-20	18.9	21-23	21.4	19-20	19.5	10.5-13	11.8

Table 6.5: Seasonal Variation in Physico-chemical Characteristics of Water at Amingaon in Kamrup District (2006-2008)

Sl.No.	Pysico-chemical Parameter	Survey Station	Year	Pre Monsoon		Monsoon		Post Monsoon		Winter	
				Range	Mean	Range	Mean	Range	Mean	Range	Mean
1.	Dissolved oxygen (mg/l)	Kamrup (Amingaon)	2006-07	8.5-9.7	8.9	7.2-8.5	7.8	8.1-9.4	8.8	8.4-9.5	9.2
			2007-08	8.0-9.1	8.7	8.2-8.5	8.3	9.0-9.5	9.2	8.5-8.9	8.6
2.	Dissolved free carbon-di- oxide (mg/l)		2006-07	2.5-2.8	2.6	2.0-2.5	2.2	3.0-3.5	3.2	2.7-2.9	2.7
			2007-08	2.1-2.5	2.3	1.8-2.8	2.3	2.5-3.0	2.7	2.5-3.1	2.8
3.	Alkalinity (mg/l)		2006-07	35-45	39.1	42-47	44.4	40-46	43.2	32-39	35.6
			2007-08	35-43	39.0	39-45	41.8	40-45	42.7	35-40	37.6
4.	Hardness (mg/l)		2006-07	17-18	17.5	10-12	11.2	14-18	16.0	20-23	21.5
			2007-08	15-20	17.6	13-14	13.4	13-19	16.2	21-23	21.8
5.	Chloride		2006-07	11.5-12.3	11.9	17.5-17.0	17.2	14. 2-14.9	14.5	11.2-11.7	11.4
			2007-08	12.0-12.5	12.2	17.1-17.8	17.4	14.5-15.0	14.8	10.9-11.3	11.0
6.	pH		2006-07	6.8-7.2	7.0	7.5-7.8	7.6	7.9-8.4	8.1	6.7-7.1	6.8
			2007-08	6.6-7.2	6.9	7.4-7.7	7.5	7.9-8.1	8.0	6.8-7.4	7.1
7.	Temperature		2006-07	18-20	19.0	20-23	21.5	18-19	18.6	10-15	12.3
			2007-08	18-21	19.4	21-23	21.8	18-20	18.9	10.5-15	12.4

Table 6.6: Seasonal Variation in Physico-chemical Characteristics of Water of Palashbari Ghat in Kamrup District (2006-2008)

Sl.No.	Pysico-chemical Parameter	Survey Station	Year	Pre Monsoon		Monsoon		Post Monsoon		Winter	
				Range	Mean	Range	Mean	Range	Mean	Range	Mean
1.	Dissolved oxygen (mg/l)	Kamrup (Palashbari)	2006-07	7.5-8.7	8.1	7.5-8.8	8.1	7.1-8.7	7.9	8.0-9.5	8.7
			2007-08	7.8-9.5	9.9	7.2-8.4	8.4	8.1-8.5	8.3	8.5-9.3	10.1
2.	Dissolved free carbon-di- oxide (mg/l)		2006-07	2.1-3.0	2.8	2.1-2.8	2.4	3.0-3.5	3.1	2.2-2.7	2.6
			2007-08	2.1-3.1	3.3	2.0-2.7	2.5	2.9-3.5	3.0	2.4-3.0	2.8
3.	Alkalinity (mg/l)		2006-07	40-45	39.7	38-42	40.8	40-46	43.6	38-40	36.2
			2007-08	37-43	41.3	39-45	40.5	43-47	42.9	34-38	36.5
4.	Hardness (mg/l)		2006-07	16-19	17.8	11-13	11.6	14-19	16.2	19-22	21.5
			2007-08	16-20	18.2	13-15	13.9	14-20	16.9	20-23	22.0
5.	Chloride		2006-07	12.0-12.3	12.2	16.8-17.3	17.2	14.5-15.2	14.5	10.8-11.5	10.5
			2007-08	11.8-12.2	12.2	17.0-17.3	17.2	14.5-15.2	14.5	10.5-11.2	10.5
6.	pH		2006-07	6.5-7.2	6.8	7.1-7.5	7.6	7.5-8.4	8.1	6.2-7.0	6.9
			2007-08	6.0-7.0	7.1	7.2-7.5	7.5	7.9-8.4	7.9	6.8-7.5	7.1
7.	Temperature		2006-07	18-20	18.5	20-23	22	15-17	17.3	9-12	11.5
			2007-08	18.3-20.2	19.5	21-23.5	22.1	16-19	19	11.2-13	11.7

Table 6.7: Seasonal Variation in Physico-chemical Characteristics of Water at Kasari Ghat in Goalpara District (2006-2008)

Sl.No.	Pysico-chemical Parameter	Survey Station	Year	Pre Monsoon		Monsoon		Post Monsoon		Winter	
				Range	Mean	Range	Mean	Range	Mean	Range	Mean
1.	Dissolved oxygen (mg/l)	Goalpara (Kachari ghat)	2006-07	8.0-9.1	9.9	8.2-8.5	8.4	9.0-9.5	9.4	8.5-8.9	10.1
			2007-08	8.5-9.8	9.4	9.4-9.9	8.5	9.5-9.7	9.3	9.1-10.5	10.1
2.	Dissolved free carbon-di-oxide (mg/l)		2006-07	2.5-2.8	2.6	2.0-2.5	2.3	3.0-3.5	3.3	2.7-2.9	2.7
			2007-08	2.3-3.0	2.8	2.5-2.9	2.6	2.8-3.2	3.1	2.5-3.1	2.6
3.	Alkalinity (mg/l)		2006-07	35-43	41.3	39-45	40.5	40-45	42.9	35-40	36.5
			2007-08	40-45	39.7	38-42	40.8	40-46	43.6	38-40	36.2
4.	Hardness (mg/l)		2006-07	12-15	13.6	13-15	13.8	10-14	11.9	18-23	21.6
			2007-08	13-18	15.2	12-17	14.7	13-16	14.2	16-21	19.5
5.	Chloride		2006-07	12.0-12.5	12.2	16.0-17.0	16.6	15. 0-15.9	15.5	11.0-12.0	11.6
			2007-08	11.8-12.5	12.3	17.0-17.5	17.2	14.2-15.3	14.7	11.0-11.7	11.2
6.	pH		2006-07	6.3-8.0	7.4	6.9-7.3	7.1	7.6-8.0	7.7	7.0-7.3	7.0
			2007-08	6.8-7.2	7.0	7.3-7.6	7.4	6.8-7.2	7.1	6.9-7.3	7.1
7.	Temperature		2006-07	11-13	12.0	18-21	20.0	13-15	14.0	9 -14	11.4
			2007-08	9-14	12.4	19-21	19.8	13-17	15.2	10-13	10.8

Table 6.8: Seasonal Variation in Physico-chemical Characteristics of Water of Jogighopa Ghat in Goalpara District (2006-2008)

Sl. No.	Pysico-chemical Parameter	Survey Station	Year	Pre Monsoon		Monsoon		Post Monsoon		Winter	
				Range	Mean	Range	Mean	Range	Mean	Range	Mean
1.	Dissolved oxygen (mg/l)	Goalpara (Jogighopa ghat)	2006-07	8.0-9.0	8.5	7.9-8.1	8.0	8.0-9.1	8.5	8.0-10.0	9.1
			2007-08	8.8-10.1	9.3	8.0-8.7	8.3	8.1-8.5	8.2	8.5-10.3	9.3
2.	Dissolved free carbon-di-oxide (mg/l)		2006-07	2.1-2.7	2.4	2.3-2.5	2.3	3.0-3.5	3.3	2.7-2.9	2.6
			2007-08	2.0-2.8	2.4	2.5-3.0	2.7	2.1-2.7	2.4	2.0-3.0	2.5
3.	Alkalinity (mg/l)		2006-07	31-34	32.5	34-37	35.9	37-41	38.5	28-30	28.8
			2007-08	30-34	31.9	35-37	36.1	38-40	39.3	25-29	26.1
4.	Hardness (mg/l)		2006-07	16-18	17.0	13-15	14.2	10-13	11.3	20-25	23.3
			2007-08	15-20	17.5	13-18	15.3	12-16	13.7	20-23	21.8
5.	Chloride		2006-07	11.8-12.2	11.9	16.5-17.0	16.7	15. 2-15.8	15.4	11.2-11.5	11.2
			2007-08	11.9-12.5	12.0	17.0-17.5	17.1	15.2-15.5	15.1	11.0-11.5	11.3
6.	pH		2006-07	6.4-6.7	6.5	7.0-7.8	7.4	7.4-7.9	7.5	6.1-7.0	6.6
			2007-08	6.6-6.8	6.6	7.1-7.6	7.3	7.2-7.8	7.6	6.0-7.5	7.1
7.	Temperature		2006-07	12-13	12.4	19-22	20.7	21-24	22.8	11-13	11.3
			2007-08	13-15	14.1	20-24	22.1	20-21	20.0	12-15	13.5

The ichthyofaunal diversity of the studied area is explained under the three broad categories – major, intermediate and minor fish group. In zone I the major group comprised of 16 species, intermediate group 31 species and minor group 37 species Whereas in zone II and III major group comprised of 14 species, intermediate group 30 species and minor group 37 species. The species composition indicates that the *Cyprinidae* is the most diversified family of the major and minor fish group. The present status of ichthyofaunal composition indicates that the minor group fish population dominates over the major and intermediate fish group (minor > major > intermediate).

Major Fish Group

The major fish group was constituted by 16 species (Tables 6.9, 6.10) belonging to 8 families, of which the most dominant one was Cyprinidae. The family Cyprinidae includes *Labeo rohita*, *L. calbasu*, *Catla catla*, *Cirrhinus mrigala*, *Cyprinus carpio*, *Hypophthalmichthys molitrix* and *Ctenopharyngodon idella.* In addition to these fish species belonging to different families like *Chitala chitala* (Notopteridae), *Sperrata seenghala*, *S. aor*, *Rita rita* (Bagridae), *Bagarius yarrellii* (Sisoridae), *Wallago attu* (Siluridae), *Hilsa* (Tenualosa) *ilisha* (Clupeidae) and *Pangasius pangasius* (Pangasiidae) were recorded in the studied area. Besides these two Channa species namely *Channa striatus* and *Channa marulius* belonging to the family Channidae were also recorded under the major fish group in the studied catches of the stretch.

Intermediate Fish Group

Altogether 31 species belonging to the intermediate fish group (Tables 6.9, 6.10) were recorded under 11 families, of which most dominant families were Cyprinidae, Mastacembelidae and Channidae. The fish species of intermediate group, recorded under the different families were *Labeo gonius*, *L. bata* and *Cirrhinus reba* (Cyprinidae), *Nandus nandus* (Nandidae), *Mastacembelus armatus* and *Macrognathus pancalus* (Mastacembelidae), *Clarias batrachus* (Clariidae), *Heteropneustes fossilis* (Heteropneustidae), *Monopterus cuchia* (Synbranchidae), *Ompok pabo* (Siluridae), *Awaous gutum* (Gobiidae), *Anabas testudineus* (Anabantidae), *Channa striatus* and *C. marulius* (Channidae) and *Notopterus notopterus* (Notopteridae).

Minor Fish Group

Study indicates that the diversity of fish fauna of minor fish group was higher than the major and intermediate group. Minor fish group was consisting of 37 species belonging to 10 families (Tables 6.9, 6.10), of which most dominant one was Cyprinidae. The family Cyprinidae includes 6 species namely *Puntius sophore*, *P. ticto*, *P. sarana*, *Amblypharyngodon mola*, *Parluciosoma daniconius* and *Salmostoma bacaila*. The other fish species of the minor group belonging to different families were *Gudusia chapra* (Clupeidae), *Chanda nama* and *Pseudambassis ranga* (Ambassidae), *Mystus tengara*, *M. vittatus* and *M. cavasius* (Bagridae), *Glossogobius giuris* (Gobiidae), *Channa punctatus* (Channidae), *Colisa fasciatus, C. sota*, and *C. lalia* (Belonidae), *Lepidocephalus guntea*, *Botia dario* and *Aspidoparia morar* (Cobitidae), *Tetraodon cutcutia* (Tetraodontidae) and *Bedis bedis* (Nandidae).

Table 6.9: Fish Diversity of Kamrup and Goalpara District

	Name of the Species
	Family – Cyprinidae
1.	*Labeo rohita* (Ham-Buch)
2.	*L. gonius* (Ham-Buch)
3.	*L. calbasu* (Ham-Buch)
4.	*Catla catla* (Ham-Buch)
5.	*Cirrhinus mrigala* (Ham-Buch)
6.	*Cyprinus carpio* (Linnaeus)
7.	*Hypophthalmichthys molitrix* (Valenciennes)
8.	*Ctenopharyngodon idella* (Valenciennes)
9.	*Chagunius chagunio* (Ham-Buch)
10.	*Labeo bata* (Ham-Buch)
11.	*Cirrhinus reba* (Ham-Buch)
12.	*Puntius sophore* (Ham-Buch)
13.	*P. ticto* (Ham-Buch)
14.	*P sarana* (Ham-Buch)
15.	*P. terio* (Ham-Buch)
16.	*Amblypharyngodon mola* (Ham-Buch)
17.	*Parluciosoma daniconius* (Ham-Buch)
18.	*Salmostoma bacaila* (Ham-Buch)
19.	*Pseudambassis ranga* (Ham-Buch)
20.	*Aspidoporia morar* (Ham-Buch)
21.	*Aspidoporia jaya* (Ham-Buch)
22.	*Brachidanio rerio* (Ham-Buch)
23.	*Danio aequipinnatus* (McClelland)
24.	*Danio devario* (Ham-Buch)
25.	*Rasbora rasbora* (Ham-Buch)
26.	*Chela laubuca* (Ham-Buch)
27.	*Parluciosoma daniconius* (Ham-Buch)

(Contd...)

	Family: Engrauilididae
28.	*Setipinna phasa* (Ham-Buch)
	Family - Channidae
29.	*Channa punctatus* (Bloch)
30.	*C. striatus* (Bloch)
31.	*C. marulius* (Ham-Buch)
	Family - Pangasiidae
32.	*Pangasius pangasius* (Ham-Buch)
	Family - Mastacembelidae
33.	*Mastacembelus armatus* (Lacepede)
34.	*Macrognathus pancalus* (Ham-Buch)
35.	*Macrognathusn aculatus* (Ham-Buch)
	Family: Chacidae
36.	*Chaca chaca* (Ham- Buch)
	Family: Aplocheilidae
37.	*Aplocheilus panchax* (Ham-Buch)
	Family: Mugilidae
38.	*Sicamugil cacasia* (Ham-Buch)
39.	*Rhinomugil corsula* (Ham-Buch)
	Family: Cobitidae
40.	*Lepidochephalus guntea* (Ham-Buch)
41.	*Botia dario* (Ham-Buch)
	Family – Siluridae
42.	*Wallago attu* (Schneider)
43.	*Ompok bimaculatus* (Bloch)
44.	*Ompok pabda* (Ham- Buch)
45.	*Ompok pabda* (Ham- Buch)
	Family - Bagridae
46.	*Sperata seenghala* (Sykes)
47.	*S. aor*
48.	*Mystus bleekri* (Day)
49.	*M. tengara* (Ham-Buch)
50.	*M. vittatus* (Bloch)
	Family – Notopteridae
51.	*Chitala chitala* (Ham-Buch)
52.	*Nototpterus notpterus*(Ham-Buch)

(Contd...)

	Family – Clupeidae
53.	*Tenualosa ilisha* (Ham-Buch)
54.	*Gudusia chapra* (Ham-Buch)
	Family: Sisoridae
55.	*Bagarius yarrelli* (Sykes)
56.	*Conta conta* (Ham-Buch)
57.	*Gagata gagata* (Ham-Buch)
58.	*Hara hara* (Ham-Buch)
59.	*Hara jerdoni* (Misra)
60.	*Sisor rhabdophorus* (Ham-Buch)
	Family: Schilbeidae
61.	*Ailia coilia* (Ham-Buch)
62.	*Clupisoma garua* (Ham-Buch)
63.	*Eutrpichthys vacha* (Ham-Buch)
64.	*Pseudotropius atherinoides* (Bloch)
65.	*Silonia silondia* (Ham-Buch)
	Family - Clariidae
66.	*Clarias batrachus* (Linnaeus)
	Family - Heteropneustidae
67.	*Heteropneustes fossilis* (Bloch)
	Family - Synbranchidae
68.	*Monopterus cuchia* (Ham-Buch)
	Family – Gobiidae
69.	*Glossogobius gutum*
70.	*Glossogobius giuris* (Ham-Buch)
	Family – Belontidae
71.	*Colisa fasciatus* (Schneider)
72.	*C. sota* (Ham-Buch)
73.	*C. lalia* (Ham-Buch)
	Family – Belonidae
74.	*Xenentodon cancila* (Ham-Buch)
	Family – Tetraodontidae
77.	*Tetraodon cutcutia* (Ham-Buch)
	Family – Nandidae
78.	*Nandus nandus* (Ham-Buch)
79.	*Badis badis* (Ham-Buch)
	Family: Balitoridae
80.	*Nemacheilus botia* (Ham- Buch)
	Family: Anguilidae
81.	*Anguila bengalensis bengalensis* (Gray)

Table 6.10: Fish Diversity of Dhubri District (July 2006-June 2008)

	Name of the Species
	Family – Cyprinidae
1.	*Labeo rohita* (Ham-Buch)
2.	*L. gonius* (Ham-Buch)
3.	*L. calbasu* (Ham-Buch)
4.	*L. pangusia* (Ham-Buch)
5.	*Catla catla* (Ham-Buch)
6.	*Cirrhinus mrigala* (Ham-Buch)
7.	Tor putitora (Ham-Buch)
8.	*Cyprinus carpio* (Linnaeus)
9.	*Hypophthalmichthys molitrix* (Valenciennes)
10.	*Ctenopharyngodon idella* (Valenciennes)
11.	*Chagunius chagunio* (Ham-Buch)
12.	*Cyprinion semiplotum* (McClelland)
13.	*Labeo bata* (Ham-Buch)
14.	*Cirrhinus reba* (Ham-Buch)
15.	*Puntius sophore* (Ham-Buch)
16.	*P. ticto* (Ham-Buch)
17.	*P sarana* (Ham-Buch)
18.	*P. terio* (Ham-Buch)
19.	*Amblypharyngodon mola* (Ham-Buch)
20.	*Parluciosoma daniconius* (Ham-Buch)
21.	*Salmostoma bacaila* (Ham-Buch)
22.	*Pseudambassis ranga* (Ham-Buch)
23.	*Aspidoporia morar* (Ham-Buch)
24.	*Aspidoporia jaya* (Ham-Buch)
25.	*Brachidanio rerio* (Ham-Buch)
26.	*Danio aequipinnatus* (McClelland)
27.	*Danio devario* (Ham-Buch)
28.	*Rasbora rasbora* (Ham-Buch)
29.	*Chela laubuca* (Ham-Buch)
30.	*Parluciosoma daniconius* (Ham-Buch)
	Family: Engrauilididae
31.	*Setipinna phasa* (Ham-Buch)

(Contd...)

	Family - Channidae
32.	*Channa punctatus* (Bloch)
33.	*C. striatus* (Bloch)
34.	*C. marulius* (Ham-Buch)
	Family - Pangasiidae
35.	*Pangasius pangasius* (Ham-Buch)
	Family - Mastacembelidae
36.	*Mastacembelus armatus* (Lacepede)
37.	*Macrognathus pancalus* (Ham-Buch)
38.	*Macrognathusn aculatus* (Ham-Buch)
	Family: Chacidae
39.	*Chaca chaca* (Ham- Buch)
	Family: Aplocheilidae
40.	*Aplocheilus panchax* (Ham-Buch)
	Family: Mugilidae
41.	*Sicamugil cacasia* (Ham-Buch)
42.	*Rhinomugil corsula* (Ham- Buch)
	Family: Cobitidae
43.	*Lepidochephalus guntea* (Ham-Buch)
44.	*Botia dario* (Ham-Buch)
	Family - Siluridae
45.	*Wallago attu* (Schneider)
46.	*Ompok bimaculatus* (Bloch)
47.	*Ompok pabda* (Ham-Buch)
48.	*Ompok pabda* (Ham-Buch)
	Family - Bagridae
49.	*Sperata seenghala* (Sykes)
50.	*S, aor*
51.	*Mystus bleekri* (Day)
52.	*M. tengara* (Ham-Buch)
53.	*M. vittatus* (Bloch)
	Family – Notopteridae
54.	*Chitala chitala* (Ham-Buch)
55.	*Nototpterus notpterus*(Ham-Buch)
	Family – Clupeidae
56.	*Tenualosa ilisha* (Ham-Buch)
57.	*Gudusia chapra* (Ham-Buch)

(Contd...)

	Family: Sisoridae
58.	*Bagarius yarrelli* (Sykes)
59.	*Conta conta* (Ham-Buch)
60.	*Gagata gagata* (Ham-Buch)
61.	*Hara hara* (Ham-Buch)
62.	*Hara jerdoni* (Misra)
63.	*Sisor rhabdophorus* (Ham-Buch)
	Family: Schilbeidae
64.	*Ailia coilia* (Ham-Buch)
65.	*Clupisoma garua* (Ham-Buch)
66.	*Eutrpichthys vacha* (Ham-Buch)
67.	*Pseudotropius atherinoides* (Bloch)
68.	*Silonia silondia* (Ham-Buch)
	Family - Clariidae
69.	*Clarias batrachus* (Linnaeus)
	Family - Heteropneustidae
70.	*Heteropneustes fossilis* (Bloch)
	Family - Synbranchidae
71.	*Monopterus cuchia* (Ham-Buch)
	Family – Gobiidae
72.	*Glossogobius gutum*
73.	*Glossogobius giuris* (Ham-Buch)
	Family – Belontidae
74.	*Colisa fasciatus* (Schneider)
75.	*C. sota* (Ham-Buch)
76.	*C. lalia* (Ham-Buch)
	Family – Belonidae
77.	*Xenentodon cancila* (Ham-Buch)
	Family - Tetraodontidae
78.	*Tetraodon cutcutia* (Ham-Buch)
	Family – Nandidae
79.	*Nandus nandus* (Ham-Buch)
80.	*Badis badis* (Ham-Buch)
	Family: Balitoridae
81.	*Nemacheilus botia* (Ham-Buch)
	Family: Anguilidae
82.	*Anguila bengalensis bengalensis* (Gray)

The fish species found in the study area ideally suit in the obtained range of physico-chemical parameters (ecological requirement) of water. The diversity of River Brahmaputra is found fairly good, suggesting that the water quality is not much affected. Increased domestic and industrial pollution, siltation due to accelerated deforestation in the periphery of the river and lack of a comprehensive management policy with adequate institutional arrangements for tackling increased anthropogenic pressure facing the river are the major factors adversely affecting the ecology and fisheries of this part of the river.

IMPORTANT ICHTHYO-FAUNA OCCURRING IN THE STUDY AREA

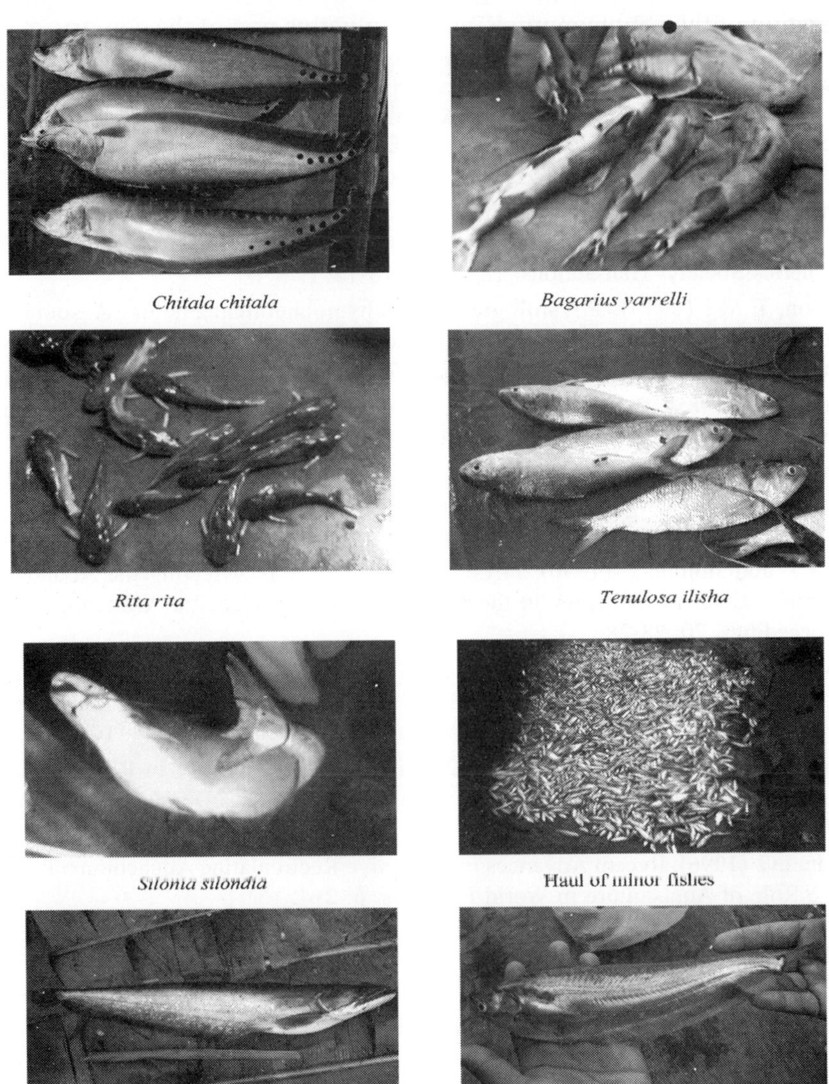

Chitala chitala

Bagarius yarrelli

Rita rita

Tenulosa ilisha

Silonia silondia

Haul of minor fishes

Wallago attu

Ompok bimaculatus

CONCLUSION

It is thereby concluded that the obtained range of water quality can be considered as the suitable ecological criteria for the said fish species found in the lower stretch of the River Brahmaputra. The result of the study provides a baseline information for establishing predictions of fish population changes with the ecological changes due to various anthropogenic causes in the lower stretch of the Brahmaputra River. At the very least, continuation of water quality monitoring is justified in order to record environmental fluctuations over time and to make biotic predictions possible. Studies like this may contribute to guide environmental management and efforts on conservation of the Brahmaputra River basin in this part of the country.

REFERENCES

APHA. (1992). Standard Methods for the Examination of Water and Waste Water, 19th Edition. American Public Health Association, New York, USA.

Braaten, P.J.; Guy, C.S. (1999). Relation Between Physicochemical Factors and Abundance of Fishes in Tributary Confluences of the Lower Channelized Missouri River. American Fisheries Society. Transactions, 128(6): 1213-1221.

Donaldson, E.M., (1975). Physiological and Physiochemical Factors Associated with Maturation and Spawning. Food and Agriculture Organisation of the United Nations. European Inland Fisheries, Issue No. 25: 53-71.

Goswami, D.C. (1985). Brahmaputra River, Assam, India: Physiography, Basin Denundation and Channel Aggradation. Water Resources Research 21, 959-978.

Matthews, W.J. (1998). Disturbance, Harsh Environments, and Physiochemical Tolerence. pp. 318-379 IN: Patterns in Freshwater Fish Ecology; Kluwer Academic Publishers; PO Box 17, 3300 AA Dordrecht, Netherlands].

Reash, R.J. and Jimmie P. (1990). Physicochemical Factors Affecting the Abundance and Species Richness of Fishes in the Cimarron River. Oklahoma Academy of Science. Proceedings, 70: 23-28.

Sabo, M.J.; William E.K.; C. Frederick B. and D. Allen R. (1991). Physicochemical Factors Affecting Larval Fish Densities Mississippi River Floodplain Ponds, Louisiana (U.S.A.). *Regulated Rivers: Research and Management,* 6(2): 109-116.

Whiteside, B.G. and McNatt, R. M. (1972). Fish Species Diversity in Relation to Stream Order and Physicochemical Conditions in the Plum Creek Drainage Basin. American Midland Naturalist. 88 (1): 90-101.

Woiwode, J.G. (1996). Recent Advances in Predictive Recirculating Aquaculture Technology. The Role of Aquaculture in World Fisheries. 6: 214.

7

Plankton Dynamics in Freshwater Fish Ponds in India

Madhumita Das; Biswajit Dash and Loveson L. Edward

ABSTRACT

The culture of Indian major carps in freshwater ponds involves use of chemical fertilizers and organic manures to enhance the photosynthetic food chain for planktivorous carps. Planktons include both phyto and zooplanktons are the natural food item in freshwater fish ponds. Study on diversity of both phytoplankton and zooplankton community gives an idea on the trophic status of a fishpond ecosystem. Plankton compositions in freshwater fish ponds can be categorized as Chlorophyceae, Bacillariophyceae, Dinophyceae and Myxophyceae as phytoplankton whereas zooplanktons are categorized as Copepoda, Cladocera, Rotifera, Ostracoda and Protozoa. Further studies are essential to study plankton dynamics in freshwater ponds through enrichment of autotrophic and heterotrophic pathways to enhance fish production of different production systems.

Keywords: Plankton dynamics, India, Fish pond, Production system.

INTRODUCTION

Plankton, apart from being the basic units of production, plays an important role in transferring energy from a given trophic level to the next higher, leading to fish, the target energy harvest unit in aquatic systems. Planktonic community structure in a fish pond is regulated by the availability of nutrients and predation.

There are two general sources of nutrients in waters, natural and manmade. Nutrients that leach from soil and atmospheric deposition are natural sources and fertilizer, animal wastes, domestic sewage and industrial wastes are manmade sources (Rai and Gaur, 2001).

Pond fertilization practices using animal wastes are widely used in many countries to sustain productivity at low costs (Gupta and Noble, 2001; Majumder *et al.*, 2002) since soluble organic matter supplied to ponds by using manure stimulate phytoplankton growth. Animal wastes lead to increased biological productivity of ponds through various pathways, which result in an increase in fish production (Dhawan and Kaur, 2002). Planktonic organisms are potential bioindicators and their quality and quantity indicate the levels of fish pond ecosystems. Plankton populations in ponds have been studied by different workers throughout the world (Almazan and Boyd, 1978; Burford and Pearson, 1998; Wetzel and Linkens, 2000; Terziyski *et al.*, 2007). Scientific carp culture in fish ponds started in India at the Pond Culture Division of CIFRI, Cuttack, Odisha with the composite culture of three species of Indian major carps and three species of exotic carps (Alikunhi and Sukumaran, 1964; Lakshmanan *et al.*, 1971; Choudhuri *et al.*, 1974).

Phytoplanktons constitute a large and diverse group of autotrophic organisms ranging from unicellular to multicellular forms. They are photosynthetic organisms that occur in marine, freshwater, desert sands, hot boiling springs, snow and ice. Physico-chemical parameters and quantity of nutrients in water play significant role in the distributional patterns and species composition of different phytoplanktons in the aquatic systems. They are main source of food directly or indirectly for various animal groups. Phytoplankton is one of the main feed of silver carp and grass carp. Zooplanktons occupy an intermediate position in the food and are food of both fish fry and adults. The seasonal changes in zooplankton species are closely related to the physico-chemical and biological regime of aquatic ecosystems. Plankton dynamics in freshwater fish ponds in India were studied by Datta and Bandopadhyay (1987), Bhatish (1992) and Rajgopal *et al.* (2010).

SAMPLING AND SAMPLE PROCESSING

The plankton samples are collected from the surface waters of the fish ponds by filtering 50 litres of water through plankton net made of bolting silk cloth (No. 25; # 64 mm) and then samples are preserved in 5% formaldehyde solution. Total number of phytoplankton and zooplankton are estimated by the 'direct census method' using a Sedgewick Rafter plankton-counting cell (APHA, AWWA, WPCF, 1998; Yijian, 1990).The plankton counts are expressed as no./l and percentages of phytoplankton and zooplankton fractions are calculated.

PHYTOPLANKTON AND ZOOPLANKTON SPECIES RICHNESS AND COMPOSITION

The biomass and species composition of plankton in an aquatic ecosystem gives an insight of the nutrient status. Phytoplanktons are the major primary producers in fish pond ecosystems which are grazed by zooplanktons. Phytoplankton community includes Chlorophyceae, Bacillariophyceae, Dinophyceae and Myxophyceae (Rao, 1975; Prasad and Srivastava, 1992). Zooplankton plays a crucial role not only in converting plant food to animal food but also themselves as a source of food for higher organisms especially in the fish pond ecosystem. Zooplankton community includes Copepoda, Cladocera, Rotifera, Ostracoda and Protozoa. The availability and adaptations depends on the surrounding environmental factors. Plankton density of fish ponds mainly depends upon the temperature, photoperiod and pH, which elicit a significant correlation. Variation in plankton density relates to the physical structure of pelagic environment of a pond ecosystem.

PHYTOPLANKTON

Chlorophyceae

The Chlorophyceae are one of the classes of green algae, distinguished mainly on the basis of ultrastructural morphology. They are usually green due to the dominance of pigments chlorophyll a and chlorophyll b. The chloroplast may be discoid, plate-like, reticulate, cup-shaped, spiral or ribbon shaped in different species. Most of the members have one or more storage bodies called pyrenoids located in the chloroplast. Pyrenoids contain protein besides starch. Some algae may store food in the form of oil droplets. Green algae usually have a rigid cell wall made up of an inner layer of cellulose and outer layer of pectose. Temperature plays an important role in the periodicity of blue green algae as emphasized by Mahar *et al.* (2004).

BACILLARIOPHYCEAE

Bacillariophytes are called "Diatoms" which are major group of algae and are among the most common types of phytoplankton. Diatoms are a widespread group and can be found in the oceans, in freshwater, in soils and on damp surfaces. The photosynthetic pigment of diatoms is brown, and occurs usually in the form of two identical plastids running the length of the cell and in the centric diatoms in the form of numerous sometimes clumped granules. Most diatoms are unicellular, although they can exist as colonies in the shape of filaments or ribbons, fans, zigzags or stars. Planktonic forms in open water usually rely on turbulent mixing of the upper layers by the wind to keep them suspended in sunlit surface waters. The siliceous skeleton common to all varieties is frequently described as structured like a pill box or petridish and offers two possible views — the valve view (as in viewing a petridish from the top) and the side or girdle view. Some species actively regulate their buoyancy with intracellular lipids to counter sinking. When conditions turn unfavourable, usually upon depletion of nutrients, diatom cells typically increase in sinking rate and exit the upper mixed layer ("bust").

Hawkes (1969) examined the thermal tolerance of different groups of algae and suggested that diatoms grow best at temperatures below 25°C and blue-green algae at temperatures above 30°C. Tucker (1985) studied the diatoms of Mississippi channel catfish ponds. Ecological study of diatoms of a freshwater pond of Ranchi, Bihar was studied by Bose (1987).

DINOPHYCEAE

Dinoflagellates are unicellular and possess two dissimilar flagellae arising from the ventral cell side. The class Dinophyceae is of uncertain origin. Some scientists even considered the Dinophyceae to be mesokaryotes (intermediate between the prokaryotes and the eukaryotes), however, this view is no longer accepted. Roughly half of the species in the group are photosynthetic (Gaines and Elbrächter 1987), the other half is exclusively heterotrophic and feeds via osmotrophy and phagotrophy. They are important components of freshwater ecosystems. Frequent dinoflagellate blooms occur in freshwater bodies. Frempong (1984) studied the seasonal sequence of diel distribution patterns of *Ceratium hirundinella* in a eutrophic lake. Ki and Han (2008) recorded *Peridinium umbonatum* from Togyo Reservoir, Korea.

MYXOPHYCEAE OR CYANOPHYCEAE

They are large group of prokaryotic, mostly photosynthetic organisms. Cyanobacteria are organisms with some characteristics of bacteria and some of algae. Though classified as blue-green algae or photosynthetic bacteria, they resemble the eukaryotic algae in many ways, including some physical characteristics and ecological niches and were at one time treated as algae. They contain certain pigments, which with their chlorophyll, often give them a blue-green colour, though many species are actually green, brown, yellow, black, or red. They are common in soil and in both salt and freshwater, and they can grow over a wide range of temperatures, from Antarctic lakes under several metres of ice to Yellowstone National Park's hot springs in the U.S. Cyanobacteria are often among the first species to colonize bare rock and soil (Desikachary, 1959). Some are capable of nitrogen fixation and others contain pigments that enable them to produce free oxygen as a by-product of photosynthesis. Under proper conditions (including pollution by nitrogen wastes) they can reproduce explosively, forming dense concentrations called blooms, usually coloured an opaque green. Cyanobacteria played a large role in raising the level of free oxygen in the atmosphere of early Earth. Despite their name, different species can be red, brown, or yellow, blooms (dense masses on the surface of a body of water) of a red species are said to have given the Red Sea its name. Nitrogen-fixing cyanobacteria need only nitrogen and carbon dioxide to live. Toxic cyanobacteria are found worldwide in inland. *Microcystis*, are almost always toxic, but non-toxic strains do occur.

Temperature plays an important role in the periodicity of blue green algae as emphasized by Mahar *et al*., (2004). Genus *Oscillatoria* has been found to be very tolerant to pollution and frequently grows in polluted waters (Rai & Kumar, 1976).

Bloom of Cyanophycean algae in lake is an obvious signe of cultural eutrophication which is basically caused by addition of sewage effluents (Horn and Goldman, 1994).

ZOOPLANKTON

Copepods

Copepods are a group of small crustaceans found in the sea and nearly every freshwater habitat. Some species are planktonic (drifting in sea waters), some are benthic (living on the ocean floor), and some continental species may live in limno-terrestrial habitats and other wet terrestrial places, such as swamps, under leaf fall in wet forests, bogs, springs, ephemeral ponds and puddles, damp moss, or water-filled recesses (phytotelmata) of plants such as bromeliads and pitcher plants. Many live underground in marine and freshwater caves, sinkholes or stream beds. Copepods are sometimes used as bioindicators. Copepods form a subclass belonging to the sub phylum Crustacea (crustaceans). Copepods are divided into ten orders. Some 13,000 species of copepods are known, and 2,800 of them live in freshwaters.

Copepods are typically 1 to 2 millimetres long, with a teardrop-shaped body and large antennae. Although like other crustaceans they have an armoured exoskeleton, they are so small that in most species this thin armour, and the entire body, is almost totally transparent. Some polar copepods reach 1 centimetre. Most copepods have a single median compound eye, usually bright red and in the centre of the transparent head, subterranean species may be eyeless. Like other crustaceans, copepods possess two pairs of antennae; the first pair is often long and conspicuous. Copepods typically have a short, cylindrical body, with a rounded or beaked head. The head is fused with the first one or two thoracic segments, while the remainder of the thorax has three to five segments, each with limbs. The first pair of thoracic appendage is modified to form maxillipeds, which assist in feeding. The abdomen is typically narrower than the thorax, and contains five segments without any appendages, except for some tail-like "rami" at the tip. About 70% of its dry weight is fat. Planktonic copepods are important to global ecology and the carbon cycle. They are usually the dominant members of the zooplankton and are major food organisms for small fish, whales, seabirds and other crustaceans such as krill in the ocean and in freshwater. Some scientists say they form the largest animal biomass on earth (Boxhall and Defaye, 2008). Predation of copepods on larger species of phytoplankton will favour gelatinous colonial species of Cyanobacteria and green algae thus causing an increase in their abundance, as observed in enclosure experiments by Sommer *et al.* (2003).

CLADOCERANS

Cladocerans commonly called "Water Fleas" are primarily-freshwater small-sized (0.2-6 mm, and up to 18 mm in single case of (*Leptodora kindtii*) branchiopod crustaceans, inhabiting pelagic, littoral and benthic zones. Four Cladoceran orders are recognised (Fryer, 1985): Anomopoda, Ctenopoda, Onychopoda, and the monotypic Haplopoda. Most species occur in continental fresh or saline waters, although two ctenopods and several onychopods from the family Podonidae are truly marine and a few more ctenopod, anomopod and onychopod species occur in brackish waters. Seven known species may be regarded as true inhabitants of subterranean environment, and a few others (of the family Chydoridae) live in semi-terrestrial conditions. The trunk and appendages of most Cladocerans (Anomopoda and Ctenopoda) are enclosed in a bivalved carapace. Tagmosis of the body is obscure (except in *Leptodora kindtii*, the single representative of Haplopoda), and a single eye and ocellus are usually present. Antennules are uniramous, while antennae are biramous (except in females of Holopedium), natatory, with 2-4 segments per branch. Four to six pairs of trunk limbs are either mostly similar in shape (Ctenopoda, Onychopoda, Haplopoda) or modified individually for various functions (Anomopoda). Cladocera is an ancient group of Palaeozoic origin. About 620 species are currently known, but we estimate that the real number of species is 2-4 times higher.

ROTIFERS

Rotifera or wheel animalcules are one of the most interesting groups of freshwater invertebrates. They belong to the subphylum Trochhelminthes, *i.e.* they are worms, although their bodies share no resemblance with typical worms such as oligochaets. Remane (1929-33) believed they were larvae of unknown worms that remained in the larval stage, but recent investigators (Clement, 1980) confirm their origin in Platyhelminthes. Having no paleontological evidence, we presume that rotifers are a very old group of invertebrates, a product of the aerobic phase in the development of our planet.

Rotifers are characterized by a corona (a ciliated area or a funnel-shaped structure at the anterior end) and a specialized pharynx called a mastax, which serves as a jaw. the most The rotifers ordinarily encountered are amictic females, *i.e.* they parthenogenetically produce diploid eggs. Usually in the autumn mictic haploid eggs are formed from which, without fertilization, males appear. They are known only in a minority of species and are reduced in size and in organs. A digestive system is totally absent and males perish within some hours or few days. From the fertilized eggs special resting ('winter') eggs evolve, having a thick protective cover resistant to desiccation, freezing and other unfavourable factors. The next spring, females hatch from these resting eggs and start a new amictic generation. Species having males once per year are monocyclic, twice per year, dicyclic and several times per year, polycyclic. In the order Bdelloidea, where no males occur, they are acyclic. Rotifers possess no respiratory organs and respire by their whole body surface. For this reason they are unable to live in an anaerobic milieu. Only few very resistant species tolerate tnicroaerobic habitats, e.g. *Rotaria neptunia* and *R. rotatoria*. There exist about 2000 species of rotifers. Pennak (1953) indicated 1700 species, less than 5% of which are restricted to brackish and marine environments.

OSTRACODS

Like the copepods, the ostracods are very much frequent in both freshwater and marine environments. They are microcrustaceans and about 2000 living species exists in the world. The larger marine species are also known as "Mussel shrimps" or "Seed shrimps", but the freshwater ostracods are usually smaller than a millimetre. In freshwater ponds they are usually found scuttling around among the submerged plants and debris at the shallow edges and less commonly in the open waters. They swim smoothly with appendages extended from between the two halves of their carapace. When disturbed, they withdraw their limbs and clamp the halves of their tiny shells tightly together. They are perhaps less attractive creatures than the other small crustaceans due to the opaque and sometimes strongly patterned shell which makes it difficult to see their internal structure. Young specimens are the most rewarding for microscopical examination, as their shells are generally more transparent than those of the adults. Ostracods are very similar in appearance, making it less than easy for the non-expert to distinguish one species from another or even one genus from another.

Study of ostracods was initiated in the 18th Century (Oertli 1982), regionally only the Holarctic fauna of freshwater ostracods is considered reasonably well documented (Meisch 2000; Martens *et al.*, 2008). Their narrow environmental preferences define them as potential bioindicators for monitoring of recent freshwater conditions (Külköylüoðlu 2004). The development of either a single species or an ostracod assemblage is influenced by physical–chemical properties of waters (salinity, temperature, pH, and dissolved oxygen), hydraulic conditions, bottom grain sizes or sedimentation rates. Harshey *et al.* (1987) reported abundance and high density of ostracoda in hard water.

PROTOZOANS

Protozoa are a diverse group of unicellular eukaryotic organisms. Protozoa commonly range from 10 to 52 micrometers, but can grow as large as 1 mm and are seen easily by microscope. The largest protozoa known are the deep-sea dwelling xenophyophores, which can grow up to 20 cm in diameter. They were considered formerly to be part of the Protista family. The protozoa of the freshwater environment range in size from about 1mm in the case of Stentor and some of the multinucleate amoebae, down to 5μm or so in the case of the smaller flagellates and they are extremely varied in both appearance and lifestyle. Protozoa exist throughout aqueous environments and soil, occupying a range of trophic levels (Honigberg *et al.*, 1964).

The seasonal distribution and variations in plankton populations in different water bodies including fish ponds have been investigated (Talling, 1987; Pradhan *et al.*, 2008). In the Indian subcontinent also, this biotic community has received due attention by several workers, with regard to its ecology, productivity and enhancement measures (Nasar, 1977; Ayyappan and Gupta, 1982). Among the biological parameters planktons are considered to be bio-indicators of water quality. The quality of both phytoplankton and zooplankton is influenced by various environmental factors (Jana and De, 1983) as well as nutrient levels (Das and Jana, 1996).

Phytoplankton constitute major fraction of primary producer in water bodies. They play important role in biosynthesis of organic matter in fish pond ecosystems. Phytoplankton primary productivity was studied by Atay and Demir (1998). Arvola (1984) observed a positive correlation between primary production and phytoplankton population. Chowdhury and Mamum (2006) studied the responses of phytoplankton on nutrient additions. A relationship between phytoplankton biomass and phosphate concentrations was studied by Gruendling (1983). Paloheimo and Zimmerman (1983) analyzed the factors influencing phosphorus-phytoplankton relationship. Phytoplankton dynamics was studied by Patralekh (1991) that was apparently regulated by zooplankton predation. Riemann (1983) compared phytoplankton primary production with bacterial secondary production. Further, Currie (1990) reported algal abundance determined by phosphorus availability to be influencing bacterial populations in the water medium.

Zooplankton constitute the organisms of the secondary trophic level which consume the food material synthesized by phytoplankters and transfer the energy to the next trophic level in the pond ecosystem. They also occupy a central position between autotrophs and other heterotrophs and are important link between food web of freshwater ecosystem. The importance of zooplanktons as fish food both for adults and fry has been stressed by different workers (Geiger, 1983). The presence and dominance of zooplankton species play very significant role in the functioning of freshwater ecosystems. These animals are usually filtrators, sedimentators or predators (Karabin, 1985). There are several studies regarding distribution, abundance and seasonal succession of zooplankton (Vasisht and Sharma, 1975; Arshaduddin and Khan, 1991). The biomass of zooplankton was estimated by Rosen (1981). The effects of physico-chemical factors on the seasonal abundance of zooplankton in a pond at Punjab, India, were analyzed by Bhatish and Kumari (1986). The aspects of population dynamics and ecology of rotifers have been studied by Neill (1984). The effects of filter-feeding zooplankton on phytoplankton in fish ponds were studied by Vyhnalek (1983).

Strong relationships exist between phytoplankton and zooplankton. Selective grazing by zooplankton is an important factor affecting the structure of zooplankton communities. However phytoplankton structure also influences the taxonomic composition and dominance of zooplankton. Interrelationships between phytoplankton and zooplankton populations have been analyzed by Saran and Adoni (1985). A study on algal diversity of a small eutrophic bog pond was made by Estep and Remsen (1985). Spodniewska (1979) observed phytoplankton as the indicator of Lake Eutrophication. Pandey *et al.* (1992) studied the species composition of phytoplankton and zooplankton communities. The variations in percentage compositions of major groups of phytoplankton and zooplankton during seasonal cycles were studied by Singh (1990).

Plankton dynamics of carp polyculture ponds (0.04 ha each) manured with cow manure and biogas slurry was studied by Das (1996). The mean plankton counts in the surface waters of comprising four treatments: *(i)* cow manure at 10t/ha/yr, urea at 100 kg N/ha/yr and single super phosphate at 50 kg P/ha/yr, *(ii)* biogas slurry at 15t/ha/yr and inorganic fertilizers as in the previous treatment, *(iii)* biogas slurry at 30t/ha/yr and iv) and biogas slurry at 30t/ha/yr with supplementary feed were in the ranges of 740-1900, 1060-2160, 960-3740 and 1170-3860/l. Higher counts were observed during March-June in all the treatments. Treatment 4 showed higher plankton counts followed by treatments 3, 2 and 1, the respective mean counts being 2550, 2220, 1480 and 1420/l. The composition of phytoplankton in the net plankton were higher in slurry applied ponds with corresponding means of 53.6, 52.6, 54.7 and 60.6%, indicating an increase in slurry applied ponds, the rest being the zooplankton contribution attributing to heterotrophy and mineralized nutrient availability. The phytoplankton comprised Myxophyceae, Chlorophyceae, Bacillariophyceae and Dinophyceae, the generic representations being *Oscillatoria, Anabaena* in Myxophyceae; *Pediastrum, Kirchneriella, Bulbochaete, Selenastrum, Botryococcus, Ankistrodesmus* in Chlorophyceae; *Cyclotella, Nitzschia, Synedra, Navicula, Amphora, Gomphonema, Pinnularia* in Bacillariophyceae and *Ceratium* in Dinophyceae. The zooplankton comprised Protozoa, Rotifera, Cladocera, Ostracoda and Copepoda with the generic representations being *Arcella, Euglena* in Protozoa; *Asplanchna, Filinia, Brachionus, Keratella, Hexarthra* in Rotifera; *Bosmina, Moina, Daphnia, Ceriodaphnia, Macrothrix* in Cladocera; *Cypris* in Ostracoda and *Diaptomus, Cyclops* in Copepoda.

Strong relationships exist between phytoplankton and zooplankton and selective grazing by zooplankton is an important factor affecting the structure of phytoplankton communities. One of the important phenomenons manifested by plankton is the diurnal vertical migration. Both phytoplankton and zooplankton show vertical migration. Sometimes the zooplankton escapes predation by fish through vertical or horizontal migration. The vertical distribution of plankton varies with the time and season and lower plankton counts are recorded in manured fish ponds during afternoon hours due to vertical migration (Lauridsen and Lodge, 1996). Daily and seasonal diel variations of plankton in Indian waters have been studied by Ayyappan *et al.* (1988) and Das (1996).

Fig. 7.1: Application of Biogas Slurry in Fish Ponds

ROLE IN FISH POND ECOSYSTEM

Fish ponds are multipurpose fish culture systems as they can be used for brood stock stocking and maturation, breeding by various methods, nursery rearing of fry and grow out culture. Extensive fish farming production system, semi-intensive production system, intensive and super intensive systems are the different fish farming production systems categorized according to the degree of intensification. Two patterns of food webs exist in a fish pond ecosystem. One is direct where phytoplankton is directly consumed by herbivorous or omnivorous fish and in the indirect one phytoplankton is consumed by zooplankton which is further consumed by carnivorous and omnivorous fishes. Phytoplankton produces large amounts of organic matter through photosynthesis and release large quantities of oxygen into pond waters. Respiration and photosynthesis of phytoplankton affects the pH, carbon dioxide concentration and dissolved oxygen and play a central role in maintaining water quality in fish ponds.

Extensive fish farming production system is mainly based on the plankton produced in the ecosystem. Pond fertilization through organic and inorganic sources is a regular management protocol in aquaculture (Bhakta *et al.*, 2006). Almost all extensive and the majority of semi- intensive aquaculture operations in India are dependent on the use of chemical fertilizers and organic manures (De Silva and Hasan, 2007). The purpose of pond fertilization is to augment fish production through autotrophic and heterotrophic pathways (Jha *et al.*, 2008). Natural food supply is enhanced by using organic and inorganic fertilizers and low-cost supplemental feeds derived agricultural by-products which enhances the photosynthetic food chain through algal-zooplankton interactions (Schroeder *et al.*, 1990; Halwart *et al.*, 2002). It is well known that high fish yield can be achieved by higher abundance of plankton in culture systems (Jha *et al.*, 2004). Even though the number of studies is already large, serious problems remain in understanding and managing interrelations among fish stock, zooplankton and phytoplankton interrelations to attain the optimal balance.

CONCLUSION

The plankton compositions in fish ponds can be categorized as Chlorophyceae, Bacillariophyceae Dinophyceae and Myxophyceae in case of phytoplankton and Copepoda, Cladocera, Rotifera, Ostracoda and Protozoa in zooplankton. In India carps cultured in fish ponds are planktivorous in nature and the study of their diversity is of paramount significance. Planktons are the most important component of a trophic system, a thoughtful utilization of the plankton community in a pond ecosystem with proper management practices will certainly enhance the levels of fish production. Further work is needed for diversification and enhancement of freshwater fish production and to study the plankton diversity in different freshwater fish pond ecosystems.

REFERENCES

Alikunhi KH and Sukumaran KK (1964). Preliminary Observations on Chinese Carps in India. *Ind. Acad. of Science.* 60: 171-188.

Almazan G and Boyd CE (1978). Plankton Production and Tilapia Yields in Ponds. *Aquaculture*, 15: 75-77.

APHA (American Water Works Association and Water Pollution Control Federation) (1998). Standard Methods for the Examination of water and Wastewater, 19th ed. American Public Health Association, Washington, DC.1038 pp.

Arshaduddin MD and Khan MA (1991). Rotifer Fauna of Some Seasonal Ponds of Osmania University Campus, Hyderabad (AP). India. *Indian J. microbial Ecol.*, 2: 29-40.

Arvola L (1984). Diel Variations in Primary Production and the Vertical Distribution of Phytoplankton in a Polyhumic Lake. *Arch. Hydrobiol.*, 101(4):503-519.

Atay D and Demir N (1998). The Effects of Chicken Manure on the Phytoplankton Primary Production in Carp Ponds. *Acta Hydrobiologica*, 40: 215-225.

Ayyappan S and Gupta TRC (1982). Limnology of Ramasamudra tank- Phytoplankton. Proc. 69th Session of Indian Sci. Congr., Mysore, 3-8 January, 1982.

Ayyappan S, Shakuntala K, Parameswaran S, Sukumaran PK and Raghavan SL (1988). Diel Variations in Water Quality, Primary Production and Plankton of a Peninsular Tank. *J Inland Fish. Soc. India*, 20(1): 13-25.

Battish SK (1992). Freshwater Zooplankton of India, Oxford and IBH Publishing Co. Pvt. Ltd, Calcutta. pp. VI + 233.

Bhatish SK and Kumari P (1986). Effect of Physico-chemical Factors on the Seasonal Abundance of Cladocera in Typical Pond at Village of Ragba, Ludhiana. *Indian Journal of Ecology*, 13(1): 146-151.

Bhakta NJ, Bandyopadhyay KP and Jana BB (2006). Effect of Different Doses of Mixed Fertilizer on Some Biogeochemical Cycling Bacterial Population in Carp Culture Pond. *Turkish Journal of Fisheries and Aquatic Sciences*, 6: 165-171.

Bose SK (1987). *Ecological Study of diatoms of a freshwater pond of Ranchi, Bihar India.* J Inland Fish. Soc. India, 28-31.

Boxhall Geoff A and Defaye Danielle (2008). Global Diversity of Copepods (Crustacea: Copepoda) in Freshwater. In E. V. Balian, C. Lévêque, H. Segers & K. Martens. Freshwater Animal Diversity Assessment. *Hydrobiologia*, 595 (1): 195-207.

Burford MA and Pearson DC (1998). Effect of Different Nitrogen Sources on Phytoplankton Composition in Aquaculture Ponds. *Aquatic Microbial Ecology*, 15: 277-284.

Choudhuri H, Chakrabarty RD, Rao GS, Janaki Ram K, Chatterjee DK and Jena S (1974). Record Fish Production with Intensive Culture of Indian and Exotic Carps. *Current Science*, 43: 303-304.

Chowdhury AH and Mamum AA (2006). Physico-chemical Conditions and Plankton Population of Two Fish Ponds in Khulna.Univ. *J. zool. Rajashahi Univ*., 25, 41-44.

Clement P (1980). Phylogenetic Relationships of Rotifers, as Derived from Photoreceptor Morphology and Other Ultrastructural Analyses. *Hydrobiologia*, 73: 93-117.

Currie DJ (1990). Large Scale Variability and Interactions Among Phytoplankton, Bacterioplankton and Phosphorus. *Limnol. Oceangr*., 35(7): 1437-1455.

Das M (1996). Microbial Ecology and Biological Productivity of Fish Ponds Fertilized with Biogas Slurry. Ph.D. Thesis, Utkal University, 389 pp.

Das SK and Jana BB (1996). Pond Fertilization Through Inorganic Sources: an Overview. *Indian Journal of Fisheries*, 43, 25-43.

Datta NC, Mandal N and Bandyopadhyay BK (1987). Seasonal Abundance of Rotifer in a Perennial Freshwater Pond in Calcutta. *J. Environ. Biol.,* 8(1): 63-71.

Desikachary TV (1959). Cyanophyta. ICAR. New Delhi, pp. 686.

De Silva SS and Hasan MR (2007). Feeds and Fertilizers: The Key to Long-term Sustainability of Asian Aquaculture. In: M.R. Hasan, T. Hecht, S.S. De Silva and A. G.J. Tacon (eds.). Study and Analysis of Feeds and Fertilizers for Sustainable Aquaculture Development. FAO Fisheries Technical Paper, No. 497, Rome, FAO, pp. 19-47.

Dhawan A and Kaur S (2002). Pig Dung as Pond Manure: Effect on Water Quality, Pond Productivity and Growth of Carps in Polyculture System. NAGA, the ICLARM Quarterly, 25(1):11-14.

Estep KW and Remsen CC (1985). Influence of the Surface Microlayer on Nutrients, Chlorophyll and Algal Diversity of a Small Eutrophic Bog Pond. *Hydrobiologia*, 121: 203-213.

Frempong E (1984). A Seasonal Sequence of Diel Distribution Pat-terns for the Planktonic Dinoflagellate *Ceratium hirundinella* in a Eutrophic Lake. *Freshwater Biol*., 14, 401-421.

Fryer G (1985). Crustacean Diversity in Relation to the Size of Water Bodies: Some Facts and Problems, *Freshwater Biology*, 15: 347-361.

Gaines G and Elbrächter M (1987). Heterotrophic Nutrition. In Taylor, F.J.R., ed. The Biology of Dinoflagellates. Botanical Monographs Volume 21, Blackwell Scientific Publications, Oxford.

Geiger JG (1983). A Review of Ponds Zooplankton Productions Fertilization for the Culture of Larval and Fingerlings. *Aquaculture*, 36: 353-360.

Gruendling GK (1983). The Distribution and Abundance of Phytoplankton and the Relationship to Phosphorus Concentrations in Lake Champion. Proc. 26th Conf. Great Lakes Res., May 23-27, 1983. p. 37.

Gupta MV and Noble F (2001). Integrated Chicken-fish Farming. M. Halwart, J. Gonsalves and M. Prein (Eds.), Integrated Agriculture-aquaculture: A primer, FAO Fisheries Technical Paper 407, FAO, Rome, pp. 49-53.

Halwart M , Smith SF and Moechl J (2002). The Role of Aquaculture in Rural Development. FAO Fisheries Department, Rome, Italy.

Harshey DK, Shrivastav, AK and Patil SG (1987). Studies on Ecology of Freshwater Ostrocoda. Part II Population Ecology in Balsagar Tank, Jabalpur M.P. India. *J. Curr. Biosci*, 4: 127-134.

Hawkes HA (1969). Ecological Changes of Applied Significance from Waste Heat. In *Biological* Aspects of Thermal Pollution, (eds Krenkel & Parker), pp. 15-53. Vanderbilt University Press.

Honigberg BM, Balamuth W, Bovee EC, Corliss JO, Gojdics M, Hall RP, Kudo RR, Levine ND, Lobblich AR and Weiser J (1964). A Revised Classification of the Phylum Protozoa. *Journal of Eukaryotic Microbiology*, 11 (1): 7-20.

Horn AJ and Goldman CR (1994). Limnology. 2nd McGraw-Hill, Inc., pp. 1-576.

Jana BB and De UK (1983). Primary Productivity of Phytoplankton, Environmental Covariates and Fish Growth in West-Bengal Ponds Under a Polyculture System. Int. Revue ges. *Hydrobiol.*, 68: 45-58.

Jha P, Sarkar K and Barat S (2004). Effect of Different Application Rates of Cowdung and Poultry Excreta on Water Quality and Growth of Ornamental Carp, *Cyprinus carpio* Var. Koi, in Concrete Tanks. *Turkish Journal of Fisheries and Aquatic Sciences*, 4: 17-22.

Jha P, Barat S and Nayak CR (2008). Fish Production, Water Quality and Bacteriological Parameters of Koi Carp Ponds Under Live-food and Manure Based Management Regimes. *Zoological Research*, 2: 165-173.

Karabin A (1985) Pelagic Zooplankton (Rotatoria+Crustacea) Variation in the Process of Lake Eutrophication. II. Modifying Effect of Biotic Agents. *Ekol. Pol.*, 33, 617-644.

Ki Jang-Seu and Han Myung-Soo (2008). New Record of the Freshwater Dinoflagellate *Peridinium umbonatum* Stein (Dinophyceae) from Togyo Reservoir, Korea. *Algae,* Volume 23(2): 115-118.

Külköylüoðlu O (2004). On the Usage of Ostracods (Crustacea) as Bioindicator Species in Different Aquatic Habitats in the Bolu Region, Turkey. *Ecol. Ind.*, 4: 139-147.

Lakshmanan MAV, Sukumaranan KK, Murty DS, Chakraborty DP and Philipose MT (1971). Preliminary Observations on Intensive Fish Farming in Freshwater Ponds by the Composite Culture of Indian and Exotic Species. *J. Inland Fish. Soc. India*, 3: 1-21.

Lauridsen TL and Lodge DM (1996). Avoidance by *Dapnia magna* of Fish and Macrophytes: Chemical Cues and Predator Mediated Use of Macrophyte Habitat. *Limnol. Oceanogr.*, 41: 794-798.

Mahar MA, Jafri, SIH Leghari SM and Khuhawar MY (2004). Environmental Degradation of Manchhar Lake (Distt. Dadu) Sindh, Pakistan. Proc. Nat. Sem. Env., Soc. and Cult. Impact of water Scarcity in Sindh.

Majumder S, Biswas S and Barat S (2002). Abundance of Ammonifying and Heterotrophic Bacterial Populations in the Water Manured with Cowdung and Distillery Sludge in Outdoor Model Tanks. *Asian Journal of Microbiology, Biotechnology and Environmental Science*, 4: 229-233.

Martens KI Schön, Meisch C and Horne DJ (2008). Global Diversity of Ostracods (Ostracoda, Crustacea) in Freshwater. *Hydrobiologia*, 595: 185-193.

Meisch C (2000). Freshwater Ostracoda of Western and Central Europe. Spektrum Akademischer Verlag, Heidelberg, Berlin. 522 pp.

Nasar SAK (1977). Investigations on the Seasonal Periodicity of Zooplankton in a Freshwater Pond in Bhagalpur, India. *Acta Hydrochem. Hydrobiol.*, 5: 577-584.

Neill WE (1984). Regulation of Rotifer Densities by Crustacean Zooplankton in an Oligotrophic Montana Lake in British Columbia. *Oecologia*, 61(2): 175-181.

Oertli, HJ (1982). Early Research on Ostracoda and the French Contribution. In: R.H. Bate, E. Robinson & L.M. Sheppard(Eds), Fossil and Recent Ostracods. Ellis Horwood Limited, Chichester. 454-478.

Paloheimo JE and Zimmerman AP (1983). Factors Influencing Phosphorus-phytoplankton Relationships. *Can. J Fish. Aquat. Sci.*, 40(10): 1804-1812.

Pandey BN, Lal RN, Mishra PK and Jha AK (1992). Seasonal Rhythm in the Physico-chemical Properties of Mahananda River, Katihar, Bihar. *Environ. Ecol.*, 10(2): 354-357.

Patralekh LN (1991). Phytoplankton Periodicity in a Perennial Pond of Bhagalpur, India. *Environ. Ecol.*, 9(2): 356-358.

Pennak RW (1953). Freshwater Invertebrates of the United States. Ronald Press, New York, 769 pp.

Pradhan A, Pranami P, Das S, Mishra M, Khanam S, Hoque BA, Mukherjee I, Thakur AR and Chaudhuri SR (2008). Phytoplankton Diversity as Indicator of Water Quality for Fish Cultivation. *American Journal of Environmental Sciences*, Volume 4, Issue 4, 406-411.

Prasad BN and Srivastava MN (1992). Fresh Water Algal Flora of Andaman and Nicobar Islands. Vol. 1. B. Singh, Dehradun, India, 369 pp.

Rai LC and Guar JP (2001). Algal Adaptation to Environmental Stresses. Springer-Verlag; Berlin Heidelberg, New York.

Rai LC and Kumar MD (1976). Systematic and Ecological Studies on Algae of Some Habitats near Sahupuri Varabasum. India. *Nova. Medcoifia.*, 27: 805-812.

Rajagopal TA, Thangamani SP, Sevarkodiyone M, Sekar and Archunan G (2010). Zooplankton Diversity and Physicochemical Conditions in Three Perennial Ponds of Virudhunagar District, *Tamil Nadu Journal of Environmental Biology*, 31: 265-272.

Rao VS (1975). An Ecological Study of Three Ponds of Hyderabad, India III. The Phytoplankton, Volvocales, Chroococcales and Desmids. *Hydrobiologia*, 47(2): 319-337.

Remane A (1929-32). Rotatoria, Gastrotricha und Kinorhyncha. In: Bronn's Klassen und Ordnungen des Tierreichs Bd. IV, Abt. II, 1. Buch, Lief. 1-4, Unvollendet. 1-576.

Riemann B (1983). Biomass and Production of Phyto and Bacterioplankton in Eutrophic Lake, Tystrup. *Freshwater biology*, 13: 389-398.

Rosen G (1981). Phytoplankton Indicators and Their Relations to Certain Chemical and Physical Factors. *Limnologica,* 13(2): 262-290.

Saran HM and Adoni AD (1985). Limnological Studies on Seasonal Variations in Phytoplankton Variations in Phytoplanktonic Primary Productivity in Sagar Lake. *Bull. Bot. Soc. Sagar*, 32: 71-76.

Schroeder GL, Wohlfarth G, Alkon A, Halevy A and Krueger H (1990). The of Dominance Algal-based Food Webs in Fish Ponds Receiving Chemical Fertilizers Plus Organic Manures. *Aquaculture*, 86: 219-229.

Singh RK (1990). On the Seasonal Abundance of Phytoplankton in Relation to Ecological Conditions of Undasa Pond. *Comp. Physiol. Ecol.*, 15(3): 91-95.

Spodniewska I (1979). Phytoplankton as the Indicator of Lake Eutrophication. *Ekol. Pol.*, 27(3): 481-496.

Sommer U, Sommer F and Santer B (2003). Daphnia Versus Copepod Impact on Summer Phytoplankton: Functional Compensation at Both Trophic Levels. *Oecologia*, 135, 639-647.

Talling JF (1987). The Phytoplankton of Lake Victoria (East Africa). *Arch. Hydrobiologia*, 25: 229-256.

Terziyski D, Grozev G, Kalchev R and Stoeva A (2007). Effect of Organic Fertilizer on Plankton Primary Productivity in Fish Ponds. *Aquaculture International*, Volume 15, Issue 3-4, pp. 181-190.

Tucker CS (1985). A Checklist of Phytoplankton (Exclusive of Diatoms) from Mississippi Channel Catfish Ponds.Technical Bulletin - Mississippi Agricultural and Forestry Experiment Station.Vol. 126.

Vasisht HS and Sharma BK (1975). Ecology of a Typical Urban Pond in Ambala City of the Haryana. *Ind. J. Ecology*, 2(1):79-86.

Vyhnalek V (1983). Effect of Filter-feeding Zooplankton on Phytoplankton in Fish Ponds. *Int. Rev. Ges. Hydrobiol.* , 68(3): 397-410.

Wetzel RG and Likens GE (2000). Limnological Analyses, Third Edition, Springer (India) Private Limited, New Delhi, India. xvi+426.

Yijian L (1990). Experimental Observation on Nitrous Oxide Accumulation during Nitrification in a Freshwater Lake. *Japanese Journal of Limnology*, 51(4):237-248.

8

Bioremediation
A Novel Tool for Environment Friendly Shrimp Aquaculture

Shubhadeep Ghosh; M.V. Hanumantha Rao; Ritesh Ranjan
Biji Xavier; Loveson L. Edward; Muktha Menon
Pralaya Ranjan Behera and N Rajendra Naik

ABSTRACT

Organic matter contains three main energy nutrients, viz., proteins, carbohydrates and fats which microorganisms efficiently utilize to synthesize their cell structure and the energy for their life processes. Microorganisms play an important role in nutrient recycling in aquatic environment. N_2 - Cycle, C - Cycle, S – Cycle and P - Cycle are the major nutrient cycling process going on in the aquatic ecosystem. However, under most circumstances the appropriate species of microorganism for purifying water/ sediment and appropriate physico-chemical conditions are not always present in the aquatic environment for speedy mineralization of organic matter. The newest attempt being made to improve water quality in intensive shrimp culture is bioremediation which involves manipulation of microorganisms in ponds to enhance mineralization of organic matter and get rid of undesirable waste compounds. Bioremediation involves both intrinsic and engineered bioremediation. Engineered bioremediation includes Biostimulation and Bioaugmentation. Bioremediation (bioaugmentation) is applied in shrimp culture, but success varies greatly, depending on the nature of the products used and competition between species or strains of bacteria. The bacteria that are added must be selected for specific functions that are amenable to bioremediation and added at high enough population density, and under the right environmental *conditions. Commercial bioremediators products for aquaculture use are available in plenty and a few of these are AQUA.BACTA.AID; ACCELOBAC; Epicin; Bactaclean-ALGAE, Type 2; Alken Clear-Flo®; Sanjiban Microactive; NS Series Super SPO; Bioklean-MX 1, etc. However, their efficacy and success rates are variable as suppliers of such products often overrate their potential.*

Keywords: Bbioaugmentation, bioremediation, commercial bioremediators, mineralization, nutrient cycle, shrimp culture.

INTRODUCTION

Aquaculture plays a vital role in world economy and is fast emerging as a major food producing industry. Aquaculture is the only hope of meeting the growing need of fish for the increasing world population, as the yield from capture fisheries have come to stagnancy. Of all the kinds of aquaculture practices, the outlook for shrimp aquaculture appears quite promising all over the tropical and subtropical countries. Asia holds a predominant position in the world shrimp production by culture. This has been possible due to the spectacular technology development and the favourable environment for the utilization of farming technology in the South East Asia over the last 10 to 15 years.

Water quality and disease control are interdependent and are linked to the microbial activities in aquaculture system. Microbial processes affect water quality factors such as the levels of dissolved oxygen, NH_3, NO_2^- and sulphide (Moriarty, 1996). One of the most important factors affecting the shrimp production is the build up and toxicity of NH_3 with the intensification of shrimp culture. As with many other industries, the intensive/rapid growth in shrimp aquaculture has brought with it the problem of environmental pollution. Shrimp culture all over the world has therefore been frequently affected by the viral and bacterial diseases (Lightner, 1993). The high microbial productivity coupled with stress and unfavourable environmental conditions lead to the outbreak of shrimp diseases.

Microorganisms not only act as autotrophs (primary producers) but also as saprophytes and heterotrophs, thereby helping in rapid recycling of dead and decaying animals and plants (organic matter), which in turn keeping the aquatic ecosystem alive. The autotrophic community is limited to few photo and chemoautotrophic bacteria, diatoms and cyanobacteria. Photoautotrophic bacteria belonging to the group green sulphur bacteria and purple sulphur bacteria help in carbon dioxide (CO_2) fixation but require anaerobic conditions, sufficient light and hydrogen donors like hydrogen sulphide (H_2S) and organic acid. Chemoautotrophic bacteria like nitrifying bacteria, bacteria involved in sulphur cycle, iron and manganese cycle contribute to primary production to a small extent (Rheinheimer, 1992). Heterotrophic microorganisms consisting of bacteria and fungi, help in degradation of organic matter, if optimum conditions are prevalent, to simpler forms like CO_2 and H_2O. Moriarty (1986) observed that the heterotrophic microbial numbers in the water column were higher in most ponds receiving organic matter (feed pellets and chicken manure). Most heterotrophic bacteria were between 0.4 and 0.8 μm in diameter and 0.5 and 1.5 μm in length. Their average cell volume was 0.14 μm^3. Novitsky (1983) showed that the heterotrophic activity in the soil-water interface region was several times greater than that in the water column above and twice as high in the sediment immediately below.

Microorganisms play a major role in cleaning up the environment through rapid mineralization of organic matter present in culture ponds. Generally, in pond environment the organic matter content will be high compared to natural environment due to extraneous input like feed, excreta, fertilizer, etc. The micro organisms present in the pond such as bacteria, fungi, protozoa etc., carry out active decomposition of left our feed and metabolites to inorganic forms such as ammonia, hydrogen sulphide, carbon dioxide etc., through the process of mineralization. These nutrients will be utilized by algae for their growth and in term produce oxygen, which the microorganisms need for decomposition of organic matter. Such a natural process is called "self purification" process (Anon, 1993). In a way micro organisms and algae exist as symbiotic partners in ponds.

Many a times the appropriate species of micro organisms for purifying water/ sediment and appropriate physico-chemical conditions may not be always present in the pond to promote rapid growth and speedy mineralization. In this situation, seeding of micro organisms or manipulation of micro flora could hasten the mineralization process and bringing about rapid purification. The term bioremediation can be used to describe the process of reducing the hazardous organic wastes to environmentally safe levels through use of micro/macro organisms in ponds. Bio-remediation can broadly be classified into Engineered and Intrinsic bioremediation. Engineered bioremediation can again be divided into biostimulation and bio augmentation (Atlas and Unterman, 1999). Few of the micro organisms, which help in this process, are bacteria like *Bacillus sp, Acinetobacter sp, Pseudomonas sp, Nitrosomonas sp, Rhodopseudomonas sp* etc. As the micro organisms are fast growing (shorter generation time) and bring down levels of toxic products such as NH_3, H_2S etc, to insignificant levels, they are preferred over the micro organisms like algae, mussels, sea cucumber etc.

A variety of commercial bioremediators have been used in shrimp aquaculture to increase shrimp productivity but with varying degrees of success. There are number of reports on the positive and negative effects of the use of bioremediators in shrimp culture ponds (Boyd *et al.,* 1984; Moriarty, 1996).

DEGRADATION OF ORGANIC SUBSTANCES BY MICROBES IN SHRIMP CULTURE SYSTEMS

Microorganisms efficiently utilize the organic matter to synthesize their cell structure and the energy for their life processes. The breakdown of organic matter or mineralization is the major role played by micro organisms. If micro organisms would not have helped in degradation, the problem due to organic matter pollution would have been magnified. Even though the micro organisms can utilize organic matter, they need optimum conditions such as Temperature, pH, O_2, Oxidation, Reduction potential (Eh), proper carbon (C): Nitrogen (N_2) ratio, etc as these are major limiting factors for their growth. Organic matter usually contains three main energy nutrients, viz., Proteins, Carbohydrates and Fats.

PROTEINS

They are plenty of proteolytic micro organisms, which can utilize protein as source of energy. The decomposition of proteinaceous materials to soluble amino acids and other compounds is necessary for assimilation of this material into bacterial protoplasm. The breakdown of protein is also important for the release of nutrients from refractory compounds. Thus, generation of nitrogenous compounds is achieved. *Enterobacter, Pseudomonas* and other eubacteria and various fungi can carry out proteolyses. Proteins are primarily hydrolysed to polypeptides, oligopeptides by exo-enzymes of micro organisms. Later, they are taken up by cells, broken down, then utilized for body building, and lastly deaminated with liberation of NH_3. Zobell and Upham (1944) found that out of sixty strains of bacteria tested all could broken down peptone to NH_3 and forty seven could liquefy gelatin.

Sepers (1981) reported on number of bacteria, which can utilize amino acid as sole C, N_2 and energy source. According to him, 83% of the tested organisms were capable of utilizing 50-83% of the applied organic compounds as sole carbon and energy source. The amino acids most resistant to bacteria are methionine, taurine, threonine and glycine.

Barat and Jana (1987) studied the protein mineralizing bacteria and ammonifying bacteria in culture tanks and reported that seasonal changes of protein mineralizing bacteria were less pronounced with relatively low numbers in July than in the remaining months of the year. The ammonifying bacteria showed a small peak in autumn. The increase in intensification of the culture systems lead to increased metabolite production which supported higher population of protein mineralizing bacteria (Barat and Jana, 1987).

CARBOHYDRATES

Many eubacteria as well as actinomycetes and numerous fungi are able to degrade simple sugars to 3C compounds and finally to CO_2 and water (H_2O) under aerobic conditions. Under anaerobic conditions only fermentation is possible.

Few bacteria are capable of breaking down disaccharide such as sucrose, lactose and maltose and polysaccharides such as mannitol, rhamnose and xylose. These include *Azotobacter, Desulfovibrio, Clostridium, Klebsiella* and *Enterobacte*r (Herbert, 1975; Lakshmanaperumalsamy, 1975). Starch is an important food reserve in plants. It is polysaccharide, which is utilized by only 10% of bacteria as C, N and energy source (Sepers, 1981). *Pseudomonas, Bacillus, Actinomycetes* and higher fungi can hydrolyse starch by means of exo-enzymes (Amylase, Maltase) into glucose under aerobic conditions, where as *Clostridium* utilize starch under anaerobic conditions. Cellulose is decomposed by Myxobacteria (*Cytophaga* and *Sporocytophaga*) and higher fungi (*Ascomycetes* and *Deuteromycetes*) under aerobic conditions (Rheinheimer, 1992).

Agar and alginic acids are product of red and brown algae, respectively and are degraded by the action of many bacteria, Viz., *Achromobacter, Agarobacterium, Flavobacterium, Cytophaga, Alginomonas alginovorus, A. alginica* and others (Rheinheimer, 1992). Chitin, a skeletal component of many lower animals, fungi and crustaceans are broken down by bacteria of the genera *Pseudomonas, Vibrio* and by fungi (Rheinheimer, 1992).

FATS

Fats are esters of fatty acids with glycerol, contained in plants and animals and also in water and sediment. Zobell and Upham (1944) isolated 13 species of lipolytic bacteria belonging to genera *Pseudomonas, Vibrio, Sarcina, Serratia and Bacillus*. Bianchi et al (1992) reported that out of 20 isolates of NH_3 and Nitrite (NO_2) - oxidizing bacteria, 49% and 21% could utilize fatty acids as carbon and energy source.

ROLE OF MICRO ORGANISMS IN NUTRIENT CYCLES OF SHRIMP CULTURE SYSTEMS

Micro organisms help not only in the production and break down of organic matter but also in nutrient recycling. Nutrient cycling is an essential process in the aquatic ecosystem. N_2 - Cycle, C - Cycle, Sulphur (S) - Cycle, Phosphorus (P) - Cycle are major nutrient cycling process going on in the aquatic ecosystem and these play key role in the formation of organic materials. Carbon is the prime substance of all the organic materials; nitrogen is necessary for the synthesis of amino acids, nucleic acids and amino sugars; sulphur is essential in sulfhydryl groups of amino acids and their polymers and phosphorus is contained in nucleic acid, phosphate esters, sugar phosphates and adenosine triphosphate (Austin,1988).

NITROGEN CYCLE

Nitrogen is a major constituent of proteins, the building block of all living matter. N_2 cycle, therefore, occupies an important place in organic matter recycling. It involves N_2 fixation, ammonification, nitrification and denitrification processes carried out by different microorganisms.

Biological N_2 fixation transforms molecular N_2 to NH_3 or organic N_2 and through this process, the atmospheric N_2 enters the biosphere and gets involved in N_2 cycle in aquatic environments. It is carried out by prokaryotes referred to as "diazotrophs". Stal *et al.* (1984) cited evidence of N_2 fixation for 18 blue green algae belonging to the genera *Anabaena, Calothrix, Microchaete, Nostoc, Nodularia, Rivularia* and *Trichodesmium*. The occurrence of *Azotobacter, Clostridium, Desulfovibrio and* photosynthetic N_2 fixing bacteria in marine sediments has been documented of which *Desulfovibrio* plays an important role (Sisler and Zobell, 1951; Pschenin, 1963; Truper and Genovese, 1968; Wyne Williams and Rhodes, 1974). The nitrogenase activity is light stimulated and to some degree inhibited by O_2 (Stal *et al.,* 1984).

Green plants utilize NH_3 and Nitrate (NO_3^-) as source of N_2 for synthesis of protein (Rheinheimer, 1992). The complex proteinaceous matter is converted to free NH_3 or ammonium ion (NH_4^+) depending on pH first by protein mineralizing bacteria and then by ammonifying bacteria such as *Pseudomonas, Bacillus and Vibrio*. This process is called ammonification and is the dominant mechanism for NH_3 production (Fry, 1987). Ammonification can take place either aerobically or anaerobically in water and sediment (Fry, 1987).

Ammonia is also produced from NO_3^- by nitrate dissimilation, which is important in anaerobic sediments. Herbert (1982) showed that *Aeromonas, Vibrio, Klebsiella, Escherichia and Clostridium* were very active in NO_3^- dissimilation and they contained an enzyme NO_3^- reductase whose activity reaches maximum under anaerobic conditions. In aerobic sediments and in the water column, NH_3 gets oxidized to NO_3 by Nitrification process. The organisms involved in nitrification have been fully described (Watson *et al.,* 1981) and consist of two genera that use different respiratory mechanisms. The NH_3 oxidizers convert NH_3 to NO_2^- (nitritation); there are 5 genera of which 2 are aquatic, viz., *Nitrosomonas* (rod shaped 1xl.5 μm) and *Nitrosococcus* (coccoid, 1.5-2 μm). The NO_2^- oxidizers convert NO_2^- to NO_3^- (nitratation) and all are aquatic, viz., *Nitrobacter* (pearl shaped rod, 0.7×1.5 μm) *Nitrococcus* (coccoid, 1.7 μm) and *Nitrospina* (rod shaped 0.35x3 μm). The activity of *Nitrosomonas* and *Nitrobacter* was reported to be affected by light (Olson, 1981) with *Nitrobacter* being the most sensitive. They are also highly sensitive to sudden changes in temperature, pH below 6, reduction in available nutrients and several chemicals used for treating diseases in aquatic ecosystems (Burrows and Combs, 1968; Scott and Gillespie, 1972; Collins *et al.,* 1975; Spotte, 1979; Smith *et al.*, 1981; Bower and Turner, 1982). Nitrification, denitrification and nitrogen fixation are threatened also by contaminants such as heavy metals (Bouwman and Bloem, 2000).

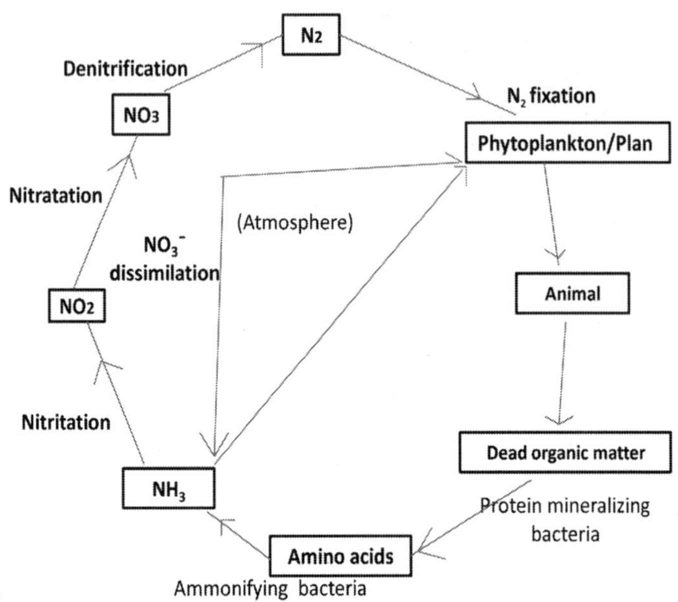

Fig 8.1: Nitrogen Cycle

Nitrosomonas sp

$$55\ NH_4^+ + 5\ CO_2 + 76\ O_2 \longrightarrow C_5H_7O_2N^- + 54\ NO_2^- + 52\ H_2O + 109\ H^+$$

NH_3-monooxygenase

Nitrobacter sp

$$400\ NO_2^- + 5\ CO_2 + NH_4^+ + 195\ O_2 + 2H_2O \longrightarrow C_5H_7O_2\ N^- + 400\ NO_3^- + H^+$$

The generation times of the autotrophic nitrifying bacteria are in the range of 10-30 h. Engel (1958) summarized that heterotrophs are also able to carry out nitrification, but to a lesser extent. The co-culture of a heterotroph *Arthrobacter* sp increased the nitrifying activity of an autotrophic *Nitrosomonas* strain possibly by reducing its lag phase (Kuenen and Gottschall, 1982; Kaplan, 1983). Bianchi *et al.* (1992) reported the ability of pseudomonads and asporogenous gram-positive rods isolated from an enclosed shrimp rearing facility to utilize NH_3. Joye and Hollibaugh (1995) reported that nitrification was rapidly and substantially reduced when 60-100 µm hydrogen sulphide (H_2S) was added to sediment slurries.

Denitrification involves reduction of NO_3 to NH_3 free N_2. Bacteria capable of denitrification are predominantly facultative anaerobes. Jetter and Ingraham (1981) listed 73 genera capable of denitrification including common aquatic heterotrophs, viz., *Pseudomonas, Vibrio and Alcaligenes*. Denitrification rates are highest in early summer and freshly anaerobic water (Nedwell, 1984). Considering denitrification to be a two step process with methanol as C and energy source, the following reactions can be written:

$$CH_3OH + 3NO_3^- \longrightarrow 3NO_2^- + CO_2 + H_2O$$

$$2NO_2^- + CH_3OH \longrightarrow N_2 + CO_2 + H_2O + 2OH^-$$

The optimum pH for denitrifying bacteria lies between 7 and 8. They are sensitive to sudden changes in temperature. Most of the N_2 cycle process occurs simultaneously in aquatic ecosystem. A well balanced microbial load would help in efficient cycling of N_2 in environment.

SULPHUR CYCLE

Sulphur is one of the most abundant elements in our planet, present at approximately 520 mg/l level in the earth's crust (Goldschmidt, 1954). Sulphur is assimilated by many microorganisms and is the second most abundant anion in sea water (Austin, 1988).

Sulphate is one of the most common forms of sulphur found in habitats. In marine sediments, sulphate (SO_4^{2-}) and H_2S are constantly recycled between oxidation and reduction steps, predominantly carried out by two main groups of bacteria, viz., SO_4^{2-} reducers and sulphide (S^{2-}) oxidizers. Sulphate (SO_4^{2-}) is assimilated by bacteria and primary producers when they grow and incorporated mainly into sulphur containing amino acids of proteins. A variety of putrefying bacteria belonging to the genera *Proteus, Mycobacterium, Chromobacter, Bacillus, Micrococcus, Flavobacterium and Vibrio* produce H_2S by degrading the sulphur containing amino acids (Wetzel, 1983).

The H_2S is also produced directly from SO_4^{2-} by sulphate reducing bacteria (SRB) (Fry, 1987). These bacteria are all strict anaerobes and use SO_4^{2-} as terminal electron acceptor to oxidize organic compounds. The SRB in marine sediments have been reported to mineralize 25 - 50% of C. These include bacteria of the genera *Desulfovibrio*, (rod, curved shaped or spiral), *Desulfotomaculum* (spore forming rod) and *Desulfococcus* (coccoid). The primary habitat of SRB is the sediment with redox potential of -100 mV or below and that SRB are active within detrital particles of 100 μm thickness (Jorgensen, 1977a, b). Sulphate (SO_4^{2-}) reduction was reported to be highest in summer and lowest in winter (Fry, 1987). Suplee and Cotner (1996) found that new ponds initially had lower levels of SRB than old ponds, but the difference was lost by 17th week of grow out.

Once formed, the H_2S is either reoxidized to SO_4^{2-} or precipitated with iron to form insoluble ferrous sulphide. Reoxidation of S^{2-} is carried out biologically by a wide range of sulphide oxidizing bacteria (SOB). The H_2S oxidizers mainly include two groups of bacteria, viz., colourless sulphur bacteria and photosynthetic bacteria.

The colourless sulphur bacteria are all aerobic or microaerophilic and oxidize H_2S to S, which they store as S globules within their cells and they can use this S later to obtain energy when H_2S is unavailable (Austin, 1988). They include bacteria of the genera *Macromonas* (rod or bean shaped, 9×20 μm), *Thiovulum* (ovoid, 20 μm), *Thiospira* (spiral 2×50 - 10 μm), *Thiobacterium* (non motile rod, 1×2 μm), *Beggiatoa* (filaments, 1-55 μm), *Thioplaca* (sheathed, 1-55 μm) and *A. chromatium* (ovoid, 30-50 μm). There are a second group of colourless sulphur bacteria that oxidize H_2S and other inorganic sulphur to produce energy and form SO_4^{2-} but, there was no intracellular S deposition in these bacteria. They include bacteria of the genera *Thiobacillus* (rod, 0.5×1-4 μm), *Thiomicrospira* (spiral, 0.2- 9.3 × 1-2 μm), *Thiosphaera* (coccoid), *Thiodendron* (vibrioid, 0.15-0.25 μm) and *Acidiphilium* (rod, 0.3-1 .2 × 0.6-4.2 μm). *Thiobacillus denitrificans* can grow in anaerobic conditions by converting NO_3^- to N_2^-. There are again a third group of colourless sulphur bacteria that require optimum temperature above 55°C for growth and thus, are of lesser importance in S cycle. They include members belonging to genera *Thermothrix* (rod), *Sulfolobus* (spherical) and *Acidianus* (spherical) (Fry, 1987).

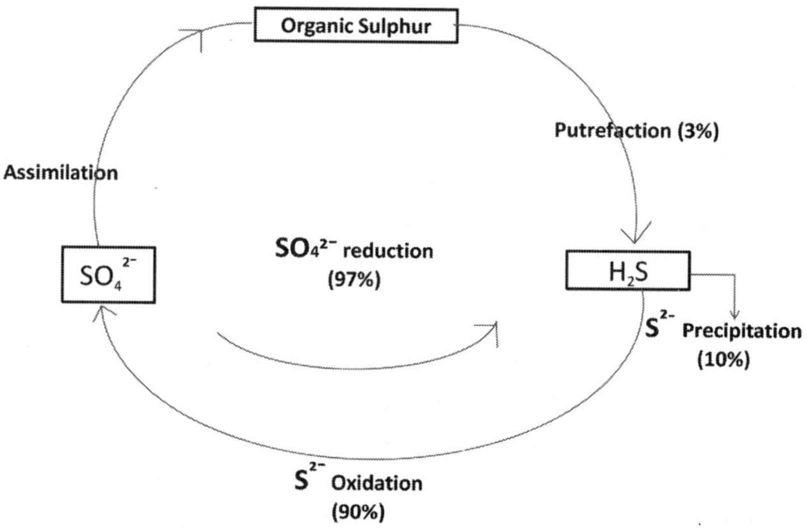

Fig. 8.2: Sulphur Cycle

Under strict anaerobic conditions and in the presence of light, photoautotrophic bacteria of the family *chlorobiaceae* [green sulphur bacteria, e.g., (i) *Chlorobium* - a non motile rod of 0.3-1.1 × 0.7-2.7 μm and (ii) Pelodictyon - a rod of 0.8 × 1.8 μm] and *Chromatiaceae* [purple sulphur bacteria, e.g. (i) *Chromatium* - an avoid rod of 1-6 × 2-15 μm and ii) *Thiopedia* - a non motile rod of 1.5 × 2 μm] oxidize H_2S efficiently to fix CO_2 phototrophically (Fry, 1987). The green sulphur bacteria grow at lowest light intensities cannot tolerate O_2 but can tolerate high H_2S concentrations. The purple sulphur bacteria need more light, are O_2 tolerant and H_2S sensitive, they always grow in a thin band just above the green sulphur bacteria and even may penetrate the oxygenated part of the H_2S/O_2 interface. Phototrophic bacteria are also found in sediments where light penetration and H_2S accumulation meet.

CARBON CYCLE

Carbon, one of the major constituents of all organic matter, undergoes recycling in nature, at the center of which stands CO_2. The earth's atmosphere contains about 0.032% (2.3 × 10^2 tons) by volume of CO_2 (Rheinheimer, 1992), but in sea water 50 times this amount is in solution. The cycle is very complex in water because many organisms are involved and many pools of different carbon compounds can be envisaged.

The C - Cycle can be divided into assimilation, i.e., synthesis and transformation of organic material into multitude of natural C compounds and dissimilation which is the stepwise breakdown of all these substances by respiration by heterotrophic plants and animals (Rheinheimer, 1992). The C-fixing bacteria including cyanobacteria, photo and chemo autotrophic bacteria, etc. synthesize organic matter by fixing CO_2 and using light and other chemical substances such as NH_3, NO_2, NO_3^- and S as their energy source (Fry, 1987). Some heterotrophs are also able to fix CO_2 in the dark and some predominantly autotrophic bacteria can use organic compounds as source of energy and C, these types are often called mixotrophs (Fry, 1987).

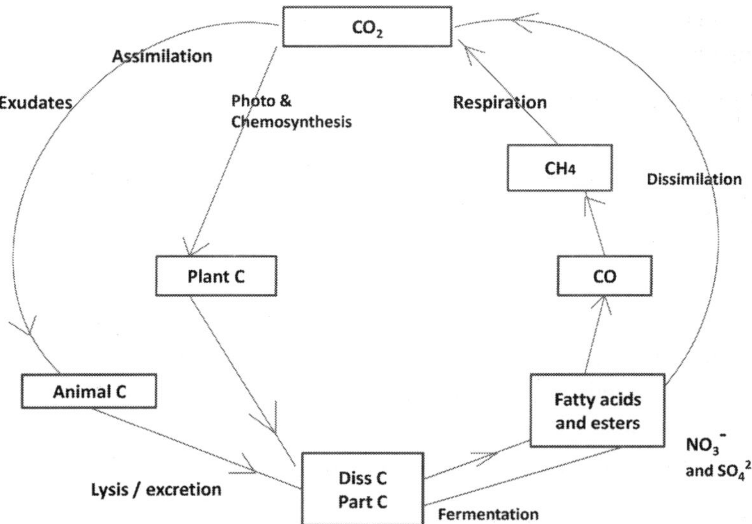

Fig 8.3: Carbon Cycle

The decomposition of primary producers, when they die by microorganisms contributed to both the dissolved organic and particulate organic carbon compound pools. Heterotrophic bacteria grow on the particulate organic carbon and secrete exoenzymes that decompose it and the decomposition products enter the dissolved organic carbon pools. Most of the dissolved organic carbon is respired by heterotrophic microorganisms to CO_2 .The wide range of heterotrophic bacteria involved in the entire process from decomposition of primary producers to production of CO_2 mainly belong to the genera of *Flavobacterium, Pseudomonas, Vibrio, Aeromonas and Alcaligenes*. Pike (1975) reported that 90-95% of bacteria in oxidation ponds are *Pseudomonas, Achromobacter and Flavobacterium,* thus demonstrating their predominance in these systems. The SRB and denitrifying bacteria are also known to mineralize carbon. The zone near the surface containing the redoxycline, is often the site of most bacterial activity when gross measures are used (Fry, 1987).

A portion of the dissolved organic carbon will be converted to methane (CH_4), probably mainly through acetate by methanogens. The CH_4 producing bacteria are morphologically diverse but physiologically similar group and most of the 7 genera are rod shaped (*Methanobacterium*) or coccoid (*Methanogenium*) but one genus (*Methanospirillum*) have spirally shaped members (Fry, 1987). All are anaerobes and grow best at redox potential of -200 mV or below. However, their growth is limited by SRB as they complete with them for acetate and hydrogen (Nedwell, 1982; 1984).

The CH_4 produced is not oxidized anaerobically in sediments by methanogens but rises into the water column and once it reaches the oxygenated layer is rapidly oxidized by methanotrophic bacteria, *Methylomonas*, *Methylcoccus* and *Methylosinus* (Fry, 1987). They are microaerophilic and use CH_4 carbon and energy source to produce CO_2 (Cappenberg, 1972; Rudd and Hamilton, 1975).

PHOSPHORUS CYCLE

Phosphate (PO_4^{3-}) is one of the most important limiting factors for plant life in many waters. Phosphorus as a vital element for all organisms is present in phospholipids, phosphorylated sugar, phytin, ATP etc and also particularly as a constituent of nucleic acids. Phosphorus cycle involves conversion of inorganic phosphorus to organic and vice versa. Phosphorus is taken up by plants as pyrophosphates, that is changed to organic P compounds and from these, PO_4^{3-} are released mainly due to action of microorganisms (Rheinheimer, 1992). During cycling P may get immobilized due to adhesion to clay particles or formation of ferric or aluminium phosphates.

Solubilization of inorganic phosphates is carried out by a wide range of micro organisms, viz., *Pseudomonas, Achromobacter, Flavobacterium, Arthrobacter, Streptomyces and Aspergillus* (Botto, 1988). This solubilized PO_4^{3-} taken up by phytoplankton and plant for production of organic substances. Mineralization of organic P is carried out by a variety of microorganisms such as *Arthrobacter, Proteus, Serratia, Streptomyces, Aspergillus* and *Rhizopus* (Botto, 1988). Although many organisms have the ability to hydrolyze phytate in vitro, this form of organic PO_4^{3-} has a very strong affinity for adsorption on clay particles, which prevent accesses by the phytases produced by the organisms. Consequently, phytate tends to accumulate and is the major form of organic phosphorus found in most soils (Botto, 1988).

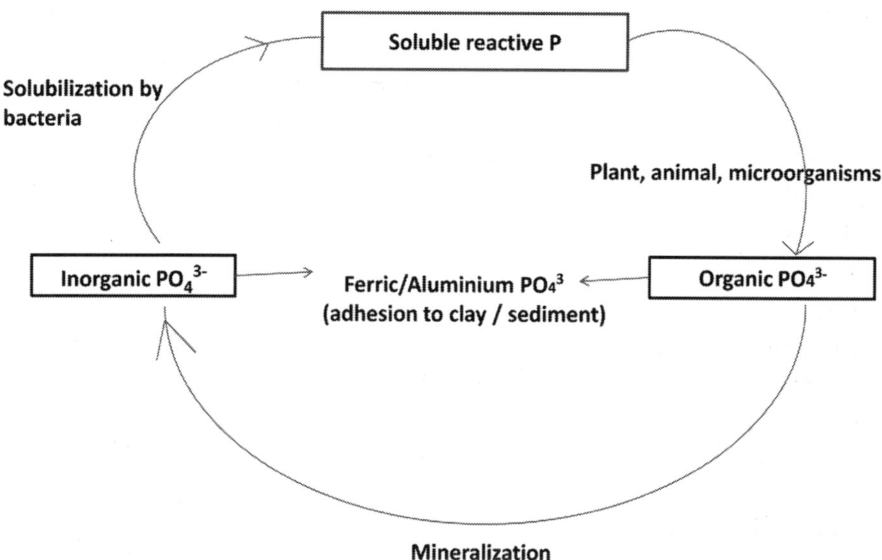

Fig. 8.4: Phosphorus Cycle

BIOREMEDIATION: A NEW CONCEPT

Bioremediation has almost become a household word these days, implying the use of biological agents to control problems of environmental pollution. A prominent example of bioremediation, often cited in popular press and scientific magazines, is that of Exxon Valdez Oil Spill, where indigenous microorganisms were supplied with an oleophilic fertilizer and allowed to proliferate and consume the spilled oil (Chakrabarty, 1992).

Bioremediation is defined as the process by which microorganisms are stimulated to rapidly degrade hazardous organic contaminants to environmentally safe levels in soils, subsurface materials, water, sludges and residues (Thomas 1992). Stimulation is achieved by the addition of nutrients and a terminal electron acceptor usually O_2, because most biological reactions occur faster under than anaerobic conditions. Under anaerobic conditions, NO_3^- has been as the terminal electron acceptor.

Bioremediation is a pollution treatment technology that uses biological systems to catalyze the destruction or transformation of various chemicals to less forms (Atlas and Unterman, 1999). Bioremediation is cost effective, environmentally sound and increasingly the preferred choice of remedial technology for clean up operation.

The objective of bioremediation programme is to immobilize contaminants (reactants) or to transform them to chemical products no longer hazardous to human health and environment. The end products of effective bioremediation are non-toxic and can be accommodated without harm to the environment and living organisms (Atlas and Unterman, 1999). The selection of most effective bioremediation strategy is based on - a) characteristic of the contaminants (toxicity, molecular structure, volatility, solubility and susceptible to microbial attack) b) the contaminated site (hydrology, geology, soil type and climate and the legal, economic and political pressures felt by the site owner and c) the microbial process that will be exploited, such as pure culture, mixed culture, their respective growth conditions and supplements.

The general approaches to bioremediation are:

1. **Intrinsic bioremediation**: Intrinsic bioremediation is the management of contaminant biodegradation without taking any engineering steps to enhance the process. It uses the innate capabilities ofnaturally occurring microbial communities to metabolize environmental pollutants. Because intrinsic bioremediation occurs in the landscape where both indigenous microorganisms and contaminants reside, this type of bioremediation necessarily occurs in situ. It may be used along or in conjunction to other remediation techniques. For intrinsic bioremediation to be effective, the rate of contaminant destruction must be faster than the rate of contaminant migration.
2. **Engineered bioremediation**: Engineered bioremediation, either accelerates intrinsic bioremediation or replaces it completely through the use of modification procedures that allow concentration of nutrients, electron acceptors, or other materials to be managed in a manner that hastens biodegradation reactions. Engineered bioremediation may be chosen over intrinsic bioremediation because of considerations of time, cost and liability. It falls into 2 categories:
   (a) Biostimulation refers to the addition of specific nutrients to a waste situation with the hope that the correct, naturally occurring microbes are present in the waste sufficient numbers and types to breakdown the waste effectively. This assumes that every organism needed to accomplish the desired treatment results present.
   (b) Bioaugmentation involves the addition of specifically formulated micro organisms to a waste situation. It allows one to control the nature of the biomass. It ensures that the proper team of microbes is present in the waste in sufficient type, number and compatibility to attack the waste constituents effectively and break them down into their most basic compounds (Burlage *et al.,* 1999)

Biodegradation of naturally occurring and synthetic organic compounds requires or is faster when several species of microorganisms are present. In instances where the indigenous microflora fails to degrade the target compounds or has been decimated by the presence of toxicants, microorganisms with specialised metabolic capabilities may be added (Thomas *et al.,* 1992).

In bioremediation, the emphasis, so far, has however, been on the use of microorganisms rather than genetically manipulated ones, because of the adverse public perception on the release of genetically engineered microorganisms as well as various regulatory constraints on their use (Chakrabarty, 1992). The major reason for using genetic selection in the decontamination of polluted environment is the fact, that in many cases, natural microorganisms have not evolved the genetic competence to utilize a synthetic compound. To generate new degradative capability against a newly made synthetic compound, a micro organism must evolve the appropriate genes encoding enzymes that would have high affinity for the target chemical or its intermediate products as substrates. Bioremediation has some definite advantages over other treatment technologies in that it can be done at site, facilitates permanent elimination of waste, biological systems are cheaper, evokes positive public acceptance, minimum site disruption, eliminates transport cost and liability and can be coupled with other treatment techniques.

The bioremediation microorganisms frequently identified as active members of microbial consortium are *Alcaligenes denitrificans, Arthrobacter globiforms, Arthrobacter sp, Bacillus sp, B. megaterium, Flavobacterium sp, Mycobacterium, M. vaccae, Methanobacteriaceae, Nitrosomonas europaea, N. corallina, N. erythropolis, Pseudomonas sp, P. aeruginosa, P. putida , P. cepacia, P. fluorescens , P. glatheri, P. mendocina, P. methanica, P. paucimobilis, P. testosteroni and P. vesicularis* (Baker and Hersan, 1994).

The requirements for an effective bioremediation is illustrated (Cookson, 1995) pyramidically as follows.

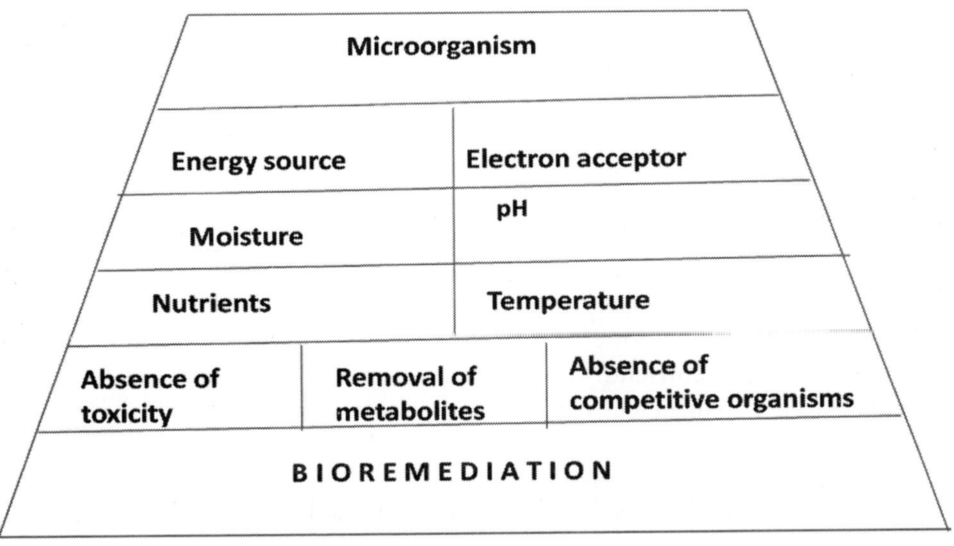

Fig. 8.5: Requirements for an Effective Bioremediation

The spectrum of compounds susceptible to bioremediation are naturally occurring, have simpler molecular structure, is non-toxic and serves as a growth substrate for aerobic microorganisms. A few examples of such compounds are inorganic ones as NO_3^-, SO_4^{2-}, PO_4^{3-} and NH_4 compounds and petroleum (xylene, toluene, benzene, ethylbenzene, alcohols and ketones). In compounds that are resistant to microbial metabolism, have complex molecular structure, low water solubility, and strong sorptive interactions, toxic and do not support the growth of microorganisms. A few examples of such compounds are halogenated aliphatic and aromatic compounds (Burlage *et al.*, 1999).

BIOREMEDIATION IN SHRIMP AQUACULTURE

The Need/Necessity

It is a golden rule that successful intensive shrimp culture requires intensive management to maintain good pond water quality. The pond water quality changes quickly because of the input of large quantities of high quality feeds. Most of these feeds eaten by shrimps are eventually excreted as metabolic wastes that add inorganic nutrients and organic matter to the bottom of ponds. According to Briggs and Funge-Smith (1994) only 21% of nitrogen and 13% of phosphorus of the feed input (at a conversion rate of 2) gets incorporated into flesh of shrimp. On the other hand, Primavera (1994) has reported only 17% incorporation of feed input by shrimp. The ponds, thus, become eutrophic with active decay and assimilation of left over feed and metabolic wastes carried out by microorganisms. As a result of microbial activity under aerobic conditions the organic matter is converted to inorganic compounds such as PO_4^{3-}, NH_3 and CO_2. The microbial process of converting organic matter to inorganic compounds is called mineralization. Some of these organic compounds serve as nutrients to stimulate algal growth, which in turn produce oxygen required for decomposition of organic matter.

Many a times the appropriate species of microorganism for purifying water/ sediment and appropriate physico-chemical conditions may not be always present in the pond to promote rapid growth and speedy mineralization. The newest attempt being made to improve water quality in intensive shrimp culture is the application of bacteria or enzymes to the ponds. This type of biotechnology is known as 'bioremediation' which involves manipulation of microorganisms in ponds to enhance mineralization of organic matter and get rid of undesirable waste compounds (Anon, 1993). Beneficial, ecofriendly bacteria are a must for healthy prawn culture. Moreover, water treatment with chlorine, iodophores and antibiotics kill the beneficial autochthonous microbes as well as pathogenic allochthonous microbes, reducing the fertility of water. Microorganisms are known to play an important role in nutrient recycling in any aquatic environment (Rheinheimer, 1992). Water quality in aquaculture system is, to a large extent, controlled by microbial biodegradation of organic residues (Avnimelech et al., 1995). Therefore, attempts are being made to improve water quality in intensive shrimp culture ponds through application of bacterial population capable of degrading organic matter in the ponds.

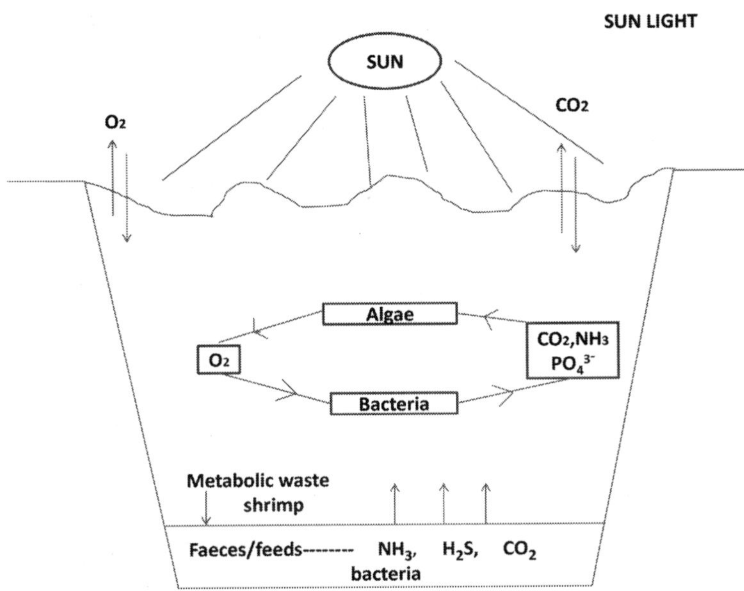

Fig. 8.6: Role of Microorganisms in the Metabolic Cycle in Shrimp Ponds

Many scientists feel that addition of bacterial seed stock is pointless. Their beliefs are based on misinterpretation of ubiquity principle. The principle of ubiquity states that bacteria may be found anywhere, it does not state that all bacteria are found everywhere all the time. The underlying assumptions of the following misconceptions are not true: (i) that the appropriate species for water purification and organic sediment decomposition are always present; (ii) that appropriate physico-chemical conditions are always present to permit rapid growth; and (iii) that bacterial growth is not limited by process such as predation (Ehrlich *et al.*, 1988). Bird and Kalff (1984) reported that addition of specific microbial mixture or manipulation of the microflora of the deteriorated environment may hasten the process of mineralization, thereby bringing about rapid purification.

The practice of bioremediation (bioaugmentation) is applied in shrimp culture, but success varies greatly, depending on the nature of the products used and the technical information available to the end users. The bacteria that are added must be selected for specific functions that are amenable to bioremediation, and added at high enough population density and under the right environmental conditions. Bioaugmentation is a significant management tool, but its efficacy depends on understanding the nature of competition between species or strains of bacteria.

APPLICATION OF BIOREMEDIAL PRODUCTS IN SHRIMP AQUACULTURE

There are many reports on the success as well as unsuccessful results of using bacterial products in aquaculture.

In the 1980's Alken-Murray Corporation changed the economic feasibility of bacterial treatment by offering highly concentrated, non-pathogenic and cost effective Alken-Clear Flo ® formulae to degrade excess nutrients, chemical pollutants and NH_3 in traditionally high volume shrimp producing pond waters. Alken-Clear Flo ® 1000 and 1002 include basic spore forming, waste degrading strains of *Bacillus* to reduce organic loadings in the water column, preventing a built of sludge on pond bottom by 60%. Alken-Clear Flo® 1100, 1200 and 1400 contain *Nitrosomonas europaea*, which degrade NH_3 to NO_2^- and *Nitrobacter winogradskyi*, which degrade NO_2^- to NO_3^- in the aerobic environment of the water column and to N_2 gas in the anaerobic environment of the bottom sludge or gravel.

Boyd *et al.* (1984) studied the effect of commercial bacterial suspension (AQUA. BACTA. AID) and found that it did not have any significant effect on water quality parameters such as total ammoniacal nitrogen (TAN) concentration, NO_2-N concentration, NO_3-N concentration, total phosphorus concentration, biological oxygen demand (BOD) and chemical oxygen demand (COD). On the other hand, Ehrlich *et al.* (1988) reported positive effects of the same bacterial consortium in its ability to accelerate nitrification, increase decomposition of organic solids (10-12 cm/month), reduce excessive algal growth, facilitate oxygenation and aid in transformation of agricultural wastes into faunal biomass.

Sanjiban Microactive is a liquid stimulator developed from complex fermentation process. It is an organic extract enriched with natural enzymes that activates and rapidly multiplies healthy organisms already present in the effluent system. In shrimp ecopond system under warm climatic conditions, the typical removal efficiency of various pollutants that have been achieved are: total suspended solids (TSS):- 80-95%, BOD: - 85-98%, COD: - 80-93%, NH4-N: - 85-95%, phosphorus: - 90-95% and E. coli: - 99%. Furthermore, production of 500-1000 kg shrimp/ha and 5000-6000 kg fish/ha can also be harvested.

Porubcan (1991a; b) reported on two attempts at bacterial treatments to improve water quality and production yield of *Penaeus monodon* - (i) floating biofilters pre-inoculated with nitrifying bacteria decreased the amounts of NH_3 and NO_2 - in the rearing water. This treatment also increased shrimp survival (Porubcan, 1991a) and (ii) the introduction of *Bacillus* sp in close proximity to pond aerators reduced COD and increased shrimp harvest (Porubcan, 1991b).

Chiayvareesajja and Boyd (1993) studied the effect of a bacterial product (ACCELOBAC) on TAN concentration and reported that treatment of pond water with up to 40 mg/1 of ACCELOBAC caused no change in TAN concentration over a 10 day period. Tucker and Lloyd (1985) found no benefits of bacterial augmentation in lowering TAN concentration or improving any other aspects of water quality.

An intensive shrimp culture pond in Thailand which use a commercial bacterial product throughout the culture period got good production of 6806 Kg/ha (FCR 1.4 and survivality 80%), demonstrating the possibility of using bacterial products to maintain good water quality (Anon, 1993). The use of 'EPICIN' a commercial bacterial product of EPICORE Network in shrimp ponds in Indonesia has produced the largest harvest ever recorded in the ponds involved and profits were up to 5 times greater than ponds not treated. The major and probably most significant effect of 'EPICIN' on water quality was in its ability to reduce NH_3 concentration. Following 'EPICIN' application, concentration of other nutrients including NO_2-, NO_3 - and H_2S were also reduced to well below than that in untreated ponds (Anon, 1995). Funge-Smith and Hawthorn (1996) tested 5 commercially available bacterial products for their efficacy in improving water quality under laboratory conditions. They reported that none of the products had significant effect on TAN as well as NO_2 -N concentrations.

Shrimp farms in Indonesia that use the Detritus Management System (DMS) - range of *Bacillus*, do not have problems from diseases caused by luminescent *Vibrio* sp (Moriarty, 1996). Chandrika (1999) reported on bioaugmentation with 10^9/g of DMS- Bacillus to mineralize and reduce the faecal matter of shrimps and left over feed in intensive aquaculture. Anon (1999) studied the effect of a bioaugmentor, viz., Bioklean MX - 1 (bacterial product) for removal of toxic NH_3 from shrimp culture systems and reported that Bioklean @ 12 ppm was effective in reducing the concentration of NH_3. They also studied the efficacy of *Pseudomonas* (1×10^6/ml) on removal of NO_2^- from shrimp culture systems and reported that 5 ml/l of Pseudomonas was effective in decreasing NO^2 concentration. They further studied effect of plant by-products and extracts on removal of NH_3 from shrimp culture system. According to them, neem seed oil @ 100 ppm, neem leaf extract @ 90 ppm and custard apple seed oil @ 90 ppm were all effective in reducing NH_3 concentration.

In China, Li Zhuojio et al. (1997) reported on the application of a mixture of several strains of photosynthetic bacteria (*Rhodomonas* sp) to improve the shrimp culture water and have achieved remarkable results. There was a total elimination of NH_3-N, H_2S and organic acids coupled with improvement in water quality and balancing of pH resulting in increase in body length and weight of shrimps. They concluded that the bacterial population might have chemical actions such as oxidation, nitrification, ammonification, denitrification, N_2 - fixation and sulphurication.

An alternative way to maintain high water quality in intensive shrimp culture is biological treatment based on the use of filters with a high surface/volume ratio, pre-colonized by microorganisms that absorb excess nutrients from the water.

A biological filter for filtration of shrimp culture water has been developed recently by Bioworld. The filter occupying a volume of 11% of water volume under production provides a large surface area (20 m^2) for many biological processes: ammonification, nitrification and denitrification. The bioremedial products offered by New China Limited, are very useful to those raising shrimp in ponds. They create larger, healthier shrimps and lessen mortality by avoiding NH_3 build up; thus increasing profits. Bacta Clean - ALGAE, Type 2 is a bioremedial product used for shrimp aquaculture pond maintenance as it prevents NH_3 build up, slime formation and algal growth. Moreover, it reduces NO_3^- added to pond water by shrimp faeces and scavenges bottom sludge materials.

Prabhu *et al.* (1999) studied the effect of a commercially available probiotic (NS series Super SPO) on the water quality parameters of 4 ponds in a shrimp farm. The product was soaked in pond water @ lg/200ml and activated by vigorous aeration for 4 h. After activation, the liquid containing the slurry was sprinkled uniformly over the surface water in each pond. The results of the experiment showed a marked decrease of NH_4-N in the concentration 3 experimental ponds with progressive days of culture (DOC); while there was a marked increase in NH_4-N concentration in the control pond. The total heterotrophic bacterial count increased by 10^4 (from 10^3 to 10^7) cfu/ml in water and by 10^5 (from 10^3 to 10^8 colony forming units (cfu)/g in sediment in the control pond, which is much more when compared to the increase by 10^3 (from 10^3 to 10^6 cfu/ml in water and 10^3 (from 10^4 to 10^7) cfu/g in sediment of experimental tanks.

Recently, Oppenheimer Biotechnology, New York, USA is co-operating with the Philippines Company Envirogenics, Inc. to evaluate the use of Oppenheimer Formula 1 product to enhance production in shrimp pond culture. The application of Oppenheimer Formula 1 to sediments and water of 2-5 acre ponds have been shown to double the normal production in the same time period. There is also evidence that microbes may reduce the mortality caused by other competing microorganisms, control algae, decrease BOD and COD, decrease NH_3, NO_2^- and NO_3^-.

Shan and Obbard (2001) from the Department of Chemical and Environmental Engineering, National University of Singapore isolated cultures of nitrifying bacteria from intensive prawn aquaculture water and enriched them using continuous and batch enrichment techniques. Cultures were immobilized on to porous clay pellets to enhance cell density and when applied to water with high TAN concentrations have been found to exhibit high TAN removal rates.

Moriarty (1996) has summarized the reasons for inefficiency of few bacterial mixtures under field conditions. According to him, the bacterial products might have lacked the sufficient number of right strains of bacteria to be effective or it was possible that the bacteria were not viable. It is apparent that many suppliers of bacterial products are unaware of the physiological and ecological requirements of their bacteria. For example, some contain purple sulphur bacteria that will remove S^{2-} only when conditions are anaerobic and light is present. Nitrifying bacteria are autotrophic and need CO_2 as their carbon source and oxidize NH_3 for their energy. They are very difficult to maintain, require oxygen and are slow growers. If these conditions are not provided, the activity of these bacteria will be inhibited.

The use of macroorganisms as effective bioremediators in shrimp culture system has led to the development of new culture models such as shrimp-shellfish (molluscs/oysters) shrimp-fish and shrimp-algae. The seaweed *Gracilaria* is an attractive species to be grown as part of polyculture with molluscs in a biological treatment system because it can remove soluble nutrients, nitrogen and phosphorus, which are not absorbed by molluscs. The culture of shrimp with fish is found to be the most successful for preventing disease occurrence. It is believed that predatory fish may eat sick or morbid shrimps, thereby eliminating the spread of diseases in shrimp culture pond. Mangroves have also been suggested to treat shrimp pond effluents in that it acts as biological filters by trapping pollutants, i.e., excess nutrients, suspended solids, heavy metals, toxic hydrocarbons, etc. (Babu *et al.*, 1998).

FUTURE DIRECTION

The significance of special groups of microorganisms with varied physiological characteristics in aquaculture systems is not well documented and also their ecology. Future studies should focus on monitoring the levels of these microorganisms with different physiological characteristics involved in nutrient cycling in different aquaculture systems. Also efforts should go into the development and evaluation of suitable bioremedial products using indigenous microflora of the culture system.

CONCLUSION

Bioremediation and its efficacy are debatable topics. However, they have potential applications in aquaculture. The challenge in maintaining a viable culture of indigenous bacteria at high cell density in active growth phase is a key factor in providing an effective treatment for shrimp culture pond water. A thorough and detailed investigation is, however, necessary to understand the behaviour as well as environmental requirements of beneficial microbes that exist in shrimp ponds. Large scale laboratory and field studies are required to clearly demonstrate the ability of the microbes as bioremediators. Viability and economics are the other vital aspects, which have to be considered before adopting these methods.

REFERENCES

Anon (1993): Bioremediation Technology for Shrimp Culture – Does it Work?. *Asian Shrimp News*, 16(4): 3.

Anon (1995): Water Treatment Booster Profits for Indonesian Shrimp Farmers. *Fish Farming International*, 22 (12): 10-11.

Anon (1999): Soil and Water Quality and Productivity Management for Sustainable Shrimp Farming. *Annual Report 1997 – 1998, Central Institute of Brackishwater Aquaculture, Chennai*, pp: 50.

Atlas, R.M. and R. Unterman (1999): Bioremediation, In: Manual of Industrial Microbiology and Biotechnology. *ASM Press*, *Washington DC.*, pp: 666-680.

Austin, B. (1988): Marine Microbiology. *Cambridge University Press*, *Cambridge*, pp: 221.

Avnimelech, Y., Mozes, N., Diab, S. and M. Kochba (1995): Rates of Organic Carbon and Nitrogen Degradation in Intensive Fish Ponds. *Aquaculture*, 134: 214-216.

Babu, B.T. and B.V.S.S.R. Subba Rao (2000): Application of Bioremediation in Sustainable Shrimp Culture. *Fishing Chimes*, 20 (7): 25-27.

Baker, K.H. and D.S. Hersan (1994): Bioremediation. *Mc-Graw Hill*, *New York*, pp: 375.

Barat, S. and B.B. Jana (1987): Effect of Farming Management on the Distribution Pattern of Ammonification Rates, Protein Mineralizing and Ammonifying Bacterial Population in Experimental Culture Tanks. *Bamidgeh*, 39(4): 120-132.

Bianchi, M., Perfettini, J. and A. Bianchi (1992): Marine Heterotrophic Bacteria Associated with Enrichment Culture of Nitrifying Bacteria Planned for Closed Aquaculture System. *Aquat.* Living *Resour.*, 5(2): 137-144.

Bird, D.F. and J. Kalff (1984): Empirical Relationship Between Bacterial Abundance and Chlorophyll Concentration in Fresh and Marine Waters. *Can. J. Fish. Aquat. Sci.*, 41: 1015-1023.

Botto, K.G. (1988): The Phosphorus Cycle, In: Mangrove Microbiology. *UNDP/UNESCO Regional Project, Research and its Application to the Mangroves of the Asia and the Pacific* (RAS/86/120).

Bouwman, L.A. and J. Bloem (2000): Microbial Indicators of Soil Quality, In: Abstracts of Intercost Workshop on Bioremediation. *Sorrento*, pp: 53-55.

Bower, C.E. and P. Turner (1982): Effect of Seven Chemotherapeutic Agents on Nitrification in Closed Seawater Culture Systems. *Aquaculture*, 29: 331-345.

Boyd, C.E., Hollerman, W.D. and Plumb, J.A. and M. Saeed (1984): Effect of Treatment with a Commercial Bacterial Suspension on Water Quality in Channel Catfish Ponds. *Prog. Fish Culturist*, 43: 36-40.

Briggs, M.R.P. and S.J. Funge-Smith (1994): A Nutrient Budget of Some Intensive Marine Shrimp Ponds in Thailand. *Aquacult. Fish. Management*, 25: 789-811.

Burlage, R.S., Atlas, R., Stahl, D., Geesy, G. and G. Sayler (1999): Theoretical and Applied Aspects of Bioremediation, In: Techniques on Microbial Ecology. pp. 356-362.

Burrows, R.E. and B.D. Combs (1968): Controlled Environment for Salmon Propagation. *Prog. Fish Culturist*, 30: 123-136.

Cappenberg, T.E. (1972): Ecological Observation on Heterotrophic, Methane Oxidizing and Sulphate Reducing Bacteria in a Pond. *Hydrobiologia*, 40: 471-485.

Chakrabarty, A.M. (1992): Bioremediation: How does the Environment Modulate Microbial Gene Evaluation?, In: Harnessing Biotechnology for the 21st Century. *American Chemical Society Conference Proceedings Series*, *American Chemical Society*, *Washington DC.*, pp: 422-426.

Chandrika, V. (1999): Incidence of Antagonistic *Bacillus* sp – an Ecofriendly Aquatic Probiotic from Aquaculture Ponds, In: Fourth Indian Fisheries Forum Proceedings. pp: 147-150.

Chiayvareesajja, A. and C.E. Boyd (1993): Effects of Zeolite, Formalin, Bacterial Augmentation and Aeration on Total Ammonia Nitrogen Concentrations. *Aquaculture*, 116: 33-45.

Collins, M.T., Gratzek, J.B., Shotts, E.B., Dawe, D.L., Campbell, L.M. and D.R. Senn (1975): Nitrification in an Aquatic Recirculating System. *J. Fish. Res. Board Canada*, 32: 2025-2031.

Cookson, J.T. (1995): Bioremediation Engineering – Design and Application. *Mc-Graw Hill, New York.*

Ehrlich, K.F., Cantin, M.C. and Horsefall (1988): Bioaugmentation: Biotechnology for Improved Aquaculture Production and Environmental Protection, In: Aquaculture Engineering Technologies for the Future. pp. 329-341.

Engel, H. (1958): Nitrification, In: Handbuch der pflangen Physiologic. *Springer, Heidelberg*, pp: 1107-1127.

Fry, J.C. (1987): Functional Roles of the Major Groups of Bacteria Associated with Detritus, In: Detritus and Microbial Ecology in Aquaculture. *ICLARM Conference Proceedings, Manila, Philippines*, pp: 83-122.

Funge-Smith, S. and S. Hawthorn (1996): The Effect of Bacteria Remediation Products on Water Quality in the Presence of Shrimp Sediments. *Abstracts of World Aquaculture Society*, pp: 133.

Goldschmidt, V.M. (1954): Geochemistry. *Clarendon Press, Oxford, UK.*

Herbert, R.A. (1975): Heterotrophic Nitrogen Fixation in Shallow Estuarine Sediments. *J.Experiment. Mar. Biol. Ecol.*, 18: 215-225.

Herbert, R.A. (1982): Nitrate Dissimilation in Marine and Estuarine Sediments, In: Sediment Microbiology. *Academic Press, London*, pp: 53-72.

Jetter, R.M. and J.L. Ingraham (1981): The Denitrifying Prokaryotes, In: The Prokaryotes: A Handbook on Habitats, Isolation and Identification of Bacteria. *Springer-Verlag, Berlin*, pp: 913-925.

Jorgensen, B.B. (1977a): The Sulphur Cycle of a Coastal, Marine Sediment (Limfjorden, Denmark). *Limnol. Oceanogr.*, 22: 814-832.

Jorgensen, B.B. (1977b): Bacterial Sulphate Reduction within Reduced Microniches of Oxidized Marine Sediments. *Mar. Biol.*, 41: 7-17.

Joye, S.B. and J.T. Hollibaugh (1995): Influence of Sulphide Inhibition of Nitrification on Nitrogen Generation in Sediments. *Science*, 270: 623-625.

Kaplan, W.A. (1983): Nitrification, In: Nitrogen in the Marine Environment. *Academic Press, London*, pp: 139-190.

Kuenen, R.D. and J.C. Gottschall (1982): Competition Among Chemolithotrophs and Methylotrophs and Their Interactions with Heterotrophic Bacteria, In: Microbial Interactions and Communities. *Academic Press, London*, pp: 153-188.

Lakshmanaperumalsamy, P., Chandramohan, D. and R. Natarajan (1975): Studies on the Nitrogen Fixation by Marine Nitrogen Fixing Bacteria. *Bull. Dept. Mar. Sci. Univ. Cochin*, 8: 103-116.

Li Zhuojia, Zhang Qing and Yang Huaquan (1997): The Effect of the Probiotics to the Shrimp Ponds. *Aquaculture of China*, 5: 30-31.

Lightner, D.V. (1993): Diseases of Cultured Penaeid Shrimp, In: CRC Handbook of Mariculture, 2nd edn. Vol. 1, Crustacean Aquaculture. CRC Press Inc., Boca Ratan, FL, pp: 393-486.

Moriarty, D.J.W. (1986): Bacterial Productivity in Ponds Used for Culture of Penaeid Prawns, Gelang Petals, Malaysia. *Microbiol. Ecol.*, 12: 259-269.

Moriarty, D.J.W. (1996): Microbial Biotechnology: A Key Ingredient for Sustainable Aquaculture. *Infofish International*, 4/96: 29-33.

Nedwell, D.B. (1982): The Cycling of Sulphur in Marine and Freshwater Sediments, In: Sediment Microbiology. *Academic Press, London.*

Nedwell, D.B. (1984): The Input and Mineralization of Organic Carbon in Anaerobic Aquatic Sediments. *Adv. Microb. Ecol.*, 7: 93-132.

Novitsky, J.A. (1983): Heterotrophic Activity Throughout a Vertical Profile of Seawater and Sediment in Halifax Harbour, Canada. *Appl. Environ. Microbiol.*, 45: 1753-1760.

Olson, R.J. (1981): Differential Photoinhibition of Marine Nitrifying Bacteria: A Possible Mechanism for the Formation of the Primary Nitrite Maximum. *J. Mar. Res.*, 39: 227-238.

Pike, E.B. (1975): Aerobic Bacteria, In: Ecological Aspects of Used-water Treatment, Vol. 1, The Organisms and Their Ecology. *Academic Press, London*, pp: 1-63.

Porubcan, R.S. (1991a): Reduction of Ammonia Nitrogen and Nitrite in Tanks of *Penaeus monodon* Using Biofilters Containing Processed Diatomaceous Earth Pre-inoculated with Nitrifying Bacteria, In: Programme and Abstracts of the 22nd Annual Conference and Exposition. *World Aquaculture Society, Baton Rouge, Louisiana.*

Porubcan, R.S. (1991b): Reduction in Chemical Oxygen Demand and Improvement in *Penaeus monodon* Yield in Ponds Inoculated with Aerobic *Bacillus* Bacteria, In: Programme and Abstracts of the 22nd Annual Conference and Exposition. *World Aquaculture Society, Baton Rouge, Louisiana.*

Prabhu, N.M., Nazar, A.R. Rajagopal, S. and S. Ajmal Khan (1999): Use of Probiotics in Water Quality Management during Shrimp Culture. *J. Aqua. Trop.*, 14 (3): 227-236.

Primavera, J.H. (1994): Environmental and Socio-economic Effects of Shrimp Farming: the Philippine Experience. *Infofish International*, 1/94: 44-49.

Pschenin, L.N. (1963): Distribution and Ecology of Azotobacter in the Black Sea, In: Symposium on Marine Microbiology. *Thomas Springfield, Illinois*, pp: 383-391.

Rheinheimer, G. (1992): Aquatic Microbiology. *4th Edition, John Wiley and Sons, Chichester*, pp: 363.

Rudd, J.W.M. and R.D. Hamilton (1975): Factors Controlling Rates of Methane Oxidation and the Distribution of Methane Oxidizers in a Small-stratified Lake. *Arch. Hydrobiol.*, 75: 522-538.

Scott, K.R. and D.C. Gillespie (1972): A Compact Recirculation Unit for the Rearing and Maintenance of Fish. *J. Fish. Res. Board Canada*, 29: 1071-1074.

Sepers, A.B.J. (1981): Diversity of Ammonifying Bacteria. *Hydrobiol.*, 83: 343-350.

Shan, S. and J.P. Obbard (2001): Ammonia Removal from Prawn Aquaculture Water Using Immobilized Nitrifying Bacteria. *Appl. Microbiol. Biotechnol.*, 57: 791-798.

Sisler, F.D. and C.E. Zobell (1951): Nitrogen Fixation by Sulphate Reducing Bacteria Indicated by Nitrogen/Argon Ratios. *Science*, 113: 511-512.

Smith, C.E., Piper, R.G. and H.R. Tisher (1981): The Use of Chinoptilolite and ion Exchange as a Method of Ammonia Removal in Fishing Culture Systems. *US Fish and Wildlife Service, Fish Cultural Development Centre, Bozeman Information Leaflet, Bozeman, Montana.*

Spotte, S. (1979): Fish and Invertebrate Culture: Water Management in Closed Systems. *2nd Edition, John Wiley and Sons, New York.*

Stal, L.J., Grossbarger, S. and W.E. Krumbein (1984): Nitrogen Fixation Associated with the Cyanobacterial mat of a marine laminated Microbial Ecosystem. *Mar. Biol.*, 82: 217-240.

Suplee, M.W. and J.B. Cotner (1996): Temporal Changes in Oxygen Demand and Bacterial Sulphate Reduction in Inland Shrimp Ponds. *Aquaculture*, 145: 141-158.

Thomas, G.M., Ward, C.H., Raymond, R.L., Wilson, J.T. and R.C. Loehr (1992): Bioremediation, In: Encyclopedia of Microbiology. *Academic Press, London*, pp: 369-385.

Truper, H.G. and S. Genovese (1968): Characterization of Photosynthetic Sulphur Bacteria Causing Redwater in Lake Faro. *Limnol. Oceanogr.*, 13: 225-232.

Tucker, C.S. and S.W. Lloyd (1985): Evaluation of Commercial Bacterial Amendment for Improving Water Quality in Channel Catfish Ponds. *Miss. State Univ. Res. Rep.*, 10: 1-4.

Watson, S.W., Valois, F.W. and J.B. Waterbury (1981): The Family of Nitrobacteriaceae, In: The Prokaryotes: A Handbook on Habitats, Isolation and Identification of Bacteria. *Springer-Verlag, Berlin*, pp: 1005-1022.

Wetzel, R.G. (1983): Limnology. *2nd Edition, W.B. Saunders, Philadelphia*, pp: 767.

Wyn-Williams, D.D. and M.E. Rhodes (1974): Nitrogen Fixation in Seawater. *J. Appl. Bacteriol.*, 37: 203-216.

Zobell, C.E. and H.C. Upham (1994). A List of Marine Bacteria Including Description of Sixty New Species. *Bull. Scripps Inst. Oceanogr.*, 5: 230-292.

9

Management and Control of Land Degradation with Special Reference to Aquaculture

Sagar C. Mandal*; Debtanu Barman
S.K. Gupta and S. Khogen Singh

ABSTRACT

Land degradation can be described as an environmental phenomenon affecting dry lands, a long-term decline in ecosystem function and productivity. Asia has been highly affected and followed by Africa, where as the Europe is the least effected. About 2.6 billion people are affected by land degradation and desertification in more than 100 countries, influencing over 33% of the earth's land surface. The natural causes of land degradation are earth quakes, tsunamis, droughts, avalanche, landslides, mud flow, volcanic eruptions, flood, tornado and wild fire. Man-made land degradations are due to land clearance, deforestation overgrazing by live stock, in appropriate irrigation and over drafting, urban sprawl and commercial development and pollution from industries, quarrying, and mining activities. Implications and effects of land degradations reduce productivity of land, migration of the people, damage to basic resources and ecosystems, food insecurity and loss of biodiversity with special reference to fisheries and aquaculture. The land degradations can be controlled by management of deforestation, managing irrigation, managing urban sprawl, managing mining and quarrying, managing agricultural intensification and land reclamation. Intensification of sustainable agriculture-aquaculture can be implemented to reduce the ecological effect without affecting the productivity. Thus it is necessary to have local and global policies and regulations to control the land degradation.

Keywords: Land degradation, biodiversity, reclamation, control, aquaculture.

INTRODUCTION

Land degradation can be described as an environmental phenomenon affecting dry lands, leads to loss of economic and biological quality of an agricultural land (Mantel & van Engelen, 1997). The Food and Agricultural Organisation (FAO) defines land degradation as a long-term decline in ecosystem function (UNEP, 2007) and productivity (Bai & Dent, 2006). It is the effect on biophysical environment by disturbing the land either by human or by natural forces. Severity of land degradation is about 30% of forestry, 20% of agricultural and 10% of grass land is undergoing degradation (Bai *et al.* 2008). Soil degradation involves a number of physical, chemical and biological processes. Soil erosion by water due to storms and soils with poor surface structural stability is the most obvious form of land degradation. The other forms of degradation seen in our state are salinisation, alkalisation, laterisation and inundation.

It is estimated that land degradation affects about 70% of the world's rangelands, 40% of rain fed agricultural lands and 30% of irrigated lands. Salinity affects about 30% of currently irrigated lands. Over ¼ of the world's land area is affected by desertification which is a potential threat to half of the world's poor people that live in dry land regions with fragile soils and unreliable rain, especially in Africa. Declining soil fertility has a severe impact globally and, in Africa, average yield losses are estimated at 8%, with up to 50% loss of productivity in certain areas. Land degradation affects water resources, reducing water availability and quality and altering the regimes of rivers and streams. Potential impacts include flooding, silting of reservoirs and estuaries, groundwater depletion, salt water intrusion into aquifers, pollution of water and salinization. Unsustainable rates of freshwater use and contamination of water and soils by urban and industrial wastes are increasing problems with environment, food safety and health implications.

Land degradation has major impacts on biodiversity through reducing land quality and its capacity to support animal, plant and microbial life and through impacts on natural ecosystems, especially fragile wetlands and extensive grazing systems in dry land areas. Many inland water ecosystems and their fishery resources and biodiversity on which large populations rely, are seriously threatened by urban and industrial growth, deforestation, agro-chemicals and sediments from runoff. Some 26% of the world's wetlands have already been lost, due largely to conversion to agriculture or diversion of water for agriculture and aquaculture. Increasing land degradation, desertification and deforestation are caused by poverty, population pressure, unsuitable land use and unsustainable agriculture, grazing and forestry practices, insecure land tenure, lack or misuse of technology, inefficient markets and other institutional, policy and legal factors.

Poverty is both a consequence of land degradation and one of the causes. Poor people deplete their resources through lack of capacity and opportunities to meet their daily needs. Efforts to increase production and improve food security and wellbeing, through intensification and new technologies have, in some cases, resulted in negative environmental and health impacts. It has been shown that economic long-term viability of technologies must be guaranteed for land users including small holders as they will only envisage involvement and investments in sustainable land use systems and better land husbandry practices if the resulting benefits will be fully appreciated and internalised. Thus land use options must be viable and socio-economic benefits must be emphasized in the promotion of good practice (income, equity, livelihood, community cohesion, environmental). In addition, to promoting good practices, satisfactory trade-offs need to be identified between the objectives of farmers and other local resource users and those of the nation. Externalities such as degradation, resource depletion, pollution and health impacts need to be identified and, as appropriate, addressed through supportive trade, financial and fiscal policies in order to encourage local management activities that also contribute to national goals, such as watershed and water resources management and biodiversity conservation.

There are two fundamental objectives of aquaculture development viz. it be environmentally sustainable and that it be economically viable. These issues are closely tied. It has been proved in numerous other human activities that if development is not sustainable then it is not viable. For any proposed aquaculture development, proponents must pay attention to planning principles, assess potential effects, and establish processes to minimize these effects through good aquaculture practices.

ISSUES AND FUTURE CHALLENGES

The ever increasing population growth and increased demands of urban and rural populations are influencing land use, the status of land and water resources and their potential to sustain the livelihoods and well-being of present and future generations. Global trends and key factors of land use change in terrestrial ecosystems include deforestation and fragmentation of forests, intensification of agriculture and its expansion into marginal areas and fragile ecosystems, as well as urban expansion and infrastructure development. Land degradation seriously affects land resources in many tropical, subtropical and dry land regions of the world, with severe impacts on much of the world's population whose livelihoods depend on agriculture, fisheries and land as well as on urban and rural food security. The magnitude of these trends is inducing changes in global systems and cycles that underpin the functioning of ecosystems and represent major environmental threats. Such changes include global warming from the build-up of greenhouse gases and its potential impacts; emissions that cause acid rain and threaten watersheds, as well as disruption of the global nitrogen and carbon cycles through burning of fossil fuels, logging and land degradation and extensive use of chemicals and fertilizers.

HOW LAND DEGRADATION IS AFFECTED GLOBALLY

According to the estimates of global extend of land degradation shows that Asia has highly affected and followed by Africa, where as the Europe is the least effected (Zika & Erb, 2009). United Nations Development Programme (UNDP) estimates $42 billion in income and 6 million hectares of productive land are lost every year. As per UNDP the conditions in Africa are worsening with dust storms, damaged water sheds, lost of forests and lower agriculture productivity, which is linked to human poverty, migration and instability (WMO, 2005). In Botswana also under threat because of soil erosion and unsustainable use of renewable natural resources, where the most of population are depends on agriculture. Pakistan also facing the threat of land degradation, by decreasing soil fertility and floods. In the case of Sudan the population is depends on the livestock for their subsistence. It is estimated that 2.6 billion people are affected by land degradation and desertification in more than a hundred countries, influencing over 33% of the earth´s land surface (Adams & Eswaran, 2000). The detailed degraded lands in dry areas as per the continents have been given in Table 9.1.

Table 9.1: Estimates of All Degraded Lands (in million km^2) in Dry Areas (Dregne & Chou, 1994)

Continent	Total Area	Degraded Area	% Degraded
Africa	14.33	10.46	73
Asia	18.81	13.42	71
Australia and the Pacific	7.01	3.76	54
Europe	1.46	0.94	65
North America	5.78	4.29	74
South America	4.21	3.06	70
Total	51.60	35.92	70

EFFECTS OF LAND DEGRADATION

The effect of land degradation is such that in the Philippines, it is estimated that soil erosion carries away a volume of soil equivalent to one meter deep over 2,00,000 ha every year. In India, about 144 million ha of land are affected by either wind or water erosion. Similarly, in Pakistan, 8.1 million ha of land have been lost to wind erosion and 7.4 million ha to water erosion. The deforestation is also very common. During 1980s, it is estimated that 4.0 million ha of forest were lost each year in Asia and the Pacific. The destruction of the forests is mainly a result of clearance for agriculture. The search for fuel wood, as well as the growing frequency and severity of forest and bush fires, are also taking their toll. In Nepal, excessive fuel wood harvesting and cutting for fodder have severely degraded forests-approximately 40 per cent of buffalo feed and 25 per cent of the cow feed is traditionally provided by the leaves of trees.

In India, which supports 15 per cent of the world's cattle and 46 per cent of the world's buffalo, upland forests have been severely overgrazed. Deforestation has led to a severe shortage of fuel wood and building materials in many areas. Crop residues and animal manure, which were previously returned to the soil to add valuable nutrients, are having to he burnt for fuel. The region's grasslands are also being destroyed-a matter of great economic importance since grazing is the largest land use in Asia. Grasslands are under attack from over-intensive grazing and from the incursion of marginal agriculture which often fails and then leaves a residue of degraded land. It can also be said that as grazing areas decrease, livestock numbers often increase. The grazing areas are often located at the source of important catchment areas, influencing downstream agricultural and settlement so the cost of their deterioration is high. The problem of the 'vanishing grasslands' is particularly serious in countries where grazing lands are used communally, but livestock are private property. It is virtually impossible to stop overgrazing in areas where grazing rights are not defined. No nation in the region has an effective plan of action to meet this challenge.

Land degradation is also altering hydrological conditions, where vegetative cover is removed, the soil surface is exposed to the impact of raindrops which causes a sealing of the soil surface. Less rain then infiltrates the soil. Runoff increases, stream flows fluctuate more than before, flooding becomes more frequent and extensive, and streams and springs become ephemeral. These conditions encourage erosion; as a result, sediment loads in rivers are increasing, dams are filling with silt, hydro-electric schemes are being damaged, navigable waterways are being blocked and water quality is deteriorating.

Land degradation and changed river ecology caused by inland farming are also challenges which need to be addressed to ensure production has a minimal effect on natural biodiversity and ecosystems. Commercial aquaculture posses a particular set of problems, with large-scale production and limited management in some instances leading to critical environmental dames and irreversible ecosystem degradation.

The Impacts of external environment on aquaculture may be positive or negative. Nutrient enrichment of water bodies may provide nutrients beneficial to aquaculture production in some extensive culture systems such as seaweeds and molluscs. However, excessive loadings with urban and industrial wastes can have severe consequences for aquaculture operations, particularly shellfish culture, when exposed to contamination with toxic pollutants, pathogens and phycotoxins. With the increasing aquatic pollution and physical degradation of aquatic habitats by other developments, aquaculturists can face risks of mass mortalities of farmed stock, disease outbreaks, product contamination and reduced availability of wild seed or broodstock.

TRENDS IN LAND DEGRADATION

Major trends related to land degradation and agricultural productivity globally include:

- Loss of water for agriculture and reallocation to cities and industries.
- Reduction in land quality in many different ways, leading to reduced food supplies, lower agricultural incomes, increased costs to farmers and consumers, and a deterioration of water catchment functions.
- Reduction in water quality due to pollution, water-borne diseases and disease vectors.
- Loss of farmland through conversion to non-agricultural purposes.

On average globally, only half of the nutrients that crops take from the soil are replaced, and the removal of the other half slowly depletes the soils, often to levels where productivity becomes impaired. Nutrients contained in harvested products and in food flow from farmland to settlements, and from rural areas to cities. Most of the nutrients in food consumed in cities are neither recycled nor otherwise re-used, but either accumulate unproductively or pollute rivers and seas. Urbanization, international trade and negligence of the environmental cost of soil nutrient removal reinforce this process.

LAND DEGRADATION AND WATER PRODUCTIVITY

The potential gain in water productivity through land management interventions, particularly to improve soil quality, is large and underappreciated. It is estimated that water productivity in irrigated systems can be improved by between 20 and 40%, primarily through land management approaches. In rain-fed systems in developing countries, where average crop production is very low and many soils suffer from nutrient depletion, erosion and other degradation problems, potential improvement in water productivity is even higher and may be as high as 100% in many systems. When these gains are achieved by reducing unproductive losses of water (primarily evaporation) or increasing transpiration efficiency, they represent water productivity gains at even larger scales than the farm. This potential for improvement is higher than that which can be expected through the genetic improvement of crops or water management alone in the near future. The mitigation of land degradation is therefore central to increasing water productivity and thereby preserving both terrestrial and aquatic ecosystems and their accompanying services.

STATUS OF LAND DEGRADATION IN ARID REGION IN INDIA

The land degradation under different land uses in the arid region mainly the desert of western Rajasthan and Gujarat, covering 28.5 million ha area, was mapped using remote-sensing technique. It revealed that about 76% area of western Rajasthan was affected by wind erosion, encompassing all the major land uses but mostly croplands and dunes/sandy areas, while water erosion affected about 2% area (mostly in croplands and scrublands), salinization about 2% (mostly in croplands) and vegetation degradation nearly 3% (especially in scrublands and forests). Mining activities have spoiled so far only 0.10% area, and degraded rocky areas covered 1% area. About 18% area was severely degraded and 66% slightly to moderately, while 16% area was not affected by degradation. The mapping showed that about 1.3 million ha area of croplands in western Rajasthan was under severe wind erosion (mostly un-irrigated). In arid Gujarat, water erosion was the most dominant process, affecting about 43% of the total area (mostly in croplands), followed by salinity (38%), while vegetation degradation (10%) and wind erosion (5%) covered smaller areas. About 44% area was severely affected, 53% slightly to moderately and 3% not affected. Large area under severe degradation was due to the huge area of the Great Rann of Kutch and the Little Rann that have high natural salinity.

Increasing salinisation of land and waterways in agricultural areas due to irrigation and deforest-ation is a global problem. Any aquaculture development using saline water must not increase salinisation and must minimize the release of nutrients to waterways. Consequently, the disposal of saline water from aquaculture systems needs to be carefully considered.

CAUSES OF LAND DEGRADATION

The causes of the degradation can be either natural or human. The natural causes includes earth quakes, tsunamis, droughts, avalanche, landslides and mud flow, volcanic eruptions, flood, tornado and wild fire (Reynolds, 2001). As the natural causes are uncontrollable, the human induced degradation is very important in view of sustainability. Climate change, as result of human intervention over ecology is another reason for the degradation (Barrow, 1991). Land clearance and deforestation is the one of the major reason for land degradation (Reynolds *et al.*, 2007). Many other operations like overgrazing by live stock, in appropriate irrigation and over drafting, urban sprawl and commercial development, land pollution including industrial development, vehicle-off loading, quarrying can also leads to land degradation. The vulnerability of the land like low level area, cost line area is more susceptible for degradation (Salvati & Zitti, 2009). Land degradation can leads to many issues like soil erosion, soil acidification, soil alkalinisation, soil salination, soil water logging and destruction of the structure of soil which will directly effects the fish production in the culture tanks because good aquaculture practices depends on good soil and water quality parameters. It has direct impact on the agriculture and environmental sustainability like reduced productivity, damage to basic resource and ecosystem, food insecurity, loss of biodiversity, climate change and land slide mitigation, and it can leads to a tremendous economic loss (Wasson, 1987). Desertification also leads to migration which will be threat to political economic instability (Zika & Erb, 2009). Land reclamation is the process of recovering the land that has lost its productivity and also make it use again or creation of new land from sea or river for the need of human activities.

NATURAL CAUSES OF LAND DEGRADATION

The land degradation can be either by natural or by human influenced activities. The natural causes include earthquakes, tsunamis, droughts, avalanche, landslides and mud flows, volcanic eruption, flood, tornado, etc. Research shows that direct impact of the earthquake on the land degradation and affected the agriculture in ancient period (Leroy *et al*., 2010) which leads to drastic changes in agriculture for a few years. The earthquake in 2004 in the region of Sumatra of Indonesia has caused degradation of agricultural land. The earthquake in Sichuan, China in 2008 has destroyed 0.4 million hectares of high yield rice cultivating land and the texture shows sandy to silty clay loam (Gang, 2008; Hulugalle *et al*., 2009). Drought is another reason, but quantification of its impact is most difficult factors compared to other natural disasters like tsunami or hurricanes. The effect of drought can vary from region to region even though; they are identical in intensity, duration, because of change in social characteristics. Soil can loss its structure aggregation because of drying out of top soil. This dried up top soil can easily be blown away as a result of wind and rain. So it effects the vegetation and agricultural productivity (Singh *et al*., 2007; Zhao *et al*., 2008).

HUMAN INDUCED CAUSES

Many human activities are leads to land degradation directly or indirectly, include deforestation, overgrazing by live stock, irrigation practices, urban sprawl and commercial development (Chomitz *et al*., 2007) pollution from industries, quarrying, and mining activities. The indirect activities included pressure on agricultural intensification and population growth. Increase in the population increases the need of food. About 220 million hectares of tropical forest have been degraded 1975 and 1990 mainly for food production (UNDP, 2004).

CLIMATE CHANGE

Changes is earth's atmosphere have large influence on land. Since the industrial revolution it is estimated that the global carbon emission to the atmosphere is about 136±55 GT (Gigatonne = 1 billion tone) (Anon. 2000) due to land use change and soil cultivation, with depletion of organic soil pool is about 78±12 GT (Lal, 2004). The terrestrial vegetation depends on temperature and precipitation. With decrease in rain fall, vegetation becomes thinner. High temperature and low precipitation leads to low organic matter production in soil and rapid oxidation. This leads to low aggregation and is vulnerable for erosion by wind and water. In Africa, 25% and 22% of land is prone to water and wind erosion, respectively (Reich *et al*., 2001).

The climate stress is accounting for 62.5% of the all the land stress there. Rain fall is the important factor that leads to land degradation. Less and over rain fall affect the land either by desertification or excess, this will lead to soil erosion. Other factors like flood and drought brought by climate also leads to land degradation. At most of the dry land climate, there will be minimum clouds, which will increase the intensity of the solar radiation, which eventually leads to land heating and rise in the air temperature (WMO, 2005).

DEFORESTATION

In deforestation process, certain trees are cut down and or burned for human use like timber, wood fire, industrialization and urbanization. Over population, force deforestation by demanding land for shelter and agriculture. Demand of agricultural is the one of main reason for deforestation (Kaimowitz & Angelsen, 1988). As per FAO, each year 13 million hectares, about 0.18% (FAO, 2005a) of world forest are lost by deforestation. An overview of deforestation figures around the globe has been given in Table 9.2, which shows that how serious is the deforestation. It can also reduce the content of water in soil, because fast evaporation of the soil water and dried atmosphere and less rain which will make our river system dry up and it will affect our natural fish biodiversity and germplasm as well. Therefore, deforestation will lead to soil erosion. The top layer of soil can easily be washed out and makes the soil unfertile and un-productive as well.

Table 9.2: An Overview of Deforestation Figures Around the Globe (FAO, 2005b)

Global Region	Period	Net Loss Hectare/Year
South America	2000-2005	4.3 million
Africa	2000-2005	4.0 million
Oceania	2000-2005	356000
North & Central America	2000-2005	333000
Asia	1990s	800000
Europe	1990s	Expanding

OVERGRAZING

Over grazing is abuse of grassland, due to decrease in grassland and increase in livestock numbers. The plant density will be reduced by overgrazing. It will not give the time for re-grow of the plants. It will results in soil infiltration, accelerated run off and soil erosion. The soil fertility is developed by action of microorganism. Overgrazing can reduce their action and also it increases the concentration of ammonium-N and nitrate-N which are toxic to root at higher concentrations (Czeglédi &Radácsi, 2005).

IRRIGATION PRACTICE

The quality of water using for the irrigation is more important. If the water has high salinity, it will accumulate and leads to desertification. Irrigational practice which leads to cracking the lands or bypass flow, by flooding will influence the soil structure and nitrate leaching. The crack developed during the irrigation may not close properly, can leave a U-shaped trace and upon drying these cracks can expand, will cause soil shrinkage.

URBAN SPRAWL AND COMMERCIAL DEVELOPMENT

Urban sprawl is defined as the physical pattern of low-density expansion of large urban areas mainly into the surrounding agricultural areas (European Environment Agency, 2006). Urban sprawl is consequence of increasing urban population. As the urban population increases, the infrastructure requirement like transportation, water, sewage and facilities such as housing, school, commerce, health, recreation will also increases (Ujoh *et al.*, 2010). It consumes agricultural productive areas, so the green vegetation will be replaced by concretes and wastes. It reduces the biomass production and destroys the productive land, leads to land degradation. For the development of infrastructure like roads and metro system, electricity and other requirement will leads to the destruction of fertile land (Geist & Lambin, 2002). In the developing countries like India, the major issue is lack good governance and administration in local bodies. Lack of information, keeping system and traceability of the record, is also an important issue for the governance (Sudhira & Ramachandra, 2007).

POLLUTION FROM INDUSTRIES

The industrial operation also causes the land degradation. It can be either from the waste from the industries or the exploitation of the resources. The large scale commercial farming can cause soil erosion, land salination or loss of nutrients. Exploitation of the water and land resources is the effect of green revolution. To increase the productivity and yield, application of chemical fertilizers, different pesticides causes the contaminated water and land. Whereas intensive agriculture and irrigation can contributes salination, alkalization and water logging (Indian Ministry of Finance, 1999). The small industries releasing the waste directly to the open areas will leads to serious issue in the future leads to environmental pollution. The waste may contain serious chemicals which can degrade the land fertility and productivity. The non recyclable compounds like poly bags will destroy the land capacity of the water intake, if they are dumped off without any care. They remain for several years. Many industrial wastes like solvents can kills the favorable micro organism may require to keep the soil fertility.

MINING AND QUARRYING ACTIVITIES

Mining is done for the extraction of the mineral deposit like iron, gold, silver, etc. and quarrying for generally the granite for construction works. Due to this excavation process alter the structure of the land, stacking of top soil, loss of soil due to dumping the mine wastes and also overburden cause lying on the land after mining. Tailings, the leftover material after purification of the ore like slag, slime, and leach residues are also cause land degradation (Vagholikar & Moghe, 2003). Stone and sand quarrying cause the loss of fertile top soil, degradation of forest and land. Mining also leads to fragmentation of forest and land often because diminishing the vegetation surrounded. Often the mines may be remote from the general transportation facility, required new roads construction to mining area, all leads to land degradation (Singh *et al.*, 2003; Singh & Asgher, 2003).

AGRICULTURAL INTENSIFICATION

Ever demand of the food and reducing agricultural land along with increasing population, leading to agricultural intensification by using advanced technologies including high yield crop, fertilization, irrigation, pesticides, etc. has increased the yield of production from the limited land. The frequent hoeing and plough of the soil will leads to erosion. The intensive farming by many number crops in year will cause for nutrient depletion, especially area where the nutrients are limited. So the use fertilizers are necessary, as consequences the soil become more acidic (Raut *et al.*, 2010).

EFFECTS OF LAND DEGRADATION

The effects of land degradation includes accelerated soil erosion by wind and water, soil acidification, soil alkalinisation, soil salination, soil water logging, destruction of the structure of soil (Eswaran *et al.*, 2001; Scherr & Yadav, 2001; Lu *et al.*, 2007). Soil erosion is the process of take up, transportation and deposit of soil from one place to another. The transportation media can be wind, water or ice. The main causes of increased erosion are industrial agriculture, deforestation and urban sprawl. Usage of tillage in industrial agriculture will remove the top vegetation and leads to erosion (Angelsen & Kaimowitz, 2001; Angelsen, 2007). It can be controlled under sustainable practices like terrace building, conservation tillage practice and tree planting. Soil acidification is the effect of reducing the pH of soil. This can commonly by acids such as sulfuric acid, nitric acid, or compounds like aluminium sulfate or compounds from fertilizer nitrogen like ammonia. The major reason for soil acidity are from nitrogen leaching process, addition of excess nitrogenous fertilizers and build up of organic matter. If the water containing high amount sodium bicarbonate will increases the pH of the soil. Soil salination is a natural phenomenon, the soil with high level of salt, climate favourable accumulation and can be by human activities like aquaculture activities, land clearing or salting the road. Soil water logging, saturation of soil with water is another effect of land degradation. Irrigation can change the soil structure. The porosity can be blocked by clay during irrigation. High level of sodium content also can cause change soil aggregation.

IMPLICATIONS AND EFFECTS

Reduced Productivity

As the land quality reduced as effect of land degradation the productivity also reduces. Impacts of change in soil quality like erosion are leads to less productive land. Water erosion is most common phenomenon which is leading to low productivity of the land. As result of soil erosion the soil fertility gradually decreases.

MIGRATION

Land degradation will leads to migration of the people from one are to another, especially the dry area to near place either for short term of long term. It can lead to suboptimal land-use and further degradation of land. It can also create social, economic and environmental imbalance.

DAMAGE TO BASIC RESOURCES AND ECOSYSTEMS

Land is a non renewable resource, by degrading it creating damage to the basic resource and ecosystem by changing the quality of the land, temporarily or permanently, creating an imbalance to the eco system. The leached nitrogen can contaminate the water sources can make it as non drinkable as high level of nitrate or it can leads to development of phytoplankton on excess level, and then reduces the dissolved oxygen level.

FOOD INSECURITY

Land degradation will leads to reduction in productivity or turn the land in to non productive land. As the problem is more common in developing countries, increasing population along with reduced productivity will leads to food insecurity.

LOSS OF BIODIVERSITY

The process like deforestation and desertification process will leads to loss of flora and fauna. Most of the species cannot adapt in to new modified environment. Change in pH of the soil can leads to destruction of the microbes in the soil really needed for the fertilization process of the soil.

ADAPTATION

The person needs to adapt in to the new environment as consequence of land degradation. The availability of resources such as water, land will be reduced as result of degradation process.

SOLUTIONS AND REMEDIES

Management of Deforestation

Afforestation: Planting of tree is the best options to make forest in a non forest land are the one of the best option to reduce the consequences of deforestation. It can reduce the soil erosion.

Use of timber alternate: Use of mud brick for the construction instead of timbers for land reclamation.

Eco forest: System which cut only the specific tree required, create minimal damage to that particular forest area.

Green business: This includes paper recycling and using wood alternatives.

MANAGEMENT ON OVERGRAZING

Management practices like water development, placement of salt and supplements, fertilizer application, fencing, burning can control the overgrazing. By control the gap between the grazing and giving time to for re-vegetation also helps to reduce overgrazing. Keeping the livestock not more than 4 days in paddock, can reduce over grazing. The density of the livestock in a particular grazing area also needs to be controlled (Czeglédi & Radácsi, 2005).

MANAGING IRRIGATION

Irrigation system can be controlled like drip irrigation to reduce soil erosion. Using high and low salt water was most effective in maintaining the productive capacity of the clay soil. Often high irrigation leads to leach of nutrient and top fertile soil along with that water. Management of irrigation is an essential factor to keep the quality of soil (Crescimanno, 2001).

MANAGING URBAN SPRAWL

The urban planning is the most important factor, to control the urban sprawl. Appropriate government policies can also control the urban sprawling. Policies appropriate to control the urban sprawling are necessary. Fertile field near by the urbane area need to be protected by the local government rules, because of the tendency of converting such land for commercial purpose will bring more income than agriculture (Ifatimehin & Musa, 2008). So, effective policy is required to control such usage of fertile land. There should be a proper waste management system dumping of these waste generated as part of urban sprawling will degrade the land, can cause soil salinity, acidity and loss of it vegetative properties. By using the digital technologies like Geographic Information Systems (GIS), mapping and monitoring will be useful for monitoring purpose for the local authorities and governments (Sujatha *et al.*, 2000; Haboudane *et al.*, 2002; Thiam, 2003; Wessels *et al.*, 2004; FAO, 2003). Another possibility is to use System Dynamics (SD) framework, which capture the stock and flow. Development of models using Cellular Automate (CA) is helpful to visualize the impact of urban sprawl (Sudhira & Ramachandra, 2007).

MANAGING MINING AND QUARRYING

The impact can be reduced by proper management of mining process, using advanced technologies rather than conventional methods. After mining by proper back filling, spreading the soil back over the top, the land can be reclaimed (Elliott *et al.*, 2003). The refilled land after mining can be used for planting trees. The top soil can be stacked if not used and can be used later for plantation. It can be adequately protected from leaching out during raining. The use of geo-textiles, the permeable fabrics which separate, filter, reinforce, protect or drain the soil, will help the re-vegetation process (Sharma *et al.*, 2004). Policies for controlling mining activities depend on the geographical location and threat to the land can be implemented to control mining and quarrying process.

MANAGING AGRICULTURAL INTENSIFICATION

Agricultural intensification need to be managed properly to reduce the environmental effect. This can be done through proper education of the farmers. The intensification is necessary for especially in developing countries for the food security. It can be adopted with ecological friendly appropriate technologies. Implementation of integrated pest and nutrient management, policies for environmental taxes for nitrogen fertilizers, high yielding varieties, terracing, legume intercropping, contour hedgerows, cover crops, minimum tillage, selection of appropriate crops, organic and inorganic fertilizer use etc can be done for sustainable agricultural intensification (Raut *et al.*, 2010).

LAND RECLAMATION

Recovery of land's productivity, which might have lost during the past or during the creation of new land from sea or river, is called as land reclamation. The requirements are land may be damaged due to natural hazards like fire, earthquake, tsunami etc. or by human activity like poor farming methods. The land with high water content, waterlogged land, which is not suitable for agricultural activities. The increasing population in urban coastal cities, where the land scarcity is huge, it is difficult to find new land. By land reclamation it can increase available arable land or it expands the carrying capacity, control of overcrowd in urban areas, economy through new industries (Soni, 2003; Singh, 2002). The world's largest land reclamation is done at Dubai, The Palm Jumeirah, 31-square-kilometer island group costing US$ 14 billion.

India has extensive salinisation, having about 7 million ha of salinised land. Salinisation is Extensive in the Indus-Ganga Plains of North-western India and in the States of Haryana, Punjab, Rajasthan and Gujarat. The Western part of this area (Rajasthan) is arid, and the rivers are intermittent. Smaller but significant occurrences are found in irrigation areas in southern India. Surface water quality in north-western India is generally good, but ground water quality is variable. Water salinity generally increases from north to south and with depth. Very saline water (16 g/L) can be found below 200 m.

Ground waters of sufficient salinity for inland saline aquaculture are available in each country discussed, and in very large supply in waterlogged areas on deep alluvium in Pakistan, north-western India and the North China Plain. When pumped for vertical drainage or to supplement surface water supply, the water is discharged to surface drainage systems; evaporation ponds are rarely used in Asia. The extraction of saline (> 3 g/L) ground water is undesirable because of its contribution to downstream salinisation of surface water. Inland saline aquaculture could provide additional income by using water associated with lowering water tables, increasing water supplies or salt-mining, but from an agricultural and resource management point of view it appears too risky to encourage deliberate extraction of saline ground water in inland areas solely for aquaculture.

Researchers have observed that opportunities for large-scale saline aquaculture using saline ground waters appear limited. Similarly, the use of saline ground water for aquaculture is likely to have little effect on the extent of land and stream salinity. There may be small-scale opportunities for farmers to diversify their income sources and use the income generated to offset the costs of other remedial measures for land salinisation.

IMPROVING DEGRADED LAND BY WATERSHED RESTORATION IN INDIA

In 1989, World Bank sanctioned a project loan for an amount of US$100 million on integrated watershed management for the hills of northern India. The project which covered states of Punjab, Himachal Pradesh, Harayana and Jammu and Kashmir, was executed with the help of personnel from the departments of agriculture, horticulture, forestry and animal husbandry. Administrative, financial and technical functions were all vested with the project authority to avoid compartmental or fragmented solutions to achieve an integrated approach. Funds were earmarked for training and for participatory on-farm research.

(a) Joint management policy

Watershed-based solutions to land degradation involve the simultaneous management of private, common, arable and non-arable land resources. Local communities utilize many different resources but in India forest policy, used to be remote from the people who were not involved in their management. Experience at the Central Soil and Water Conservation Research and Training Institute (CSWCRTI), in Dehradun, has encouraged about 50 per cent of Indian states to declare a joint forest management policy which is community-friendly or participatory.

(b) People's participation

In 1978, the CSWCRTI began to introduce resource conservation through integrated watershed management, involving a mix of structural and vegetative measures with the help of local communities. Initially, people's involvement was low but this was built up and the projects were ultimately handed over to officially-registered community organisations. The open grazing was eliminated through 'social' fencing and biomass productivity was doubled or even tripled. The organisations operated independently of both government and local authorities, deriving their income from the sale of grass, harvested water, fuel wood and membership fees. Funds were spent in maintaining project structures, paving village roads, constructing village halls and starting up veterinary hospitals. In some cases, they leased government forest lands to increase their incomes.

CAUSES OF MANGROVE DAMAGE AND NEED FOR CONSERVATION

The value of mangroves has gone unrecognized for many years and the forests are disappearing in many parts of the world. These impacts are likely to continue and worsen, as human populations expand further into the mangroves. In regions where mangrove removal has produced significant environmental problems, efforts are underway to launch mangrove agro-forestry and agriculture projects. Mangrove systems require intensive care to save threatened areas. So far, conservation and management efforts lag behind the destruction; there is still much to learn about proper management and sustainable harvesting of mangrove forests. Even where efforts have been made to slow the destruction, remaining forests have a number of problems. In some areas, the health and productivity of the forests have declined significantly. The causes of these tragic losses differ from habitat to habitat but are generally tied directly or indirectly to human activities. Individual study is required to determine the most effective remedial measures. Where degraded areas are being regenerated, continued monitoring and thorough assessment must be done to help us understand the recovery process. This knowledge will help us develop strategies to effectively rehabilitate degraded mangrove habitats over the world.

AQUACULTURE PRACTICES IN DRY LANDS

Aquaculture in dry lands is inherently advantageous to dry land agri-culture because although aquatic organisms live in water they do not transpire it, so water losses from aquaculture are predomi-nately from evaporation rather than raised evapo-transpiration. Also, many more aquatic species than terrestrial crop spe-cies are tolerant of salinity and even thrive in it. Thus, dry land aquaculture can prosper on fossil aquifers whose high salinity greatly curtails their use by dry land agriculture. When dry land aquaculture borrows the technology of dry land greenhouses, water conservation is even greater than it is in agricultural greenhouses due to zero transpiration of aquatic organisms. At the same time, dry land aquaculture does not compete for water with dry land agriculture due to the diver-gent salinity tolerances of terrestrial plants and aquatic organisms (Kolkovsky *et al.*, 2003). Since dry land aquaculture is always more economic on land than dry land agriculture, land use as well as water use efficiencies are high. Thus, dry land aquaculture, like dry land controlled-environment cash crop agriculture, does not depend on local ecosystem services and need not cause desertifi-cation.

Dry land aquaculture is based on aquatic animals and plants or some combination of both. The produc-tivity of aquatic animals is not light and $C0_2$ dependent; hence the costs of feeding the animals are greater than those of fertilizing the plants. However, there is an added cost of water filtration due to the enrichment of the water by the surplus organic load of animal feed and animal excretions. This cost can be reduced by integrating animal and plant aquaculture, in which algae thrive on the animal waste-enriched water or the enriched water can be used for irrigation of crops. Plant aquaculture is advantageous on animal aquaculture in that feeding is not required and organic load is not a problem. Also, given that most aquatic plants are either very small or unicellular, their growth is much faster than that of terrestrial plant crops and the ratio of harvested to non-harvested biomass of the crop is much higher than that of terrestrial plants.

Dry land aquaculture of both plants and animals is more advan-tageous than aquaculture elsewhere due to the abundance of light for aquatic plants and of winter warmth for both plants and animals. An added benefit is the higher availability and hence the lower price of land in dry lands than in non-dry lands and the reduced competition with agriculture on land in the dry lands. Most of the products of dry land aquaculture are cash crops, such as ornamental fish, high-quality edible fish and crustaceans, and industrially valuable bio-chemicals produced by micro-algae, such as pigments, food additives, health food supplements, and pharmaceutical products.

CREATING LEGAL FRAMEWORK FOR CONSERVATION

In soil conservation the law has far too often been seen only as a means of enforcing unpopular measures such as the protection of forest and grazing areas. These measures, which have often deprived the rural poor of their livelihoods, have become very unpopular with the general public and have almost inevitably failed. This has led many to the unfortunate conclusion that the use of legislation is counterproductive in land conservation and rehabilitation programme. Innovative legislation can offer governments an important tool for promoting conservation. A thorough review of all relevant legislation is an essential element of a national conservation strategy. Where necessary, existing legislation should be revised and new legislation introduced. Emphasis should be placed on the introduction of measures which will encourage more productive and sustainable forms of land use, and effective stakeholder participation.

REVIEWING WORKFORCE AND TRAINING

The requirements of staff, training and facilities should all be reviewed as an important step in the development of a national programme. While doing this, special attention should be given to:

- Training technicians in how to involve rural communities in planning and managing their own conservation programmes, as well as the latest conservation techniques;
- Incorporating conservation as a vital part of all farmer training courses; and
- Organizing short seminars for administrators to sensitize them to conservation and the important role that they have in national programmes.

The importance of these needs has already been recognized by the Asia Soil Conservation Network for the Humid Tropics (ASOCON), which has promoted training for conservation staff in the region and is able to provide information on request.

RESEARCH NEEDS

As the general approach to land conservation and reclamation changes, there is a need to identify research needs, particularly adaptive research in conservation practices. These must be suited to local conditions, easily integrated into existing farming systems and readily acceptable to the land users because of the tangible benefits that they offer. Traditional conservation practices often offer a starting point for research as farmers are inclined to accept new ideas which are based on already tried practices. There are many well-known traditional conservation practices in the region, ranging from the use of log contour fences in Papua New Guinea to bench terracing in Java and a variety of agro-forestry systems in the Philippines and Sri Lanka. As populations increase and the pressure on the land intensify, traditional systems need to be adapted to the changing requirements of land users. Once research priorities have been identified, it is necessary to consider whether the research is best conducted nationally or regionally. As most countries in the region have limited facilities and a shortage of trained research workers, it is necessary to ask regional networks like Asia Soil Conservation Network for the Humid Tropics (ASOCON), to investigate conservation issues, which is common to many countries.

DEVELOPING CONSERVATION PROGRAMMES

Once government policy and strategy have been finalized, programmes need to be developed. These plans should be flexible and designed to be periodically reviewed and updated. Generally, national conservation plans need to be developed at three levels as mentioned below:

- At the national level, where government policy is combined with physical, social and economic data to produce a general national conservation programme for the next 10 to 20 years. This programme should be published as a formal government document and incorporated in the national development plan where it forms a framework for subsequent legislation, administrative action and budgeting for conservation.
- At the district or province level, more specific and detailed programmes need to be developed, based on the national programme but in the form of rolling multi-year plans which can be reviewed and updated annually. An important aspect of these plans should be the identification of the specific inputs from different government and donor agencies.
- At the local level, programmes must be framed to the individual requirements of the community and developed in collaboration with the

communities themselves. Members of the ASOCON network have already been involved in developing a methodology and planning system at this level. Once formulated, these local level plans should be referred back to the district level and provision made for technical support and any other inputs that may be needed for their implementation.

The predicted increase in the loss of land as a function of sea level rise should impact both shrimp farming and finfish culture. The adaptation measure recommended for shrimp farming entails integration Climate Change and Climate Variability (CCCV) impacts and adaptation responses into the EIA process as well as the preservation of the mangrove zone between the sea and farm infrastructure. The adaptation measures for finfish culture include the definition and implementation of a zoning scheme for cage culture and other aspects of sub-tidal aquaculture. Climate change and/or climate variability, together with the other stresses on the environment, produces actual and potential impacts. These impacts trigger efforts of mitigation, to remove the cause of the impact, or adaptation to modify the impacts. Climate change generally will exacerbate existing problems including flooding and degradation of ecosystems.

CONCLUSION

Declining of the productive capacity of the land is a serious global issue as it affects the social, economical and environmental balances across the globe. Land degradation can be caused by natural phenomenon, but human induced land degradation is most dominant cause of climate change. The population growth also leads to land degradation indirectly. As results of these human activities it can leads to soil erosion by wind and water, soil acidification, soil alkalinisation, soil salination, soil water logging, destruction of the structure of soil. The implications of the land degradation include reduced productivity, migration, damage to basic resources and ecosystems, food insecurity, loss of biodiversity and adaptation. The land degradations can be controlled by managing different human activities such as deforestation, use of timber alternate, eco forest, etc. Managing grazing practices, land management, irrigation management, control on urban sprawl and control and management on mining quarrying operations are the few solutions for reduce or prevent land degradation. Sustainable agriculture & aquaculture intensification can be implemented to reduce the ecological effect without affecting the productivity. It is necessary to have local and global policies and regulations to control the land degradation.

Land degradation is driven by the complex socio-political and economic context in which land use occurs; the same is true of solutions to land degradation. Smallholder agricultural systems are an important intervention point for measures aimed at preventing or mitigating land degradation in the developing world. Integrated solutions that support participa-tion in sustainable land management are needed to achieve balance in food produc-tion, poverty alleviation, and resource con-servation.

Aquaculture has a strong tie with the environment through its prerequisite for good water quality. Not only can it provide considerable benefits to the community in terms of jobs and economic opportunities, but it can also act as a sentinel for some of the less observable effects of human activity that affect our water catchments. Aquaculture development that is planned with good-practice principles in mind must be sustainable if it is to be viable. The scope for integrating aquaculture activities into remedial solutions for salinisation of inland agricultural lands provides a new frontier for the modern systems approach to agriculture.

REFERENCES

Adams CR, Eswaran H (2000). Global Land Resources in the Context of Food and Environmental Security, *In*: Gawande SP (Ed.), Advances in Land Resources Management for the 20th Century. New Delhi: Soil Conservation Society of India, pp. 35-50.

Angelsen A (2007). Forest Cover Change in Space and Time: Combining von Thünen and the Forest Transition. World Bank Policy Research Working Paper WPS 4117. World Bank, Washington D.C.

Angelsen A, Kaimowitz D (2001). Agricultural Technologies and Tropical Deforestation. Center for International Forestry Research (CIFOR), Bogor, Indonesia and CABI Publishing, Oxon, UK, p. 422.

Anon. (2000). Intergovernmental Panel on Climate Change, *Land Use, Land Use Change and Forestry*, Cambridge Univ. Press, Cambridge, pp.181-281.

Bai ZG, Dent DL (2006) Global Assessment of Land Degradation and Improvement: Pilot Study in Kenya. Report 2006/01, ISRIC-World Soil Information, Wageningen, p. 42.

Bai ZG, Dent DL, Olsson L, Schaepman ME (2008). Global Assessment of Land Degradation and Improvement 1. Identification by Remote Sensing. *Report 2008/01*, ISRIC,Wageningen.

Barrow CJ, (1991). Land Degradation: Development and Breakdown of Terrestrial Environments. Cambridge University Press, Cambridge, p. 295.

Chomitz KM, Buys P, De Luca G, Thomas TS, Wertz-Kanounnikoff S (2007). At Loggerheads? Agricultural Expansion, Poverty Reduction, and Environment in the Tropical Forests. World Bank, Jakarta, Indonesia, p. 284.

Crescimanno G (2001). Irrigation Practices Affecting Land Degradation in Sicily, Ph.D Thesis. Wageningen University, p. 169.

Czeglédi L, Radácsi A (2005). Overutilization of Pastures by livestock. Acta pascuorum (Grassland studies) 3: 29-36.

Dregne HE, Chou NT (1994). Global Desertification Dimensions and Costs, *In*: Dregne HE (Ed.), *Degradation and Restoration of Arid Lands*, Lubbock: Texas Technical University.

Elliott S, Navakitbumrung P, Kuarak C, Zangkum S, Anusarnsunthorn V, Blakesley D (2003). Selecting Framework Tree Species for Restoring Seasonally Dry Tropical Forests in Northern Thailand Based on Field Performance. Forest Ecology and Management 184: 177-191.

Eswaran H, Lal R, Reich PF (2001). Land Degradation: An Overview, *In*: Bridges EM, Hannam ID, Oldeman LR, Penning de Vries FWT, Scherr SJ, Sombatpanit S (Eds.), Response to Land Degradation, Science Publishers, Inc: Enfield, New Hampshire, USA, pp. 20-35.

European Environment Agency, EEA Report No. 10 (2006),_http://reports.eea.europa.eu/eea_report_2006_10/en/eea_report_10_2006.pdf.

FAO (2003). Agro-Ecological Zoning and GIS Applications in Asia with Special Rmphasis on Land Degradation Assessment in Dry Lands (LADA), *In*: Proceedings of a Regional Workshop, Bangkok, Thailand, 10-14 November (2005a), p. 137.

FAO (2005a). Global Forest Resource Assessment 2005: Progress Toward Sustainable Forest Management, FAO Forestry Paper 147, FAO, Rome, Italy, p. 320.

FAO (2005b). Deforestation Continues at an Alarming Rate. FAO News Room. 14 November, www.fao.org/newsroom/en/news/2005/1000127/index.html.

Gang H (2008). Environmental Challenges After China's Sichuan Earthquake. World Resources Institute. Accessed October 25, 2010. http://earthtrends.wri.org/updates/node/316.

Geist H, Lambin E (2002). Proximate Causes and Underlying Driving Forces of Tropical Deforestation. Bioscience 52(2): 143-150.

Haboudane D, Bonn F, Royer A, Sommer S, Mehl W (2002). Land Degradation and Erosion Risk Mapping by Fusion of Spectrally-based Information and Digital Geomorphometric Attributes. International Journal of Remote Sensing 23: 3795-3820.

Hulugalle NR, Jaya R, Luther GC, Ferizal M, Daud S, Yatiman I, Yufniati ZA, Feriyanti F, Tamrin HB (2009). Physical Properties of Tsunami-affected Soils in Aceh, Indonesia: 2½ Years After, Catena 77: 224-231.

Ifatimehin OO, Musa SD (2008). Application of Geoinformatic Technology in Evaluating Urban Agriculture and Urban poverty in Lokoja. Niger. J. Geogr. Environ. 1: 21-23.

Indian Ministry of Finance (1999). The Underlying Causes of Environmental Degradation. Economic Survey, pp. 98-99. http://indiabudget.nic.in/es98-99/chap1104.pdf.

Kaimowitz D, Angelsen A (1988). Economic Models of Tropical Deforestation — A Review. Center for International Forestry Research (CIFOR), Bogor, Indonesia and CABI Publishing, Indonesia, p. 139.

Kolkovsky S, Hulata, G, Simon Y, Segev R, Koren A (2003) Integration of Agri-Aquaculture Systems-The Israeli Experience, *In*: Gooley GJ, Gavine FM (Eds.) Integrated Agri-Aquaculture Systems, A Resource Handbook for Australian Industry Development,), Rural Industries Research and Development Corporation, RIRDC Publication, Kingston, ACT, Australia, pp. 14-23.

Lal R (2004). Soil Carbon Sequestration Impacts on Global Climate Change and Food Security. Science 304: 1623-1627.

Leroy SAG, Marco S, Bookman R, Miller CS (2010). Impact of Earthquakes on Agriculture during the Roman-Byzantine Period, Quaternary Research 73: 191-200.

Lu D, Batistella M, Mausel P, Moran E (2007). Mapping and Monitoring Land Degradation Risks in the Western Brazilian Amazon Using Multitemporal Landsat TM/ETM + images. Land Degradation & Develop 18: 41-54.

Mantel S and van Engelen VWP (1997). The Impact of Land and Degradation on Food Productivity- Case Studies of Uruguay, Argentina and Kenya. Volume 1: Main Report. Report 97/01, International Soil Reference and Information Centre (ISRIC), Wageningen, p. 52.

Raut N, Sitaula BK, Bajracharya RM (2010). Agricultural Intensification: Linking with Livelihood Improvement and Environmental Degradation in Mid-hills of Nepal. The Journal of Agriculture and Environment 11: 83-91.

Reich PF, Numbem ST, Almaraz RA, Eswaran H (2001). Land Resource Stresses and Desertification in Africa, *In*: Bridges EM, Hannam ID, Oldeman LR, Pening FWT, de Vries SJ, Scherr SJ, Sompatpanit S (Eds.), Responses to Land Degradation. Proceedings of the 2nd International Conference on Land Degradation and Desertification, Khon Kaen, Thailand. New Delhi, Oxford University Press.

Reynolds JF (2001). New Initiatives on Desertification and Land Degradation, LUCC Newsletter No. 7.

Reynolds JF, Smith DMS, Lambin EF, Turner II BL, Mortimore M, Batterbury SPJ, Downing TE, Dowlatabadi H, Fernández RJ, Herrick JE, Huber-Sannwald E, Jiang H, Leemans R, Lynam T, Maestre FT, Ayarza M, Walker B (2007). Global Desertification: Building a Science for Dryland Development. Science 316 (5826): 847-851.

Salvati L, Zitti M (2009). Assessing the Impact of Ecological and Economic Factors on Land Degradation Vulnerability Through Multiway Analysis. Ecological Indicators 9: 357-363.

Scherr SJ, Yadav S (2001). Land Degradation in the Developing World: Issues and Policy Options for 2020 (Chapter 21), *In*: Pinstrup-Andersen P, Lorch RJ (Eds.), The Unfinished Agenda: Perspectives on Overcoming Hunger, Poverty and Environmental Degradation, International Food Policy Research Institute: Washington, DC, pp. 133-138.

Sharma KD, Kumar P, Gough LP, Sanfilipo JR (2004). Rehabilitation of a Lignite Mine-disturbed Area in the Indian Desert. Land Degradation & Development 15(2): 163-176.

Singh AL, Asgher S (2003). Land Degradation Through Brick Kilns: A Case Study of Aligarh. Indian Journal of Regional Science 35 (2).

Singh AN, Raghubanshi AS, Singh JS (2002). Plantations as a Tool for Mine Spoil Restoration. Current Science 82: 1436-1441.

Singh AN, Raghubanshi AS, Singh JS (2003). Mining and Quarrying. State of the Environment Report, http://parisara.kar.nic.in/PDF/Mining.pdf.

Singh R, Singh PK, Singh G (2007). Evaluation of Land Degradation due to Coal Mining-a Vibrant Issue, First International Conference on MSECCMI, New Delhi, India, pp. 129-133.

Soni P (2003). Climate Change and Restoration of Tropical Forests. Indian Forester 129: 865-873.

Sudhira HS, Ramachandra TV, (2007). Integrated Spatial Planning Support System for Managing Urban Sprawl. Reviewed Paper # 199, in: Conference Proceedings of 10th International Conference on Computers in Urban Planning and Urban Management, Iguassu Falls, PR, Brazil.

Sujatha G, Dwivedi RS, Sreenivas K, Venkataratnam L (2000). Mapping and Monitoring of Degraded Lands in Part of Jaunpur District of Uttar Pradesh Using Temporal Spaceborne Multispectral Data. International Journal of Remote Sensing 21: 519-531.

Thiam AK (2003). The Causes and Spatial Pattern of Land Degradation Risk in Southern Mauritania Using Multitemporal AVHRR-NDVI Imagery and Field Data. Land Degradation & Development 14: 133-142.

Ujoh F, kwabe ID, Ifatimehin OO (2010). Understanding Urban Sprawl in the Federal Capital City, Abuja: Towards Sustainable Urbanization in Nigeria. Journal of Geography and Regional Planning 3(5): 106-113.

UNDP (2004). Reclaiming the Land Sustaining Livelihood. United Nations Development Programme- Lessons for the Future. Brochure, November, p. 1-20.

UNEP (2007). (United Nations Environment Programme, Global Environment Outlook (GEO-4), Nairobi, p. 572.

Vagholikar N, Moghe KA (2003). Undermining India: Impacts of Mining on Ecologically Sensitive Areas. Kalpavriksh, Pune, p. 35.

Wasson R, (1987). Detection and Measurement of Land Degradation Processes, *In*: Chisholm & Dumsday (Eds.), Land Degradation: Problems and Policies, Cambridge University Press; Cambridge; pp. 49-75.

Wessels KJ, Prince SD, Frost PE, van Zyl D (2004). Assessing the Effects of Human Induced Land Degradation in the Former Homelands of Northern South Africa with a 1 km AVHRR NDVI time-series. Remote Sensing of Environment 91: 47-67.

WMO (2005). Climate and Land Degradation, World Meteorological Organisation, WMO No. 989.

Zhao Z, Cai Y, Fu M, Bai Z (2008). Response of the Soils of Different Land Use Types to Drought: Eco-physiological Characteristics of Plants Grown on the Soils by pot Experiment. Ecological Engineering 34: 215-222.

Zika M, Erb KH, (2009). The Global Loss of Net Primary Production Resulting from Human-induced Soil Degradation in Dry Lands. Ecological Economics 69: 310-318.

10

Multiple Use of Water Through Integrated Fish Farming Systems

A.K. Prusty*; Poonam Kashyap; J.P. Singh
S.K. Gupta and D.K. Meena

ABSTRACT

Agriculture remains central to the Indian economy and it therefore receives a greater share of the annual water allocation. With population increase and economic growth, water demands for cities and for the industry are growing much faster than those of agriculture. Increasing competition for water is constraining both current availability of water for irrigation and further expansion of the irrigated area. The reduced per hectare availability will have direct influence on components of farming system. Hence, more focus should be on sustainable management of water resources for optimal agricultural production. This necessitates the exploration of opportunities for multiple use of water in agriculture through farming system approach. Integrated farming system involving multiple use of water could be an answer to resource scarce conditions in changing climatic scenario.

INTRODUCTION

Water is a vital component of agricultural production. Water has to be applied in the right amounts at the right time in order to achieve the right crop result. However, the application of water should be such that there should not be wastage of such a valuable resource. Judicious use of water will help farmers to manage water efficiently and reduce pollution risks. Economic, environmental and social considerations are playing an increasing role in agricultural production. Careful and effective water management will form part of these considerations, as well as helping the farmer to continue producing profitable production. Farmers aim to guarantee that the safety and quality of the water which they use will satisfy the highest expectations of the food industry and consumers. In addition, on-farm practices should ensure that water management is produced under sustainable economic, social, environmental conditions. Only 2.5% of 1386 million cubic kilolitres of water available on earth is freshwater and only one-third of this smaller quantity is available for human use (Postel et al., 1996). The productive utilization of available water resources is instrumental in climate resilience and risk management in changing environmental scenario.

WATER AVAILABILITY IN INDIA

In Indian conditions, the availability of water is highly uneven in both time and space. The total average annual flow per year for Indian rivers is estimated at 1953 km3. According to the National Water Policy (National Water Policy, 2002) of India, , 'Out of the total precipitation, including snowfall, of around 4000 billion cubic meters in the country, the availability of water from surface water and replenishable ground water is put at 1869 billion cubic meters. Because of topographical and other constraints, about 60% of this, i.e.690 billion cubic meters from surface water and 432 billion cubic meters from ground water, can be put to beneficial use.' According to the international norms, if per-capita water availability is less than 1700 m^3 per year then the country is categorized as water-stressed and if it is less than 1000 m^3 per capita per year, then the country is classified as water-scarce. In India, per capita surface water availability in 1991 and 2001 was 2309 and 1902 m3 respectively, and these are projected to reduce further to 1401 and 1191 m3 by the years 2025 and 2050 respectively (Sharma, 2005). Hence, there is a need for proper planning, development and management of the greatest assets of the country, namely water and land resources, for raising the standards of living of the millions of people.

With rapid increase in population and improved living standards, coupled with declining available water resources, the pressure is mounting on our water resources day by day., Country is facing frequent incidences of flood and drought due to spatial and temporal variability in precipitation. Overexploitation of groundwater is leading to low flows in the rivers, resulting in declined groundwater resources, and salt-water intrusion in aquifers in the coastal areas. Unrestricted irrigation through the canal system in some of the command areas has also contributed to water logging and salinity.

The quality of surface and groundwater resources is also deteriorating because of increasing pollutant loads from point and non-point sources. So far, the major consumptive use of water has been for irrigation. The gross irrigation potential is estimated (National Water Policy, 2002) to have increased from 19.5 million hectare (m ha) at the time of independence to about 140 m ha today. Further development of irrigation potential is required; keeping in view that the population is expected to reach around 1390 million by 2025. The drinking-water needs of people and livestock also have to be met. Demand for water for hydro and thermal power generation and for other industrial uses is also increasing substantially. As a result, water, which is already a scarce resource, will become even scarcer in future. Climate change and its projected implications would add to this already grave condition in India. Such a situation underscores the need for utmost efficiency in utilization of water and public awareness of the importance of its conservation and management, in every aspect of its use.

WATER USE AND AGRICULTURE SECTOR

Agriculture remains central to the Indian economy and it therefore receives a greater share of the annual water allocation. Irrigation, being the major water user, its share in the total demand is bound to decrease from the present 83% to 74% due to more pressing and competing demands from other sectors by 2025 A.D. The share of water allocated to irrigation is likely to decrease by 10% to 15 % in the coming decades ultimately leading to water stress in agriculture (CWC 2010). With population increase and economic growth, water demands for cities and for the industry are growing much faster than those of agriculture. Increasing competition for water is constraining both current availability of water for irrigation and further expansion of the irrigated area. In agriculture alone, staples, livestock, inland fisheries and aquaculture, and non-food crops already compete for water resources. The steady increase of inland aquaculture also contributes to the competition for water resources. Increased competition for water often translates into loss of access to water for the poor and other vulnerable groups. For millions of smallholder farmers, fishers, water is one of the most important factors of production: without water, they cannot make a living.

Hence, more focus should be on sustainable management of water resources for optimal agricultural production. It is essential to increase the efficiency of each component of irrigation system and crop production, preventing wasteful and ecologically injurious use of water. In view of these considerations, it is largely emphasized for enhancing water productivity through multiple uses. Each and every component of the farming system (crop, horticulture, animal, fishery including subsidiary enterprises like mushroom, apiary, kitchen gardening, processing and value addition etc) needs optimal allocation of water and multiple use of water by each component can increase the profitability and sustainability of the system under water stress conditions.

MULTIPLE USE OF WATER

Molden et al. (2003) estimated that by 2020 approximately 75% of the world's population will live in areas experiencing physical or economic water scarcity. The reduced per hectare availability will have direct influence on components of farming system. This necessitates the exploring opportunities for multiple use of water in agriculture through farming system approach. The main focus of farming system research is to maximize the recycling of waste of one component into input for other component and it holds good for water also. In the system mode, recycling of waste waters from animal sheds (animal urine, cleaning of animals, cleaning of sheds etc.) to crop production and fisheries , collection of runoff from crop field (during excess rainfall) in to fish pond, rearing of poultry and piggery along with fisheries are found to be promising avenues for multiple use of water. Integrated farming system involving multiple use of water could be an answer to resource scarce conditions in changing climatic scenario. In general, multiple use of water is not a new concept. It can simply be explained as use of available quantity of water for more than one purpose to achieve more crop and profit per drop of water in other words to maximize the ratio of output over the amount of water resource depleted (output per unit of water).

Integrated Farming System (IFS) holds the key for ensuring nutritional, livelihood and income security in a sustainable mode for small and marginal farmers of the country who constitute 84% of farming community. IFS based on multiple uses of water, comprising of crop, fishery, duckery, poultry, piggery, agro-forestry etc. are in practice not only in India but also in other Asian countries. Such a system results in more judicious use of water resulting in higher water productivity and also improving livelihood of resource poor farmers (Sharda and Juyal 2009; Gill et al. 2005). Small and medium size water bodies can be brought under multi-component production systems using in and around areas which will ultimately lead to improved income, nutrition and livelihood of small farm holdings. It is estimated that water productivity increases by 12 times in humid areas with pond based integrated farming systems (Vision 2030, PDFSR).

For benefit of the rural poor the approach should be "bottom-up", using the resources already available: local people, their knowledge and their natural resources. It must also seriously take into consideration, through participatory approaches, the needs, aspirations and circumstances of smallholders. Small farm holders including marginal (0.40 ha) and small (1.20 ha) category of farmers constitute more than 86% of Indian farm families and are expected to increase to the level of 96% in coming three decades. To earn a reasonable livelihood from such a small land holding to meet the needs of a 5-6 member family and equal number livestock is a serious challenge. It must be applicable under the highly heterogeneous and diverse conditions in which smallholders live and must be environmentally sustainable. In this backdrop, Integrated fish based farming systems could be regarded as an alternative for efficient utilization of available resources, waste recycling and energy saving, and for maintaining ecological balance and circulation as fisheries sector has been playing an important role in Indian economy through employment generation, contribution to food and livelihood security and foreign exchange earnings through export. This sector provides livelihood to about 14.49 million people directly or indirectly involved. India is the 3rd largest producer of fish in the World and 2nd largest producer of freshwater fishes.

What is Integrated Fish Farming (IFF)?

Integrated fish farming includes fish, crop, livestock, horticulture, sericulture, poultry etc. The wise integration of these farming system enterprises promotes full utilization of land area, recycling of wastes and by-products, minimizes operational costs in feed and fertilizer and maintains a balanced ecosystem. Integrated fish farming is a diversified and coordinated way of farming with fish as the main target along with other farm products, such as rice, vegetable, and fruits (Sinhababu and Venkateswarlu 1995; Ayinla 2003). Major objective if IFF is to increase the productivity of water, land and associated resources while contributing to increased food fish production

DEFINITION

"Integrated fish farming systems refer to the production, integrated management and comprehensive use of aquaculture, agriculture and livestock, with an emphasis on aquaculture"

Basic Principles of IFF

Basic principles of integrated fish farming systems are based on 3R's

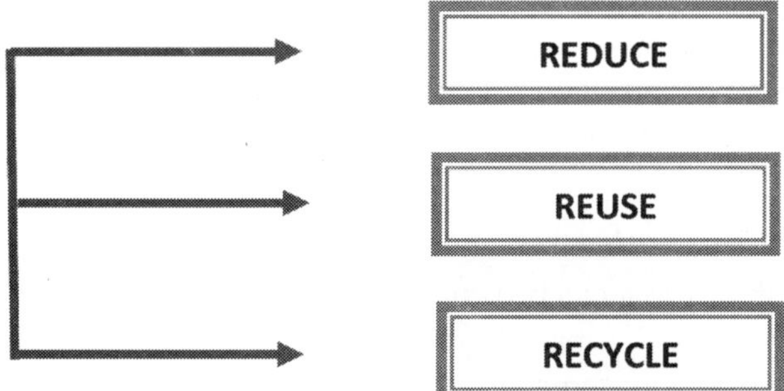

Reduce the Waste

Reduce food wastage to save water. A 50% reduction of food losses and waste at the global level would save 1,350 km3 of water.

Re-use and Recycle Water in Food Production

Drainage water, treated wastewater, brackish and desalinated water can be used in agriculture, especially in the arid and semi-arid zones and in rapidly growing peri-urban areas. Cities' wastewaters are in fact a precious source of water and nutrients for agriculture that have to be properly managed to minimize environmental and health risks. Utilizing residues and by-flows of the food sector rather than growing crops specifically to produce bioenergy would limit the pressure on water resources and competition with food crops. It would even increase water productivity: the same water would have produced food and bioenergy. Many forms of aquaculture such as cage culture, flow-through systems and integrated agri-aquaculture represent food productions systems that do not significantly increase water consumption. Recirculation of water in aquaculture can reduce water use by 90%.

The fundamental ecological and economic principle embodied in integrated farming systems is that many outputs ("wastes" or "by-products") of subsystems become basic inputs for other subsystems, rather than just additive components of the overall farm economy. A synergism is therefore created such that the total productivity of the system exceeds the sum of the individual subsystems. These results in higher yields for all the commodities produced and a wider range of products than could otherwise be obtained per unit area. Under such system, main objective is to maximize the returns from the whole system than economic results from any single component.

Integrated fish farming works in the following way:

- Trapping of solar energy and production of organic matter by primary producers.
- Utilization of primary producers by phagotrophs or tertiary consumers.
- Decomposition of primary producers and phagotrophs.
- Release of nutrients for producers

The animal waste in water body enters the food chain in 3 different ways viz. As Feed (Direct utilization of organic materials coated with bacteria and other materials), as autotrophic production (by providing nutrients for micro-flora) and as heterotrophic production (by production of micro-fauna such as protozoans and zoo planktons)

Different Types of Integrated Fish Farming Systems

Integrated fish farming can be broadly classified into two categories, namely: Crop-fish and Livestock-fish based systems. Some of the major crop-fish based systems include rice-fish systems, horticulture-fish system whereas livestock-fish system includes cattle-fish system, pig-fish system, poultry-fish system, duck-fish system, goat-fish system etc.

RICE-FISH INTEGRATION

Low lying rice fields where 30-50 cm water column could be maintained and regulated for a period of 3 months or more are suitable for making this combination functional. This system needs modification of rice fields, digging peripheral trenches, construction of dykes, pond refuge, sowing improved varieties of rice, manuring, stocking of fish at 10,000/ha and finally feeding of stocked fish with rice-bran and oilcakes at 2-3% of body weight. For the culture of fish in combination with rice, varieties such as Panidhan, Tulsi, CR260 77, ADT 6, ADT 7, Rajarajan and Pattambi 15 and 16 are suitable. These varieties possess strong root systems but and are also capable of withstanding flooded conditions. Besides, they have a life span of 180 days which provides culture duration of about four to five months for fish after their transplantation. This type of fish culture has several advantages such as: (a) economical utilisation of land; (b) savings on labour cost towards weeding and supplemental feeding; (c) enhanced rice yield; and (d) additional income and diversified harvest such as fish and rice from same plot along with some other crops on bunds. In rice-fish culture use of pesticide, insecticides or other chemicals should be avoided as they will kill the fish. Integrated rice and fish culture optimizes the benefits of scarce land and water resources through complementary use, and exploits the synergies between fish and plant. Two crops cultivated on the same field increase the farmer's income, ensuring a higher return on his investment.

HORTICULTURE-FISH INTEGRATION

In horticulture-fish integration pond embankment can be very well utilized for fruits and vegetable farming. For this top, inner and outer dykes of ponds as well as adjoining areas can be best utilized. Pond water is used for irrigation and silt, which is a high-quality manure is used for crops, vegetables and fruit bearing plants. Plants selected for embankment farming should be of dwarf type, less shady, evergreen, seasonal and highly remunerative. Dwarf variety fruit bearing plants like mango, banana, papaya, coconut and lime are suitable for horti-fish combiantion, while pineapple, ginger, turmeric, chili are grown as intercrops. Residues of vegetables cultivated are recycled into fishponds, particularly when stocked with fishes like grass carp. In mixed culture of grass carps along with rohu, catla and mrigal, in 50: 15: 20: 15 ratio at a density of 5000 fish/ha. This type of integrated system besides enhancing water productivity also fetches 20-25% higher return than fish culture alone.

LIVESTOCK-FISH INTEGRATION

Livestock-fish system includes cattle-fish system, pig-fish system, poultry-fish system, duck-fish system, goat-fish system, rabbit-fish system. In this practice, excreta of ducks, chicks, pigs and cattle are either recycled into the fish pond for use by fish to serve as direct food for fish or for plankton production which in term is used by fish as food. As a result, the expenditure towards chemical fertilisers and supplementary feeds for fish culture is reduced by 50-60%. Potential linkages between livestock and fish production is through use of nutrients (N, P and K), particularly reuse of livestock manures for fish production and use of production and processing of livestock by-products for aquaculture. Aquaculture may also provide inputs and other benefits to livestock production. A variety of aquatic plants e.g. duckweeds and the aquatic fern Azolla have proven potential as livestock feeds; and invertebrates such as snails and crustaceans can be used for poultry feeds.

In cattle fish integration cowsheds are constructed in the vicinity of fishponds and the slurry from the biogas plants may be discharged into fishponds. A unit of 5-6 cows can provide adequate manure for 1 ha of pond. In cattle fish integration, in addition to 9,000 kg of milk, about 3,000-4,000 kg fish/ha/year can also be harvested.

In pig-fish combination depending on the size of the fishponds and their manure requirements, pigsties can either be built on the dry-side of the bund or may also be constructed in a nearby place. Pigdung contains more than 70 per cent digestible feed for fish. The undigested solids present in the pigdung also serve as direct food source to tilapia and common carp. A stocking density of 60-100 pigs has been found to be enough to fertilise a fish pond of one hectare area. Fishes like grass carp, silver carp and common carp (1:2:1) are suitable for pig-fish integration.

In poultry-fish integration poultry droppings rich in nitrogen and phosphorus are utilized for fish culture. Poultry housing, when constructed above the water level using bamboo poles would fertilise fishponds directly. Rhode island or Leghorn birds are preferred in poultry-fish system for their better growth and egg laying capacity. 300-500 layers/broilers are sufficient to meet the fertilizer requirement of a 1 ha. pond.

In duck-fish integration duck dropping go directly in pond, which in turn provide essential nutrients to stimulate growth of natural food for fish. Ducks also consume frogs, tadpoles etc. making a safer environment for fishes and act as bio-aerators. In turn, fish-pond being a semi-closed biological system with several aquatic animals and plants, provide excellent disease-free environment for ducks. Most commonly used breed for this system in India is the 'Indian runners'. In the livestock-fish integrations a stocking density of 10000 fingerlings/ha. could produce 3000-5000 kg fish yield/ha/year.

Advantages of Fish Based Integrated Farming systems:

- Artificial balanced ecosystem with no waste
- Increased food supply
- Increased output and economic efficiency
- More employment and improvement in the socio-economic status
- Multiple use of water
- Cost-effective use of available water resources
- Wider range of products

CONCLUSION

Increasing demands are being placed on the Nation's finite water resources, and the choices being made influence the sustainability of these precious resources. The development of management strategies to sustain water resources requires the balancing of water needs for different competitive demands. To accomplish this requires holistic approach in farming system through multiple use of water which can lead to enhanced water productivity. Multiple water use module provides access to "small and marginal" users, for livelihood, nutritional and income enhancements. Water resource creation, management and utilization through farming system approach will help to manage the spatial and temporal water stress caused by physical availability. A multi-disciplinary approach is needed, including technological, economic, social and political aspects, which are interrelated.

REFERENCES

Ayinla OA (2003). Integrated fish farming: Averitable Tool for Poverty Alleviation/Hunger Eradication in the Niger Delta Region. In A.A Eyo and J.O Atanda (eds). Conference Proceedings of Fisheries Society of Nigeria, Owerri, Nigeria. pp. 40-41.

CWC (2010). Report on "Water and Related Statistics", December, 2010 Published by Central Water Commission (CWC), New Delhi.

Gill, M.S., Samra, J.S. and Singh, G. (2005. Integrated Farming System for Realizing High Productivity Under Shallow Water Table Conditions. Research Bulletin, Punjab Agriculture University, Ludhiana.

Molden, D., Murray-Rust, H., Sakthivadivel, R., Makin, I., (2003). A Water Productivity Framework for Understanding and Action. In: Kijne, J.W., Barker, R., Molden, D. (Eds.) Water Productivity in Agriculture: Limits and Opportunities for Improvement. CABI Publishing, Wallingford, UK, pp. 1-18.

National Water Policy, Ministry of Water Resources, New Delhi, 2002.

Postel, S.L., Daily, G.C. and Ehrlich, P.R., Human Appropriation of Renewable Freshwater. Science, (1996), 271, 785-788.

Sharda, V.N. and Juyal, G.P. (2009). Conservation Technologies for Sustaining Natural Resources. Handbook of Agriculture, pp. 323-370, ICAR, DIPA, New Delhi.

Sharma, R., Climate and Water Resources of India. Curr. Sci., 2005, 89, 818-824.

Sinhababu, D.P. and Venkateswarlu, B., (1995). Rice-fish in Rainfed Lowlands. CRRI Bidletin p. 14. Central Rice Research Institute, Cuttack/India.

Vision (2030). Vision 2030 Document, Published by Project Directorate for Farming Systems Research (PDFSR), Modipuram, Meerut, U.P. (India).

An Overview of Fisheries

Hussein Abdel-Hay Kauod

ABSTRACT

This article is an overview on fisheries; definition and management. A fishery is an area with an associated fish or aquatic population which is harvested for its commercial value. Fisheries can be ocean fisheries, fish farming and aqua farming. Modern fisheries management is often referred to as a governmental system of appropriate management rules based on defined objectives and a mix of management means to implement the rules.

Keywords: Fisheries; Ocean; Management, Policy.

INTRODUCTION

A fishery is an area with an associated fish or aquatic population which is harvested for its commercial value. Fisheries can be wild or farmed. Most of the world's wild fisheries are in the ocean.

WILD FISHERIES

Wild fisheries are sometimes called capture fisheries. The aquatic life they support is not controlled in any meaningful way and needs to be "captured" or fished. Wild fisheries exist primarily in the oceans, and particularly around coasts and continental shelves. They also exist in lakes and rivers. Issues with wild fisheries are overfishing and pollution. Significant wild fisheries have collapsed or are in danger of collapsing, due to overfishing and pollution. Overall, production from the world's wild fisheries has leveled out, and may be starting to decline. As a contrast to wild fisheries, farmed fisheries can operate in sheltered coastal waters, in rivers, lakes and ponds, or in enclosed bodies of water such as tanks. Farmed fisheries are technological in nature, and revolve around developments in aquaculture. Farmed fisheries are expanding, and Chinese aquaculture in particular is making many advances. Nevertheless, the majority of fish consumed by humans continues to be sourced from wild fisheries. As of the early 21st century, fish is humanity's only significant wild food source.

OCEAN FISHERIES

Most of the world's wild fisheries are in the ocean.

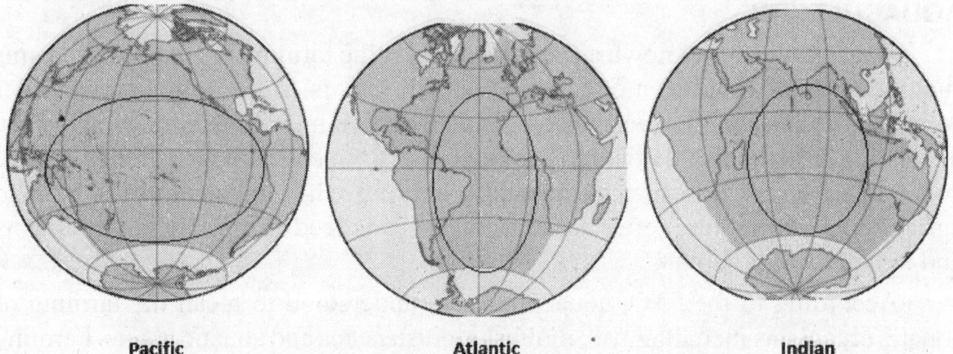

Fig. 11.1: Oceans Occupy 71 Per cent of the Earth's Surface. They are Divided into Five Major Oceans, which in Decreasing Order of Size are: the Pacific Ocean, Atlantic Ocean, Indian Ocean, Southern Ocean, and Arctic Ocean. Over 70 Per cent of the World Catch from the Sea comes from the Pacific Ocean.

Table 11.1: Area of World Oceans

Ocean	Area Million km²	%	Volume Million cu km	%	Mean Depth km	Max Depth km	Coastline km	Fish Capture Million Tonnes	%
Pacific Ocean	155.6	46.4	679.6	4.37	10.924	135.663	84,234	71.000	
Atlantic Ocean	76.8	22.9	313.4	22.5	4.08	8.605	111,866	24.045	20.3
Indian Ocean	68.6	20.4	260.3	10.6	3.03	7.258	66,525	10.107	8.6
Southern Ocean	20.3	6.1	91.5	6.7	4.51	7.235	17,968	0.147	0.1
Arctic Ocean	14.1	4.2	17.0	1.2	1.21	4.665	45,389		
Total	335.3		1370.8		4.09	10.924	356,000	118.623	

FISH FARMING

Fish farming is the principal form of aquaculture, while other methods may fall under mariculture. Fish farming involves raising fish commercially in tanks or enclosures, usually for food. A facility that releases juvenile fish into the wild for recreational fishing or to supplement a species' natural numbers is generally referred to as a fish hatchery. Worldwide, the most important fish species used in fish farming are carp, salmon, tilapia and catfish.

There is an increasing demand for fish and fish protein, which has resulted in widespread overfishing in wild fisheries. Fish farming offers fish marketers another source. However, farming carnivorous fish, such as salmon, does not always reduce pressure on wild fisheries, since carnivorous farmed fish are usually fed fishmeal and fish oil extracted from wild forage fish. The global returns for fish farming recorded by the FAO in 2008 totaled 33.8 million tones worth about $US 60 billion.

AQUACULTURE

Aquaculture, also known as aqua farming, is the farming of aquatic organisms such as fish, crustaceans, mollusks and aquatic plants. Water populations under controlled conditions, and can be contrasted with commercial fishing, which is the harvesting of wild fish. Broadly speaking, finfish and shellfish fisheries can be conceptualized as akin to hunting and gathering while aquaculture is akin to agriculture. Mariculture refers to aquaculture practiced in marine environments and in underwater habitats.

According to the FAO, aquaculture "is understood to mean the farming of aquatic organisms including fish, mollusks, crustaceans and aquatic plants. Farming implies some form of intervention in the rearing process to enhance production, such as regular stocking, feeding, protection from predators, etc. Farming also implies individual or corporate ownership of the stock being cultivated." The reported output from global aquaculture operations would supply one half of the fish and shellfish that is directly consumed by humans; however, there are issues about the reliability of the reported figures. Further, in current aquaculture practice, products from several pounds of wild fish are used to produce one pound of a piscivorous fish like salmon.

Particular kinds of aquaculture include fish farming, shrimp farming, oyster farming, alga culture (such as seaweed farming), and the cultivation of ornamental fish. Particular methods include aquaponics and integrated multi-trophic aquaculture, both of which integrate fish farming and plant farming.

Mollusks, especially bivalves such as clams and mussels, have been an important food source since at least the advent of anatomically modern humans, and this has often resulted in overfishing. Other commonly eaten mollusks include octopuses and squids, whelks, oysters, and scallops. In 2005, China accounted for 80% of the global mollusk catch, netting almost 11,000,000 tones (11,000,000 long tons; 12,000,000 short tons). Within Europe, France remained the industry leader. Some countries regulate importation and handling of mollusks and other seafood, mainly to minimize the poison risk from toxins that accumulate in the animals.

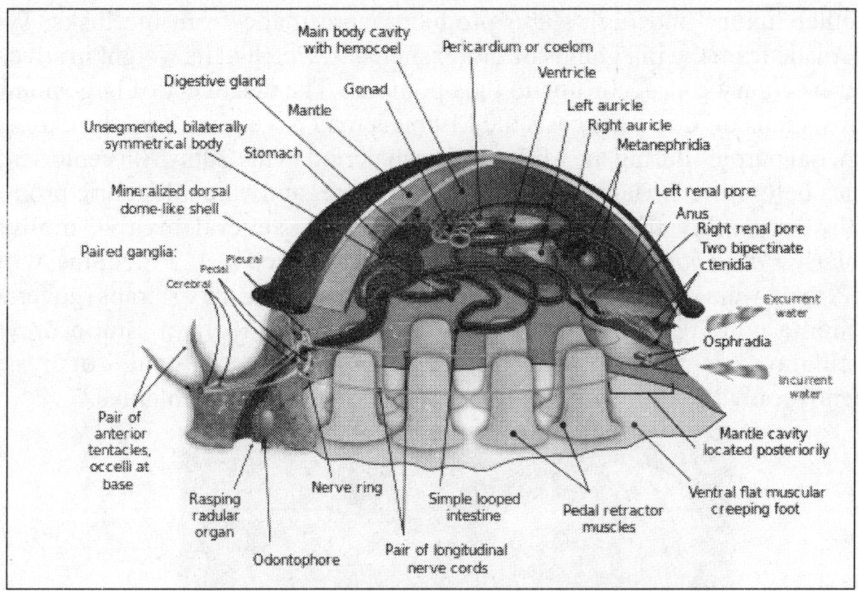

Fig. 11.2: Anatomical Structure of Mollusks

Most mollusks with shells can produce pearls, but only the pearls of bivalves and some gastropods, whose shells are lined with nacre, are valuable. The best natural pearls are produced by marine pearl oysters, *Pinctada margaritifera* and *Pinctada mertensi*, which live in the tropical and subtropical waters of the Pacific Ocean. Natural pearls form when a small foreign object gets stuck between the mantle and shell.

The two methods of culturing pearls insert either "seeds" or beads into oysters. The "seed" method uses grains of ground shell from freshwater mussels, and overharvesting for this purpose has endangered several freshwater mussel species in the southeastern USA. The pearl industry is so important in some areas; significant sums of money are spent on monitoring the health of farmed mollusks.

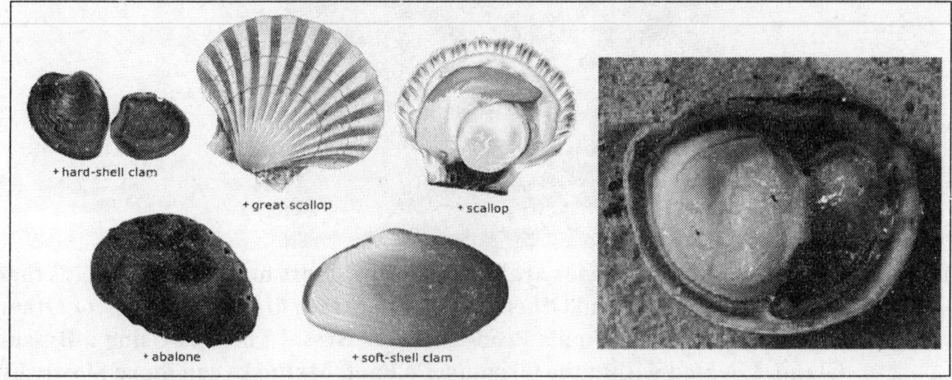

Fig. 11.3: Most Mollusks

Other luxury and high-status products were made from mollusks. Tyrian purple, made from the ink glands of murexshells, "... fetched its weight in silver" in the fourth century BC, according to the opompus. The discovery of large numbers of *Murex* shells on Crete suggests the Minoans may have pioneered the extraction of "imperial purple" during the Middle Minoan period in the 20th-18th centuries BC, centuries before the Tyrians. Sea silk is a fine, rare, and valuable fabric produced from the long silky threads (byssus) secreted by several bivalve mollusks, particularly *Pinna nobilis*, to attach themselves to the sea bed. Procopius, writing on the Persian wars *circa* 550 CE, "stated that the five hereditary satraps (governors) of Armenia who received their insignia from the Roman Emperor were given chlamys (or cloaks) made from *lana pinna* (*Pinna* "wool," or byssus). Apparently, only the ruling classes were allowed to wear this chlamys."

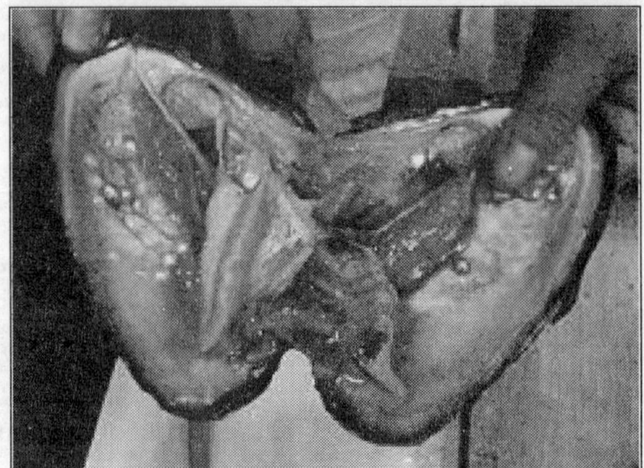

Fig. 11.4: The Best Natural Pearls are Produced by Marine Pearl Oysters, Pinctada Margaritifera and Pinctada Mertensi

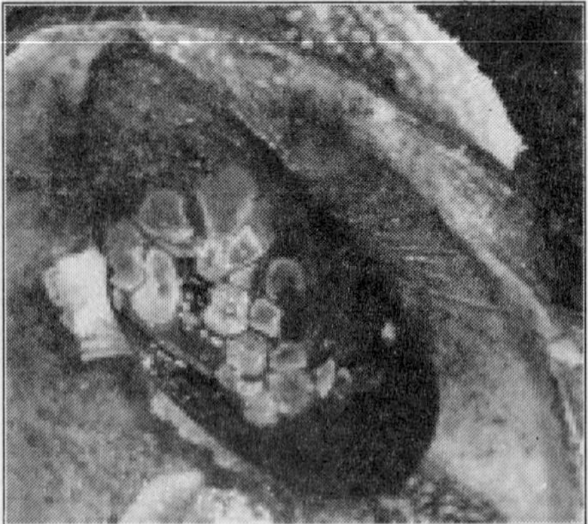

Fig. 11.5: Byssal, or Byssus Threads are Strong, Silky Fibers made from Proteins that are used by Mussels and Other Bivalves to Attach to Rocks, Pilings, or Other Substrates. These Animals Produce Their Byssal Threads Using a Byssus Gland, Located within the Organism's Foot. Mollusks can move Slowly by Extending a Byssal Thread, Using it as an Anchor and then shortening it.

Mollusk shells, including those of cowries, were used as a kind of money (shell money) in several preindustrial societies. However, these "currencies" generally differed in important ways from the standardized government-backed and -controlled money familiar to industrial societies. Some shell "currencies" were not used for commercial transactions, but mainly as social status displays at important occasions, such as weddings. When used for commercial transactions, they functioned as commodity money, as a tradable commodity whose value differed from place to place, often as a result of difficulties in transport, and which was vulnerable to incurable inflation if more efficient transport or "goldrush" behavior appeared.

Shrimp farming is an aquaculture business that exists in either a marine or freshwater environment, producing shrimp or prawns (crustaceans of the groups Caridea or Dendrobranchiata) for human consumption.

Marine shrimp farming is an aquaculture business for the cultivation of marine shrimp or prawns for human consumption. Commercial shrimp farming began in the 1970s, and production grew steeply, particularly to match the market demands of the United States, Japan and Western Europe. The total global production of farmed shrimp reached more than 1.6 million tons in 2003, representing a value of nearly 9 billion U.S. dollars. About 75% of farmed shrimp is produced in Asia, in particular in China and Thailand. The other 25% is produced mainly in Latin America, where Brazil, Ecuador, and Mexico are the largest producers; the largest exporting nation is Thailand.

Shrimp farming has changed from traditional, small-scale businesses in Southeast Asia into a global industry. Technological advances have led to growing shrimp at ever higher densities, and brood stock is shipped worldwide. Virtually all farmed shrimp are of the family Penaeidae, and just two species – *Penaeus vannamei* (Pacific white shrimp) and *Penaeus monodon* (giant tiger prawn) – account for roughly 80% of all farmed shrimp. These industrial monocultures are very susceptible to diseases, which have caused several regional wipe-outs of farm shrimp populations. Increasing ecological problems, repeated disease outbreaks, and pressure and criticism from both NGOs and consumer countries led to changes in the industry in the late 1990s and generally stronger regulation by governments. In 1999, a programme aimed at developing and promoting more sustainable farming practices was initiated, including governmental bodies, industry representatives, and environmental organisations.

A. Freshwater prawn farming is an aquaculture business designed to raise and produce freshwater prawns or shrimp for human consumption. Freshwater prawn farming shares many characteristics with and many of the same problems as, marine shrimp farming. Unique problems are introduced by the developmental life cycle of the main species (the giant river prawn, *Macrobrachium rosenbergii*). The global annual production of freshwater prawns (excluding crayfish and crabs) in 2003 was about 280,000 tons, of which China produced some 180,000 tons, followed by India and Thailand with some 35,000 tons each. Additionally, China produced about 370,000 tons of Chinese river crab *(Eriocheir sinensis)*.

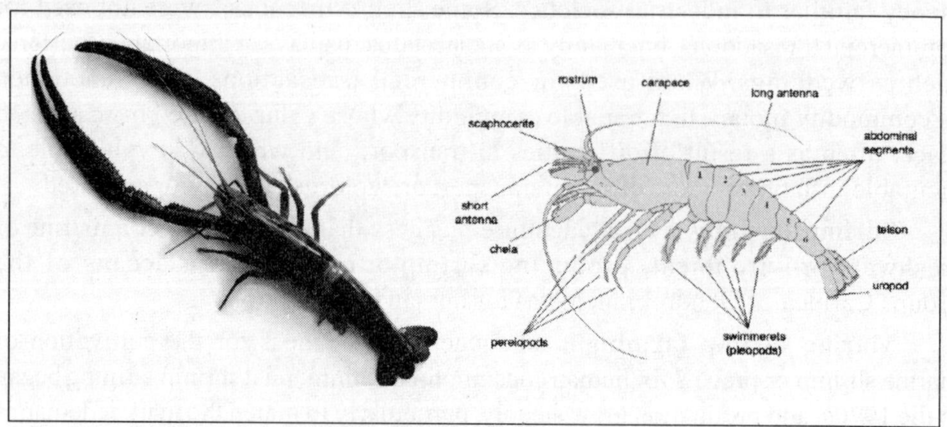

Fig. 11.6: Freshwater prawn

FISHERIES MANAGEMENT

Draws on fisheries science in order to find ways to protect fishery resources so sustainable exploitation is possible. Modern fisheries management is often referred to as a governmental system of appropriate management rules based on defined objectives and a mix of management means to implement the rules, which are put in place by a system of monitoring control and surveillance. According to the FAO, there are "no clear and generally accepted definitions of fisheries management". However, the working definition used by the FAO and much cited elsewhere is:

1. The integrated process of information gathering, analysis, planning, consultation, decision-making, allocation of resources and formulation and implementation, with enforcement as necessary, of regulations or rules which govern fisheries activities in order to ensure the continued productivity of the resources and the accomplishment of other fisheries objectives.
2. The *Fishery Manager's Guidebook* issued in 2009 by the FAO of the United Nations, advises that the precautionary approach or principle should be applied when "ecosystem resilience and human impact (including reversibility) are difficult to forecast and hard to distinguish from natural changes. The precautionary principle suggests that when an action risks harm, it should not be proceeded with until it can be scientifically proven to be safe. Historically fishery managers have applied this principle the other way round; fishing activities have not been curtailed until it has been proven that they have already damaged existing ecosystems. In a paper published in 2007, Shertzer and Prager suggested that there can be significant benefits to stock biomass and fishery yield if management is stricter and more prompt.

Table 11.2: Difference between Crabs, Lobsters and Shrimp

Differences between crabs, lobsters and shrimp		
crabs	 lobsters	shrimp
Crabs do not look like shrimp. Unlike shrimp, their abdomen is small, and they have short antennae and a short carapace that is wide and flat. They have prominent grasping claws as their front pair of limbs Crabs are adapted for walking on the seafloor. They have robust legs and usually move about the seafloor by walking sideways. They have pleopods, but they use them for intromission or to hold egg broods, and not for swimming. Whereas shrimp and lobsters escape predators by lobstering, crabs cling to the seafloor and burrow into sediment. Compared to shrimp and lobsters; the carapace of crabs are particularly heavy hard and mineralised.	Lobsters and spiny lobsters look somewhat like large versions of shrimp. Spiny lobsters lack the large claws, but have long spiny antennae and a spiny carapace. Some of the biggest decapods are lobsters. Like crabs, lobsters have robust legs and are highly adapted for walking on the seafloor, though they do not walk sideways. Some species have rudimentary pleopods, which give them some ability to swim, and like shrimp they can lobster with their tail to escape predators but their primary mode of locomotion is walking, not swimming. Lobsters are an intermediate development between shrimp and crabs.	Shrimp are slender with long muscular abdomens. They look somewhat like small lobsters, but not like crabs. The abdomens of crabs are small and short, whereas the abdomens of lobsters and shrimp are large and long. The lower abdomens of shrimp support pleopods which are well adapted for swimming. The carapace of crabs are wide and flat, whereas the carapace of lobsters and shrimp are more cylindrical. The antennae of crabs are short, whereas the antennae of lobsters and shrimp are usually long, reaching more than twice the body length in some shrimp species.

The precautionary principle or precautionary approach states that if an action or policy has a suspected risk of causing harm to the public or to the environment, in the absence of scientific consensus that the action or policy is harmful, the burden of proof that it is *not* harmful falls on those taking an action.

The principle is used by policy makers to justify discretionary decisions in situations where there is the possibility of harm from taking a particular course or making a certain decision when extensive scientific knowledge on the matter is lacking. The principle implies that there is a social responsibility to protect the public from exposure to harm, when scientific investigation has found a plausible risk. These protections can be relaxed only if further scientific findings emerge that provide sound evidence that no harm will result.

In some legal systems, as in the law of the European Union, the application of the precautionary principle has been made a statutory requirement in some areas of law.

Regarding international conduct, the first endorsement of the principle was in 1982 when the World Charter for Nature was adopted by the United Nations General Assembly, while its first international implementation was in 1987 through the Montreal Protocol. Soon after, the principle integrated with many other legally binding international treaties such as the Rio Declaration and Kyoto Protoco.

Table 11.3: Key Issues in the Conservation of Fisheries

1.	Management and conservation of fisheries are necessary, because economic forces do not usually lead to a satisfactory stable state.
2.	Conservation measures are needed permanently, not only while fisheries are in poor shape; they cannot normally be discontinued once the stocks have recovered.
3.	Technical conservation measures (such as minimum mesh sizes) are not usually sufficient on their own; direct conservation measures (restrictions on catches or fishing effort) are also needed in most cases.
4.	Closures of fisheries during the spawning season are not necessarily a very effective conservation measure.
5.	Stability of catches cannot be achieved at the same time as stability of fishing effort.
6.	Properly calculated Total Allowable Catches (TACs) and quotas do not necessarily allow the fleet to fish all year, restrictions on the fishery do not mean that the scientific assessment must be wrong.
7.	TACs and quotas are an indirect method for controlling fishing effort: direct limitation is another way of achieving the same objective.

CONCLUSION

Improved high seas policies will regulate fisheries on the global commons and prevent further declines in fish stocks. Improved diet and food security will benefit coastal residents. Successful models for sustainable fisheries management and marine protected areas (MPAs) in coastal areas will inspire replication around the world. Sustainable trade in marine ornamentals will reduce threats to coral reefs, help businesses to commit to environmental sustainability and raise awareness about the negative impacts that removing adult fish has on the health of the wider ecosystem.

International agreements and policy precedents are needed to improve regulation and enforcement in the high seas, negotiations on fisheries and ocean policy must work with country representatives in the seascapes to promote novel policy solutions for high seas fisheries.

REFERENCES

Alexei (July 26, 2009). "Chile's Antibiotics Use on Salmon Farms Dwarfs That of a Top Rival's". *The New York Times*. Retrieved 2009-08-28. Bulletin of the European Association of Fish Pathologists 22 (2): 117-125 2002 Salmon Farming Tactics Produce Unhealthy Fish Purdue Scientists: Genetically Modified Fish could Damage Ecology. "Alaska Passes Law Requiring Mandatory La.

Butterfield, N.J. (2006). "Hooking Some Stem-group "Worms": Fossil Lophotrochozoans in the Burgess Shale". *BioEssays* 28 (12): 1161-6. doi:10.1002/bies.20507.PMID 17120226.

Facts About Antibiotic Resistance UNH Aquaculture website Barrionuevo

Fedonkin, M.A., Simonetta, A. and Ivantsov, A.Y. (2007)."New data on Kimberella, the Vendian Mollusc-like Organism (White Sea region, Russia): Palaeoecological and Evolutionary Implications". *Geological Society, London, Special Publications* 286: 157-179.Bibcode:2007GSLSP.286.157F.doi:10.1144/SP286.12. Retrieved 2008-07-10.

Fedonkin, M.A.; Waggoner, B.M. (1997). "The Late Precambrian Fossil Kimberella is a Mollusc-like Bilaterian Organism". *Nature* 388 (6645): 868.Bibcode: 1997 Natur. 388..868F. doi:10.1038/42242.

Kocot KM, Cannon JT, Todt C, Citarella MR, Kohn AB, Meyer A, Santos SR, Schander C, Moroz LL, Lieb B, Halanych KM (2011) Phylogenomics Reveals Deep Molluscan Relationships. Naturedoi:10.1038/nature10382.

Mandel, Gregory N.; Gathii, James Thuo (2006). "Cost Benefit Analysis Versus the Precautionary Principle: Beyond Cass Sunstein's Laws of Fear". *University of Illinois Law Review* 2006 (5): 1037-1079.

Nick Bostrom 2003 Ethical Issues in Advanced Artificial Intelligence – Section 2Lymbery, P. CIWF Trust Report, "In Too Deep - The Welfare of Intensively Farmed Fish" (2002)

Passamaneck, Y.; Schander, C.; Halanych, K. (2004). "Investigation of Molluscan Phylogeny Using Large-subunit and Small-subunit Nuclear rRNA Sequences." *Molecular Phylogenetics & Evolution* 32 (1): 25-38.doi: 10.1016/j.ympev. 2003. 12.016. PMID 15186794.

Porter, S.M. (Jun 2007). "Seawater Chemistry and Early Carbonate Biomineralization". *Science* 316 (5829):1302301. Bibcode:2007Sci...316.1302P.doi:10.1126/science.1137284. ISSN 0036-8075.PMID 17540895.

Precautionary Principle: Origins, Definitions, and Interpretations." Treasury Publication, Government of New Zealand. 2006. http://www.treasury.govt.nz/publications/research-policy/ppp/2006/06-06/05.htm

Recuerda, M. A. (2008). "Dangerous Interpretations of the Precautionary Principle and the Foundational Values of the European Union Food Law: Risk versus Risk". *Journal of Food Law & Policy* 4 (1) Consolidated Version of the Treaty on the Functioning of the European Union article 191.

Recuerda, Miguel A. (2006). "Risk and Reason in the European Union Law". *European Food and Feed Law Review* 5.

Sachs, Noah M. (2011). "Rescuing the Strong Precautionary Principle from its Critics". *University of Illinois Law Review* 2011 (4): 1285-1338.

Sigwart; Sutton, M. D. (Oct 2007). "Deep Molluscan Phylogeny: Synthesis of Palaeontological and Neontological Data". *Proceedings of the Royal Society B: Biological Sciences* 274 (1624): 2413-2419.

Stewart, R.B. (2002). "Environmental Regulatory Decision Making Under Uncertainty". *Research in Law and Economics* 20: 76.

The Paralyzing Principle: Does the Precautionary Principle Point us in any Helpful Direction?" Goliath Business Knowledge on Demand. December 2002. http://goliath.ecnext.com/coms2/gi_0199-2593495/The-paralyzing-principle-does-the.html

Wägele, J.; Letsch, H.; Klussmann-Kolb, A.; Mayer, C.; Misof, B.; Wägele, H. (2009). "Phylogenetic Support Values are not Necessarily Informative: The Case of the Serialia Hypothesis (a Mollusk Phylogeny)". *Frontiers in zoology* 6(1): 12. doi:10.1186/1742-9994-6-12. PMC 2710323.PMID 19555513.

Wilson, N.; Rouse, G.; Giribet, G. (2010). "Assessing the Molluscan Hypothesis Serialia (Monoplacophora+Polyplacophora) Using Novel Molecular Data.". *Molecular Phylogenetics & Evolution* 54 (1): 187-193.doi:10.1016/j.ympev. 2009.07.028. PMID 19647088.

Winnepenninckx, B; Backeljau, T; De Wachter, R (December 1, 1996). "Investigation of Molluscan Phylogeny on the Basis of 18S rRNA Sequences". *Molecular Biology and Evolution* 13 (10): 1306-1317.doi:10.1093/oxfordjournals. molbev. a025577. PMID 8952075.

Index